# BLOODSHOT SALVATION

# THE BOOK OF REVENGE

JEFF LEMIRE | MICO SUAYAN | LEWIS LAROSA | BRIAN REBER | DIEGO RODRIGUEZ

# CONTENTS

*Collection Cover Art:* Kenneth Rocafort

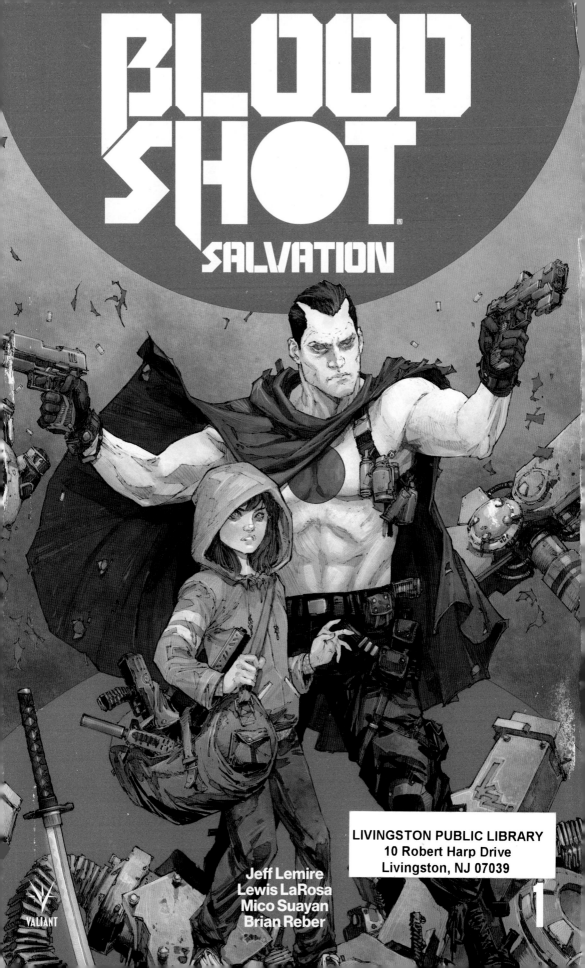

# BLOOD SHOT

## SALVATION

Jeff Lemire
Lewis LaRosa
Mico Suayan
Brian Reber

1

# BLOODSHOT®
## SALVATION

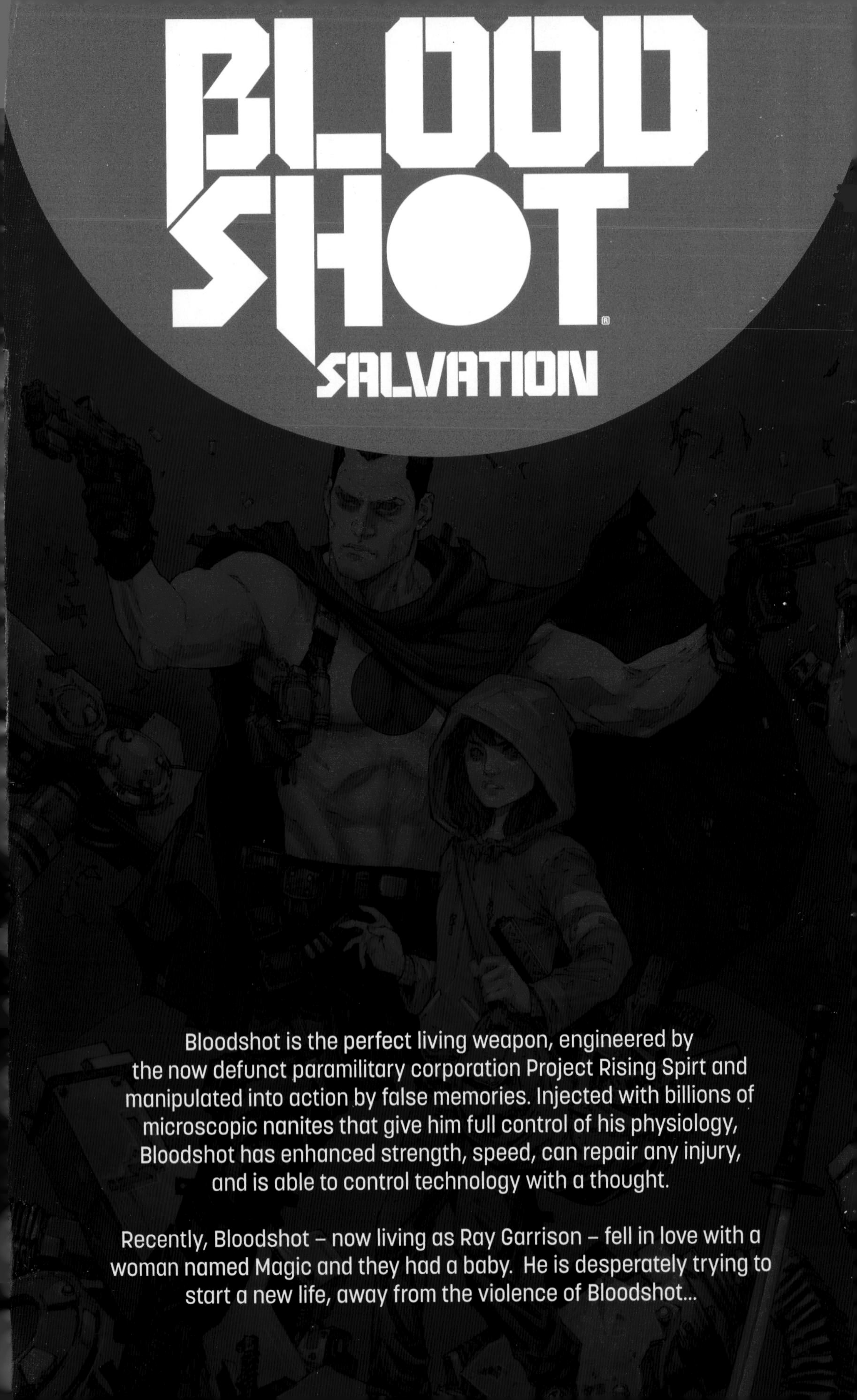

Bloodshot is the perfect living weapon, engineered by the now defunct paramilitary corporation Project Rising Spirt and manipulated into action by false memories. Injected with billions of microscopic nanites that give him full control of his physiology, Bloodshot has enhanced strength, speed, can repair any injury, and is able to control technology with a thought.

Recently, Bloodshot – now living as Ray Garrison – fell in love with a woman named Magic and they had a baby. He is desperately trying to start a new life, away from the violence of Bloodshot...

*Assistant Editor:* Benjamin Peterson
*Associate Editor:* Danny Khazem
*Editor:* Warren Simons

**VALIANT**®

Bloodshot® Salvation: The Book of Revenge. Published by Valiant
Entertainment LLC. Office of Publication: 350 Seventh Avenue, New
York, NY 10001. Compilation copyright © 2018 Valiant Entertainment
LLC. All rights reserved. Contains materials originally published in
single magazine form as Bloodshot Salvation #1-5. Copyright ©
2017 and 2018 Valiant Entertainment LLC. All rights reserved. All
characters, their distinctive likeness and related indicia featured in
this publication are trademarks of Valiant Entertainment LLC. The
stories, characters, and incidents featured in this publication are
entirely fictional. Valiant Entertainment does not read or accept
unsolicited submissions of ideas, stories, or artwork. Printed in the
U.S.A. First Printing. ISBN: 9781682152553.

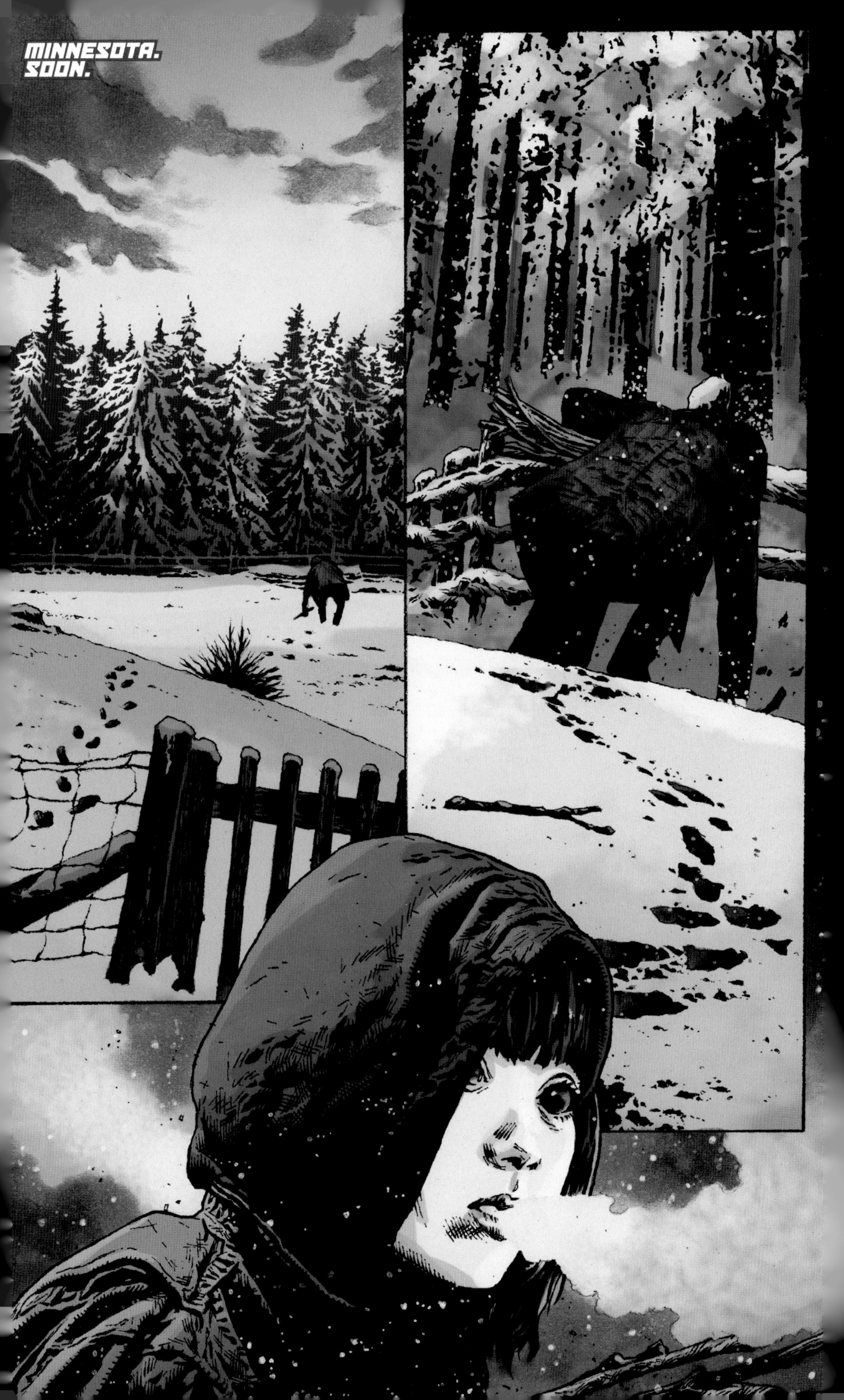
MINNESOTA.
SOON.

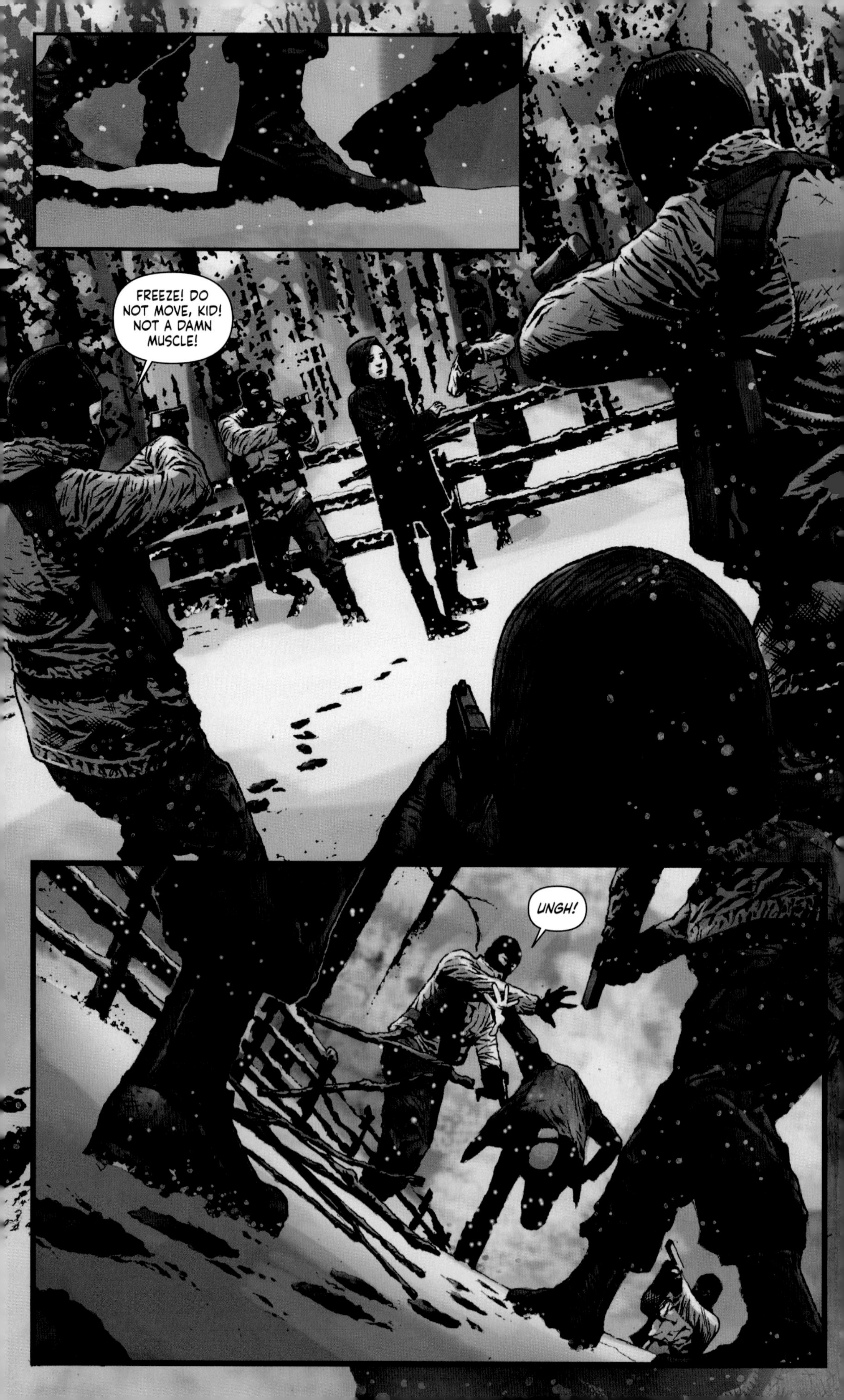
FREEZE! DO NOT MOVE, KID! NOT A DAMN MUSCLE!
UNGH!

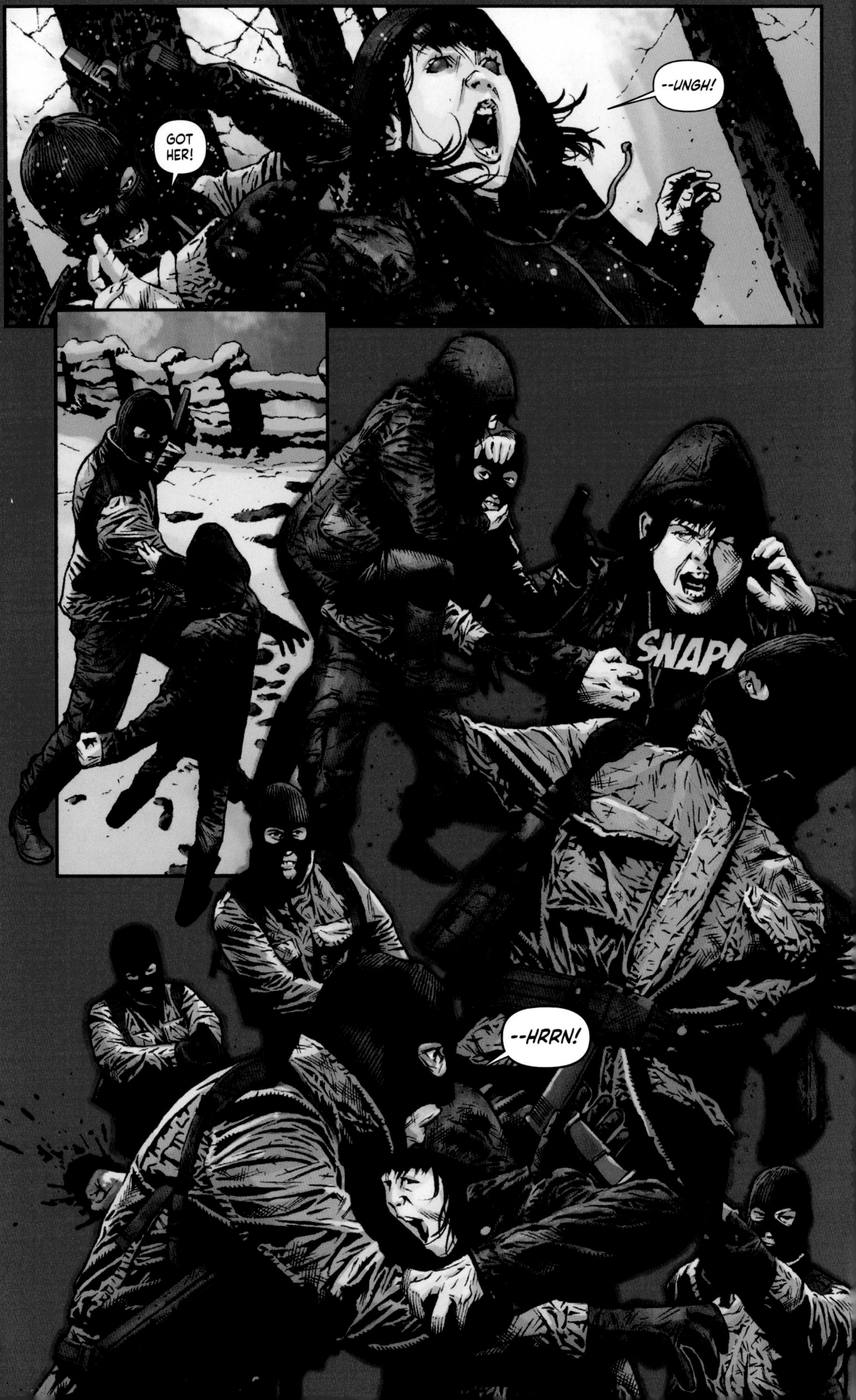
GOT HER!
--UNGH!
SNAP!
--HRRN!

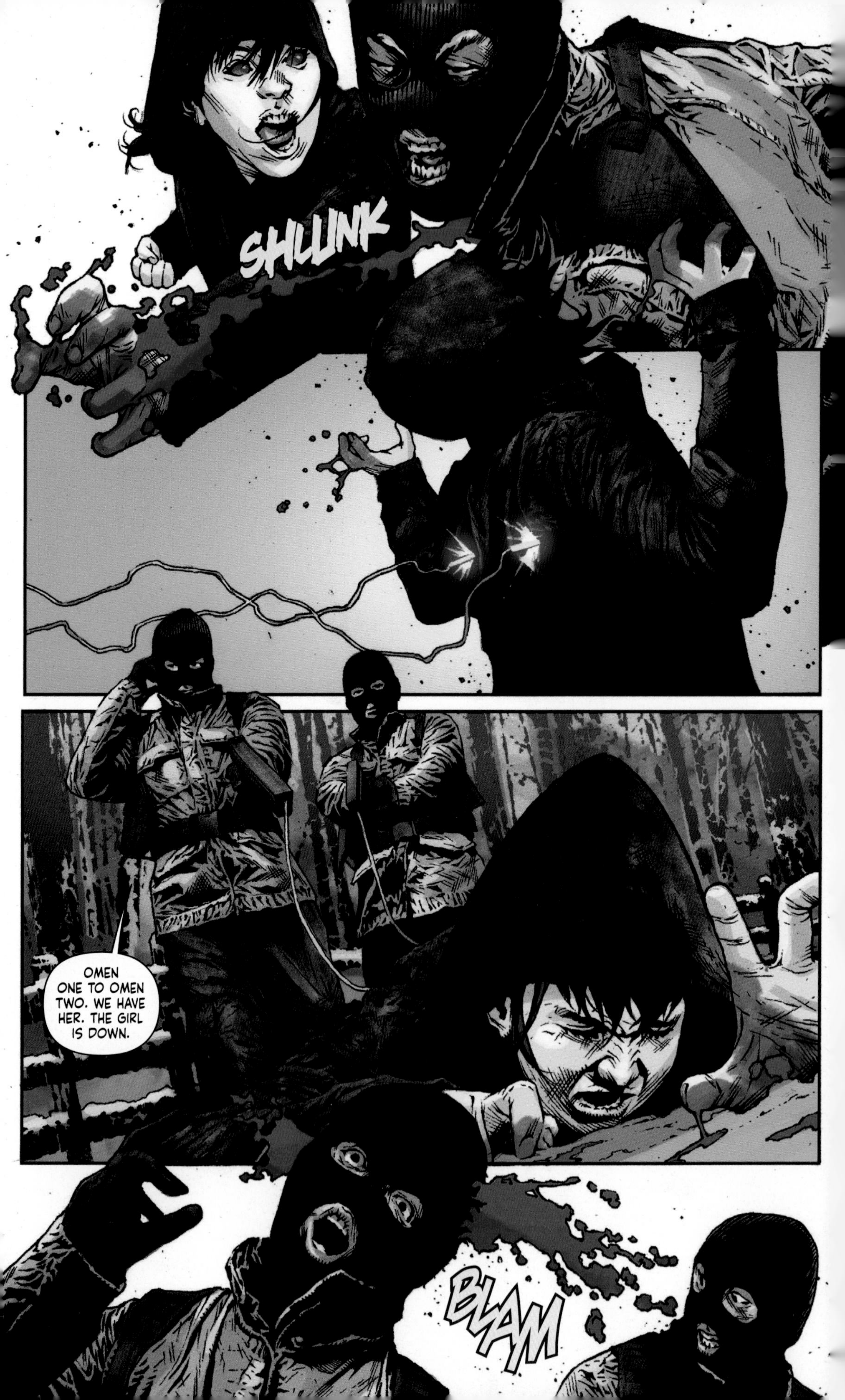
SHLUNK
OMEN ONE TO OMEN TWO. WE HAVE HER. THE GIRL IS DOWN.
BLAM

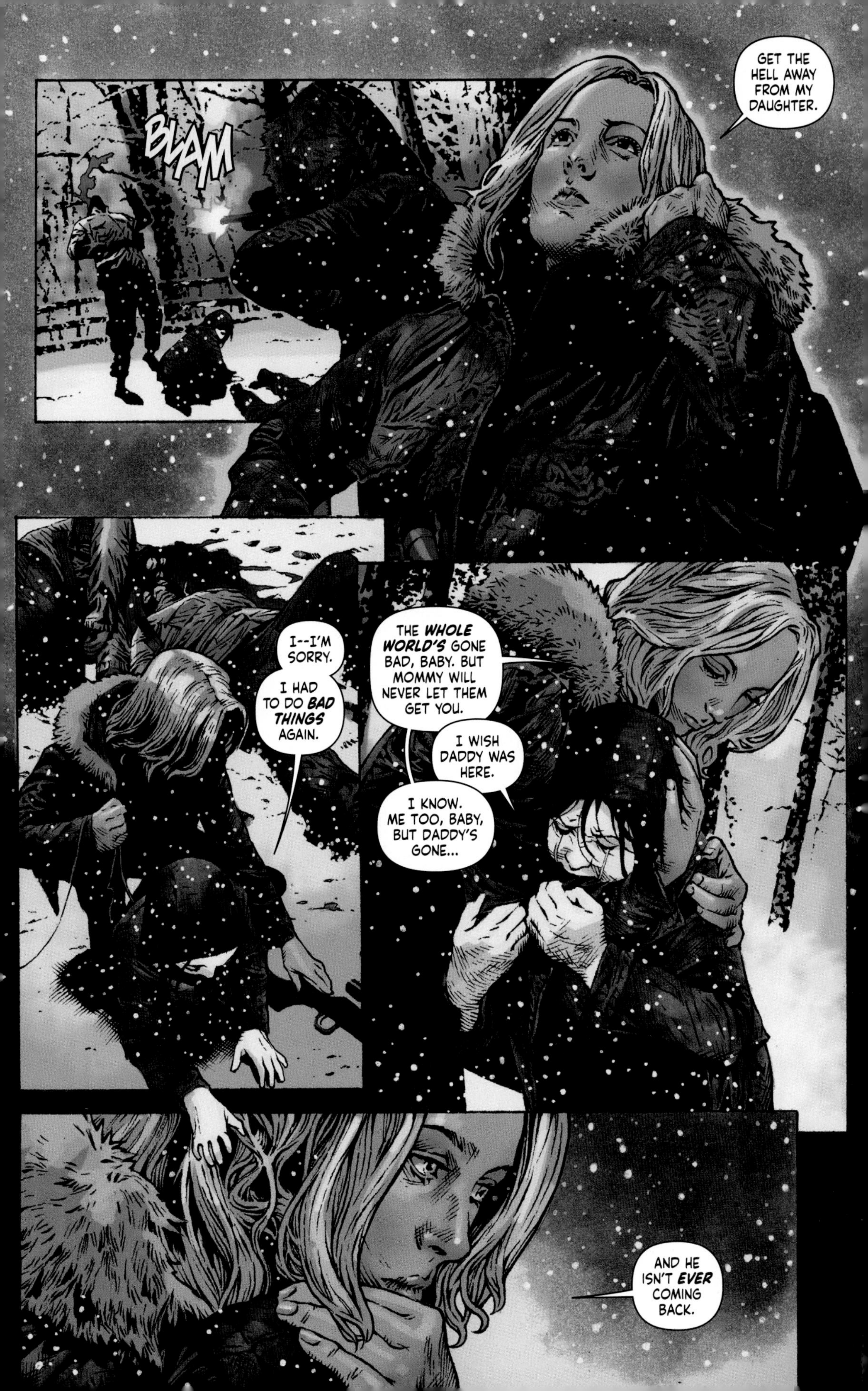
BLAM
GET THE HELL AWAY FROM MY DAUGHTER.
I--I'M SORRY.
I HAD TO DO BAD THINGS AGAIN.
THE WHOLE WORLD'S GONE BAD, BABY. BUT MOMMY WILL NEVER LET THEM GET YOU.
I WISH DADDY WAS HERE.
I KNOW. ME TOO, BABY, BUT DADDY'S GONE...
AND HE ISN'T EVER COMING BACK.

# BLOOD
# SALV

# THE BOOK (

# SHOT
## TION
## F REVENGE

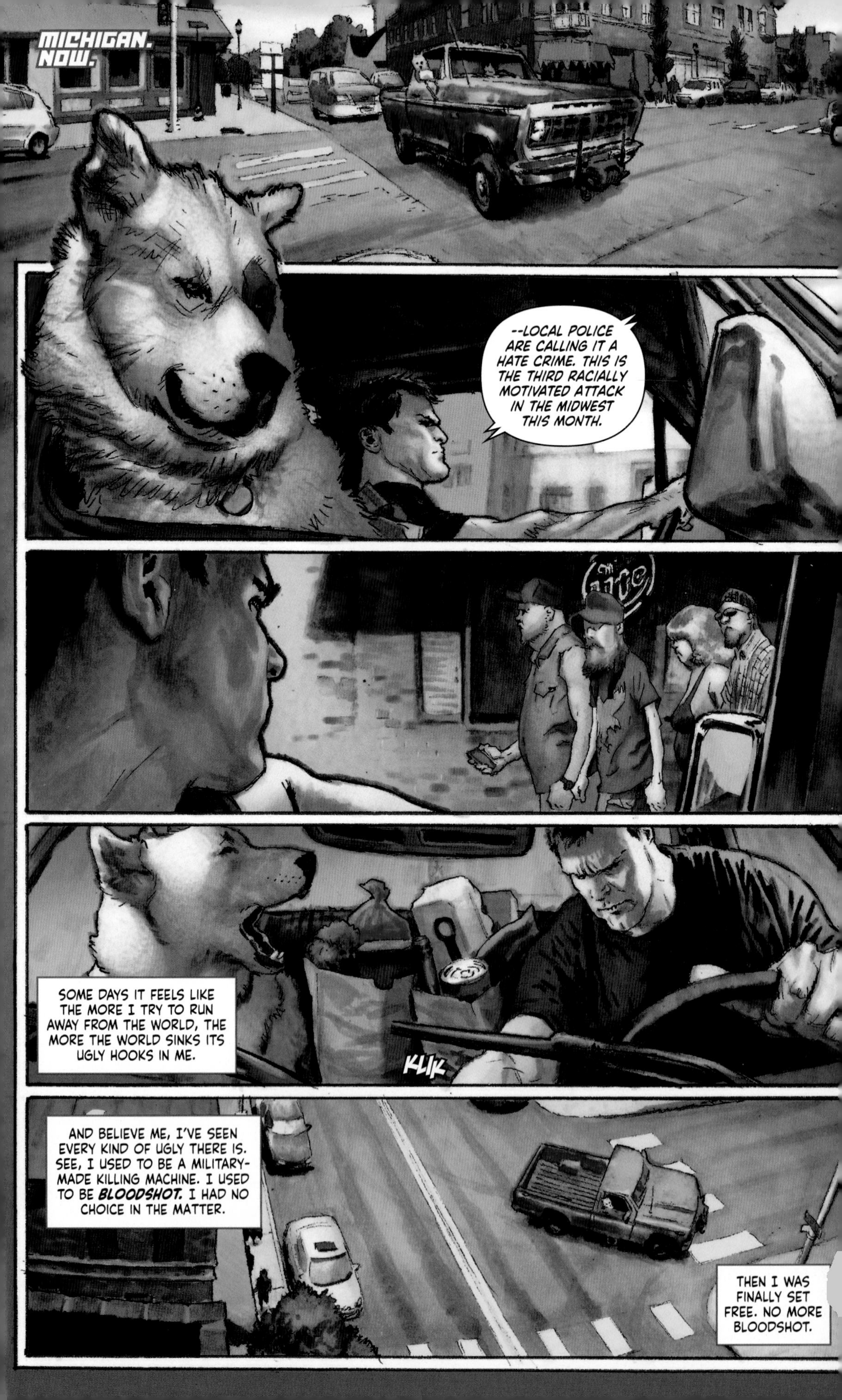
MICHIGAN. NOW.
--LOCAL POLICE ARE CALLING IT A HATE CRIME. THIS IS THE THIRD RACIALLY MOTIVATED ATTACK IN THE MIDWEST THIS MONTH.
SOME DAYS IT FEELS LIKE THE MORE I TRY TO RUN AWAY FROM THE WORLD, THE MORE THE WORLD SINKS ITS UGLY HOOKS IN ME.
KLIK
AND BELIEVE ME, I'VE SEEN EVERY KIND OF UGLY THERE IS. SEE, I USED TO BE A MILITARY-MADE KILLING MACHINE. I USED TO BE ***BLOODSHOT.*** I HAD NO CHOICE IN THE MATTER.
THEN I WAS FINALLY SET FREE. NO MORE BLOODSHOT.

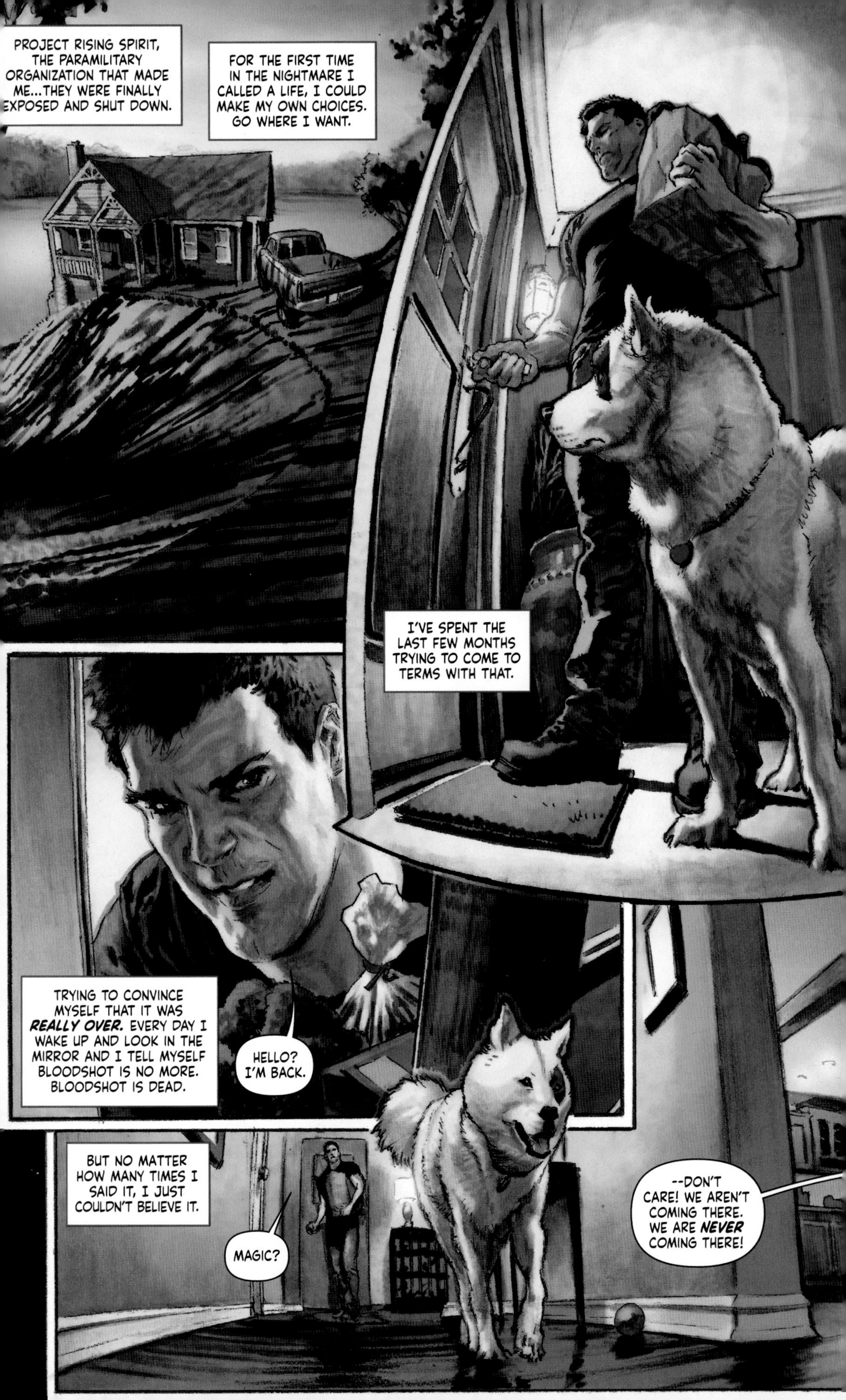
PROJECT RISING SPIRIT, THE PARAMILITARY ORGANIZATION THAT MADE ME...THEY WERE FINALLY EXPOSED AND SHUT DOWN.
FOR THE FIRST TIME IN THE NIGHTMARE I CALLED A LIFE, I COULD MAKE MY OWN CHOICES. GO WHERE I WANT.
I'VE SPENT THE LAST FEW MONTHS TRYING TO COME TO TERMS WITH THAT.
TRYING TO CONVINCE MYSELF THAT IT WAS **REALLY OVER.** EVERY DAY I WAKE UP AND LOOK IN THE MIRROR AND I TELL MYSELF BLOODSHOT IS NO MORE. BLOODSHOT IS DEAD.
HELLO? I'M BACK.
BUT NO MATTER HOW MANY TIMES I SAID IT, I JUST COULDN'T BELIEVE IT.
MAGIC?
--DON'T CARE! WE AREN'T COMING THERE. WE ARE **NEVER** COMING THERE!

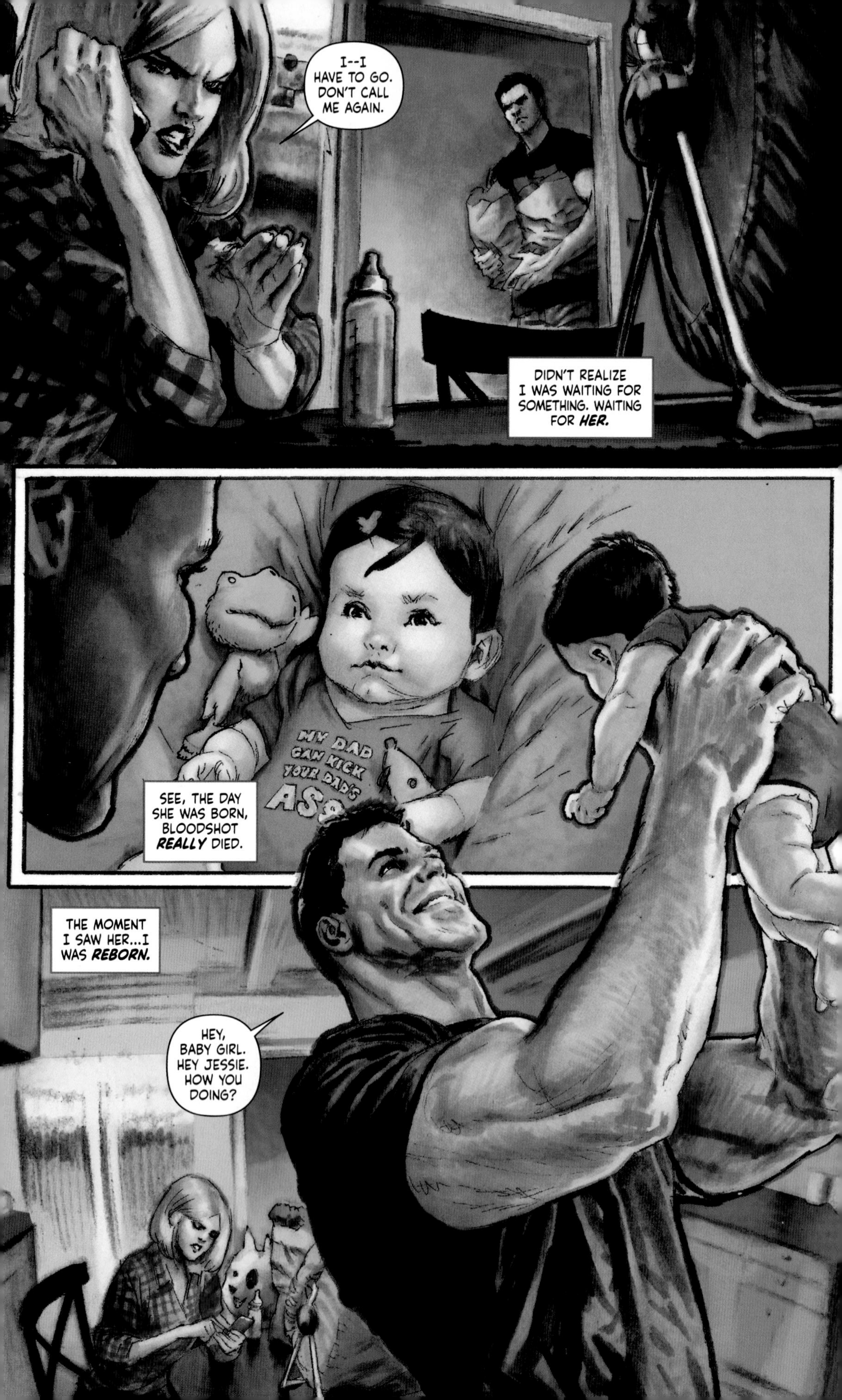
I--I HAVE TO GO. DON'T CALL ME AGAIN.
DIDN'T REALIZE I WAS WAITING FOR SOMETHING. WAITING FOR HER.
MY DAD CAN KICK YOUR DAD'S ASS
SEE, THE DAY SHE WAS BORN, BLOODSHOT REALLY DIED.
THE MOMENT I SAW HER...I WAS REBORN.
HEY, BABY GIRL. HEY JESSIE. HOW YOU DOING?

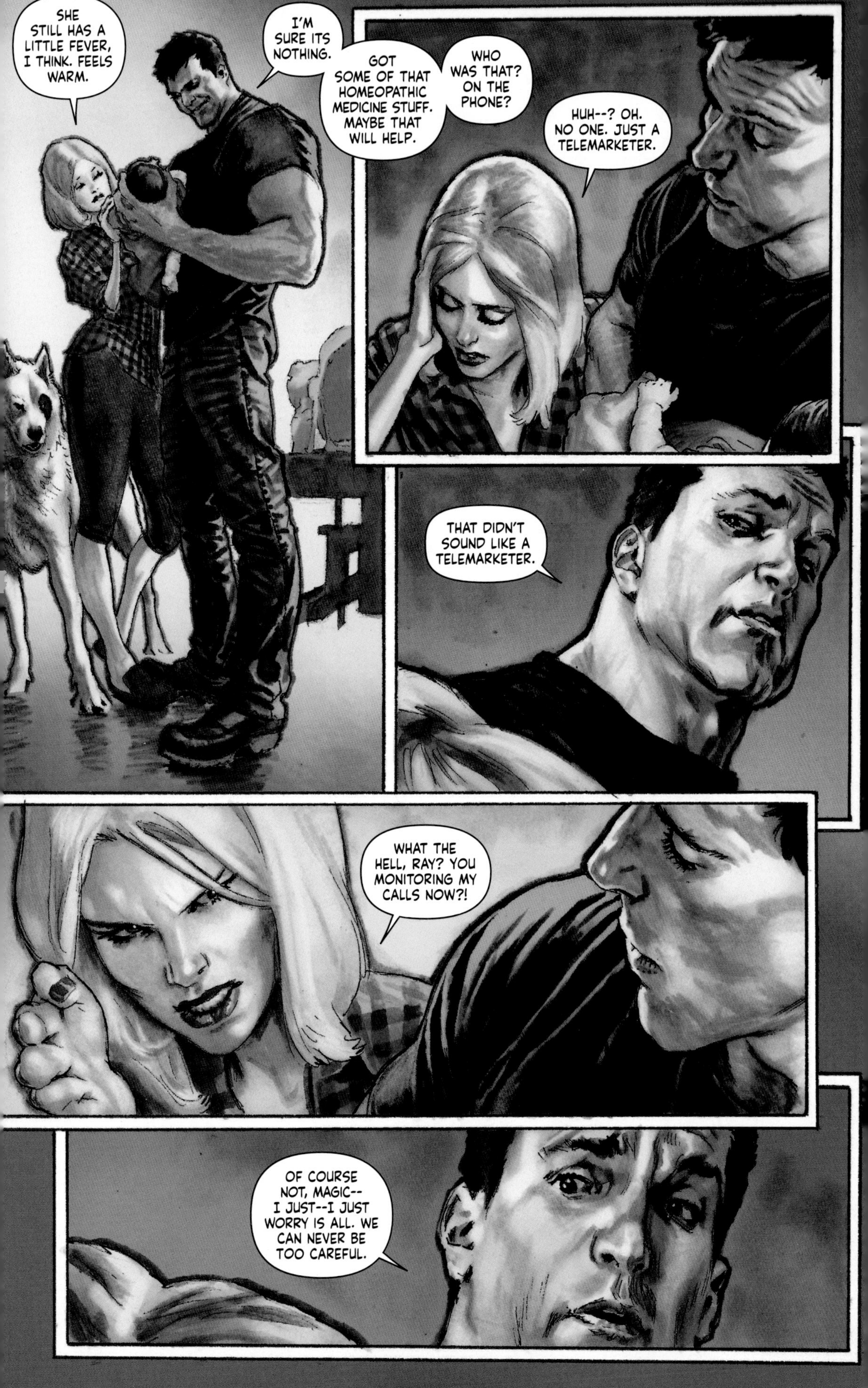

SHE STILL HAS A LITTLE FEVER, I THINK. FEELS WARM.
I'M SURE ITS NOTHING.
GOT SOME OF THAT HOMEOPATHIC MEDICINE STUFF. MAYBE THAT WILL HELP.
WHO WAS THAT? ON THE PHONE?
HUH--? OH. NO ONE. JUST A TELEMARKETER.
THAT DIDN'T SOUND LIKE A TELEMARKETER.
WHAT THE HELL, RAY? YOU MONITORING MY CALLS NOW?!
OF COURSE NOT, MAGIC-- I JUST--I JUST WORRY IS ALL. WE CAN NEVER BE TOO CAREFUL.

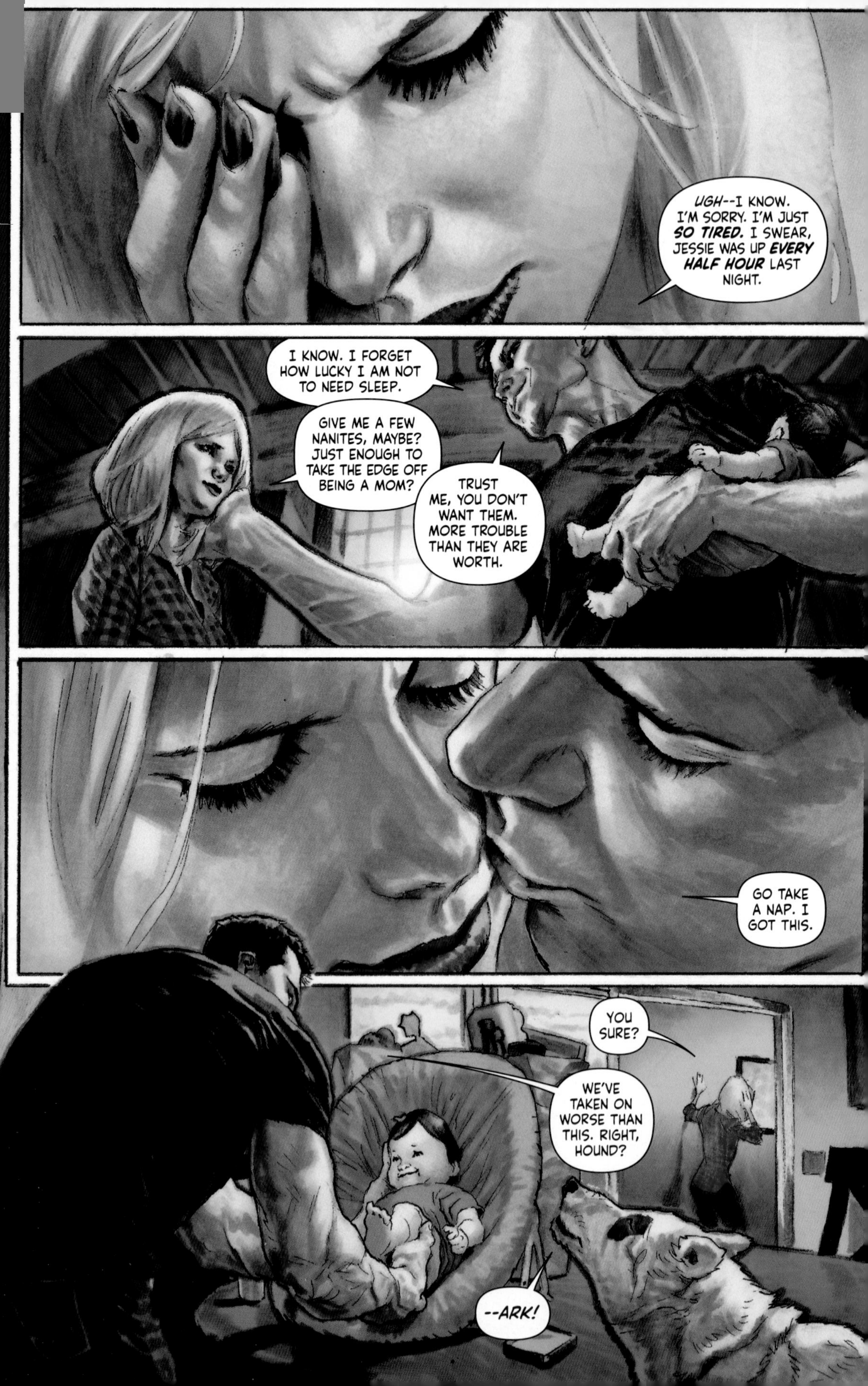
*UGH*--I KNOW. I'M SORRY. I'M JUST **SO TIRED.** I SWEAR, JESSIE WAS UP ***EVERY HALF HOUR*** LAST NIGHT.
I KNOW. I FORGET HOW LUCKY I AM NOT TO NEED SLEEP.
GIVE ME A FEW NANITES, MAYBE? JUST ENOUGH TO TAKE THE EDGE OFF BEING A MOM?
TRUST ME, YOU DON'T WANT THEM. MORE TROUBLE THAN THEY ARE WORTH.
GO TAKE A NAP. I GOT THIS.
YOU SURE?
WE'VE TAKEN ON WORSE THAN THIS. RIGHT, HOUND?
*--ARK!*

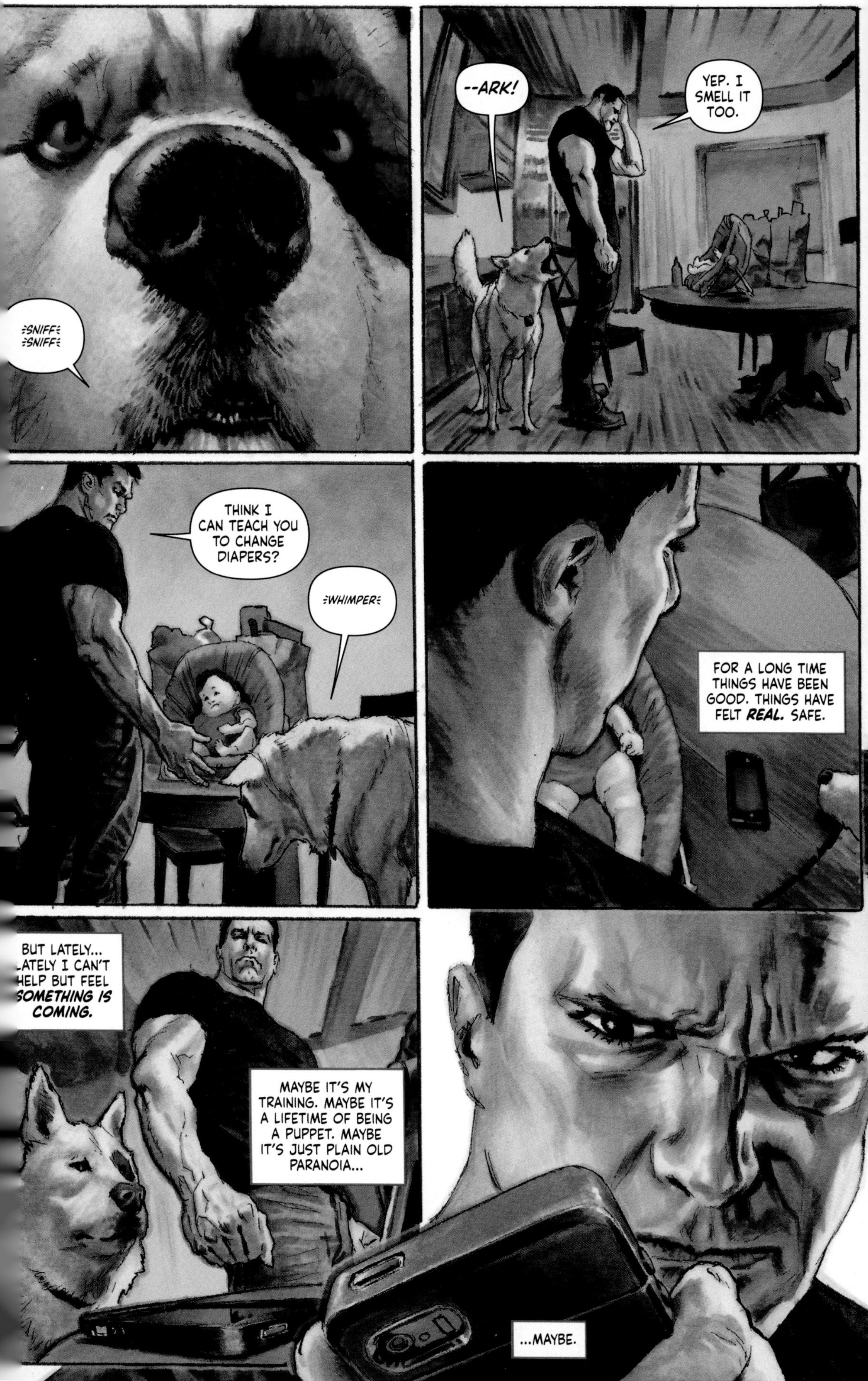

SNIFF SNIFF
--ARK!
YEP. I SMELL IT TOO.
THINK I CAN TEACH YOU TO CHANGE DIAPERS?
WHIMPER
FOR A LONG TIME THINGS HAVE BEEN GOOD. THINGS HAVE FELT **REAL.** SAFE.
BUT LATELY... LATELY I CAN'T HELP BUT FEEL ***SOMETHING IS COMING.***
MAYBE IT'S MY TRAINING. MAYBE IT'S A LIFETIME OF BEING A PUPPET. MAYBE IT'S JUST PLAIN OLD PARANOIA...
...MAYBE.

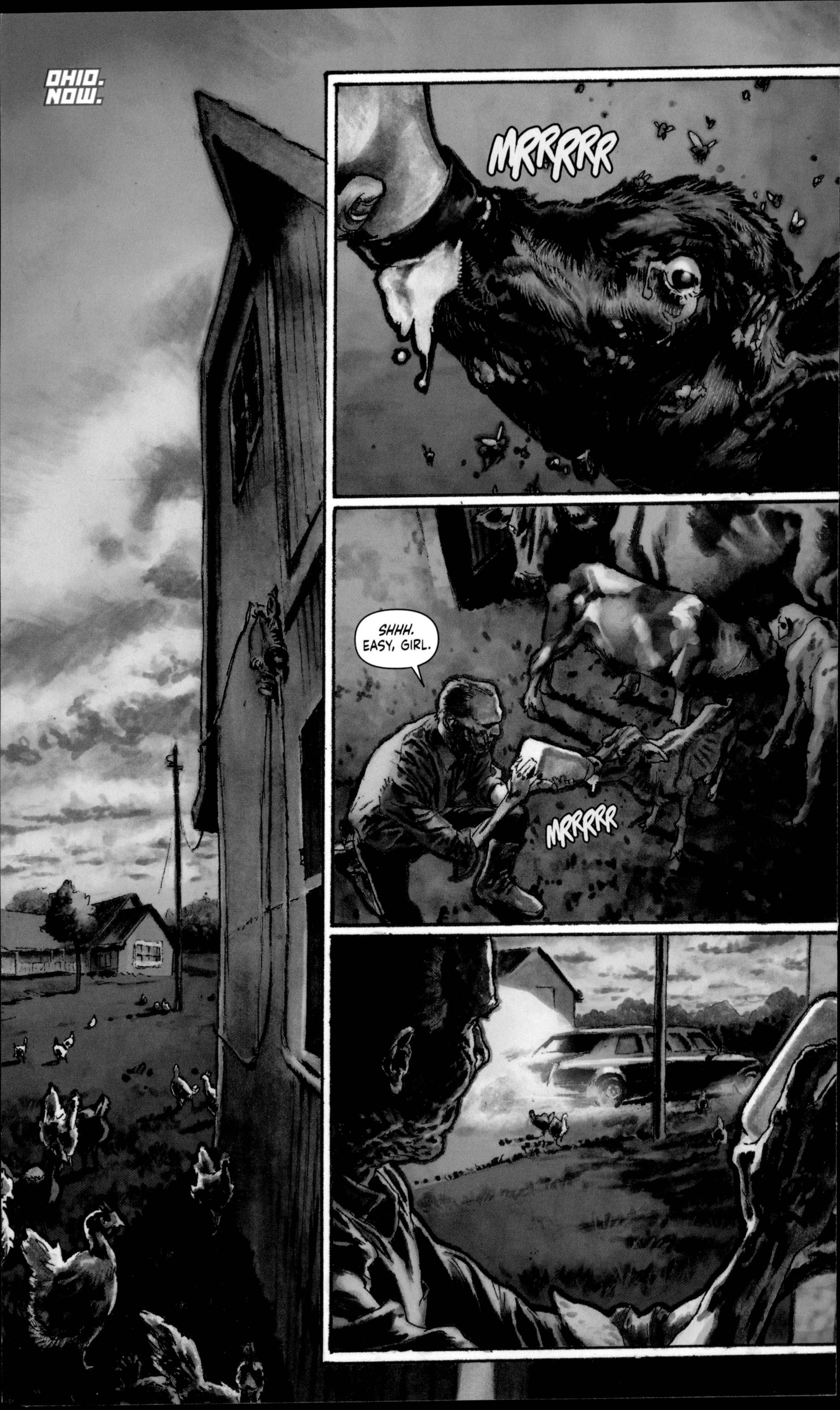

OHIO. NOW.
MRRRRR
SHHH. EASY, GIRL.
MRRRRR

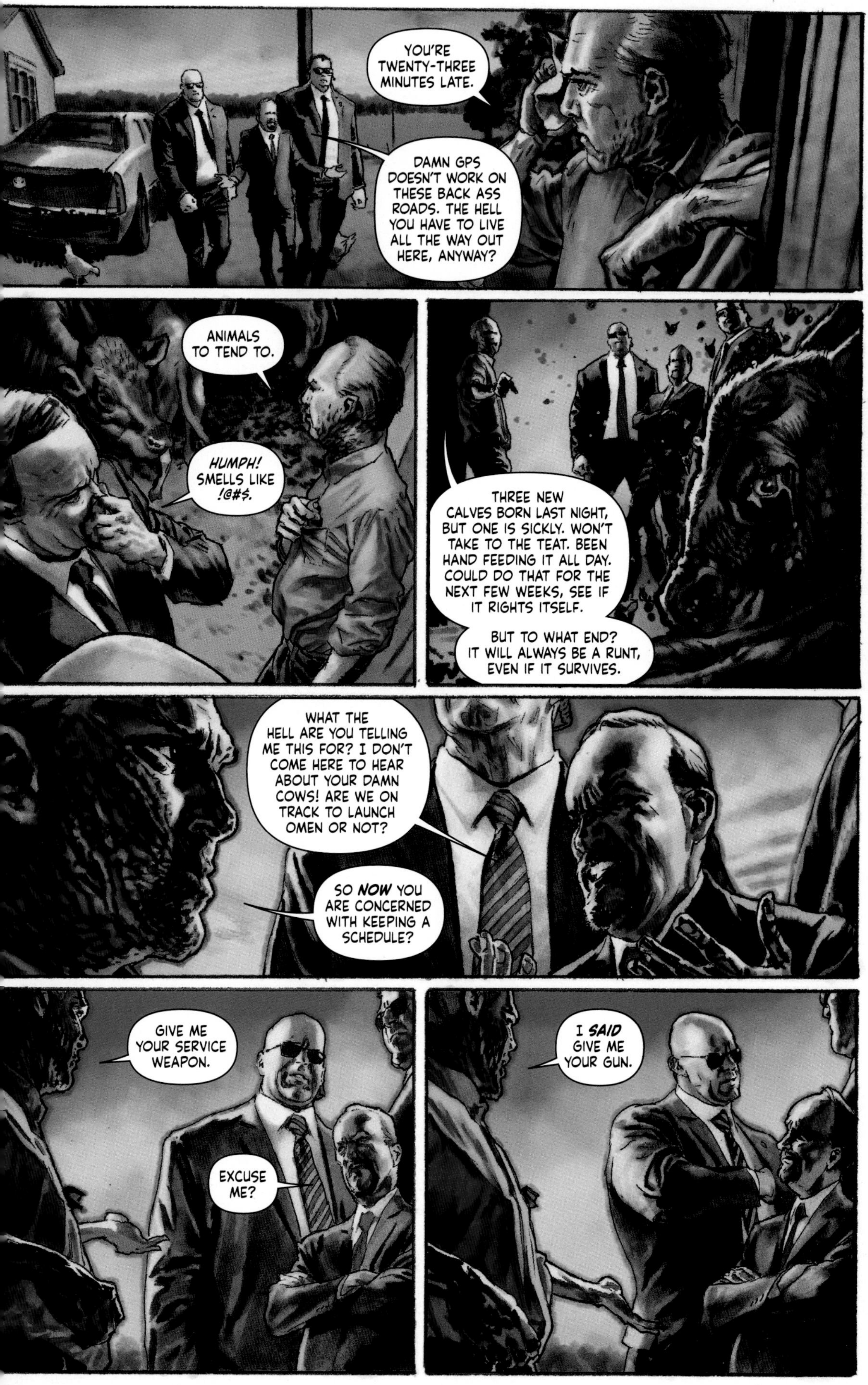
YOU'RE TWENTY-THREE MINUTES LATE.
DAMN GPS DOESN'T WORK ON THESE BACK ASS ROADS. THE HELL YOU HAVE TO LIVE ALL THE WAY OUT HERE, ANYWAY?
ANIMALS TO TEND TO.
HUMPH! SMELLS LIKE !@#$.
THREE NEW CALVES BORN LAST NIGHT, BUT ONE IS SICKLY. WON'T TAKE TO THE TEAT. BEEN HAND FEEDING IT ALL DAY. COULD DO THAT FOR THE NEXT FEW WEEKS, SEE IF IT RIGHTS ITSELF.
BUT TO WHAT END? IT WILL ALWAYS BE A RUNT, EVEN IF IT SURVIVES.
WHAT THE HELL ARE YOU TELLING ME THIS FOR? I DON'T COME HERE TO HEAR ABOUT YOUR DAMN COWS! ARE WE ON TRACK TO LAUNCH OMEN OR NOT?
SO NOW YOU ARE CONCERNED WITH KEEPING A SCHEDULE?
GIVE ME YOUR SERVICE WEAPON.
EXCUSE ME?
I SAID GIVE ME YOUR GUN.

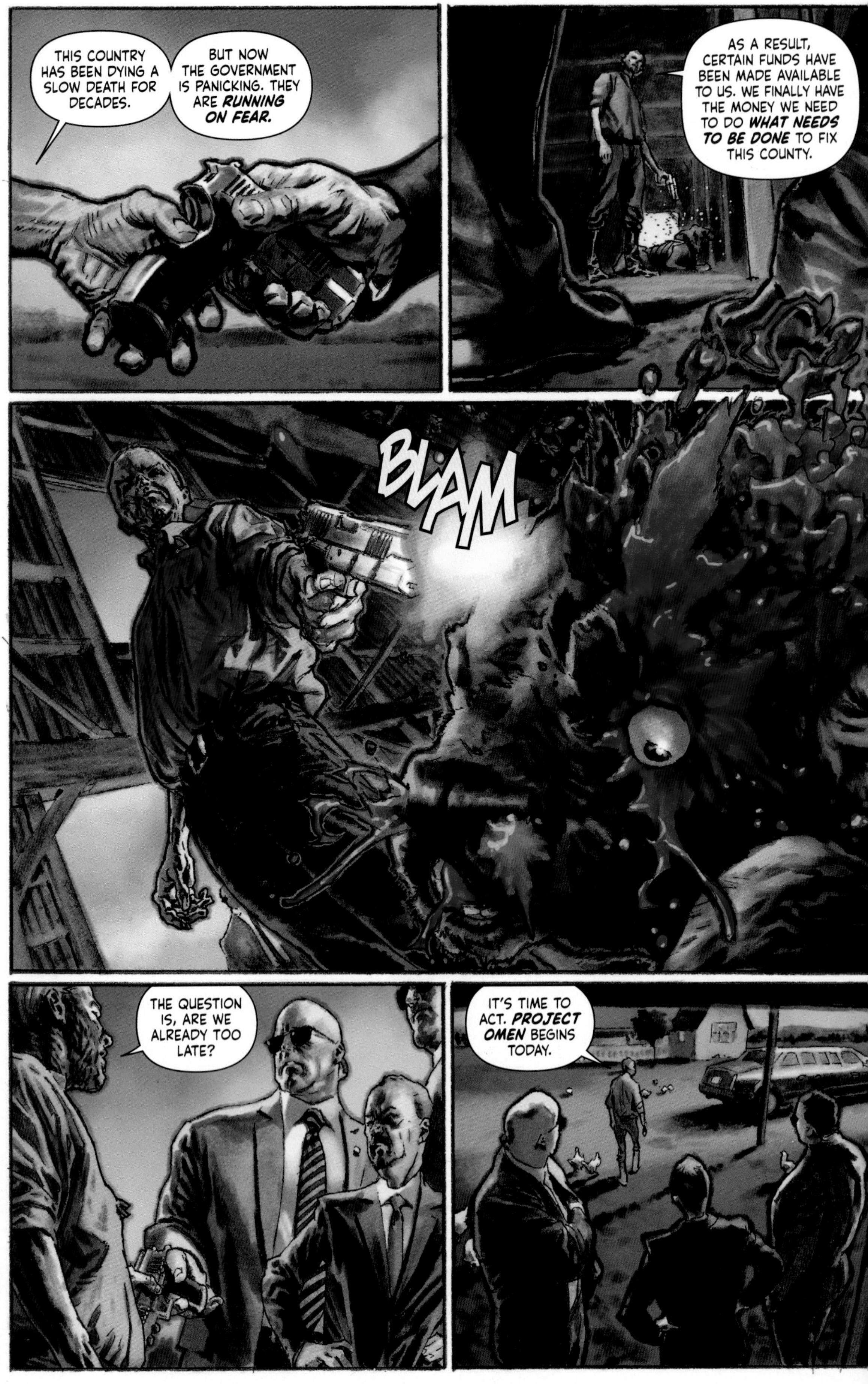
THIS COUNTRY HAS BEEN DYING A SLOW DEATH FOR DECADES.
BUT NOW THE GOVERNMENT IS PANICKING. THEY ARE *RUNNING ON FEAR.*
AS A RESULT, CERTAIN FUNDS HAVE BEEN MADE AVAILABLE TO US. WE FINALLY HAVE THE MONEY WE NEED TO DO *WHAT NEEDS TO BE DONE* TO FIX THIS COUNTY.
BLAM
THE QUESTION IS, ARE WE ALREADY TOO LATE?
IT'S TIME TO ACT. *PROJECT OMEN* BEGINS TODAY.

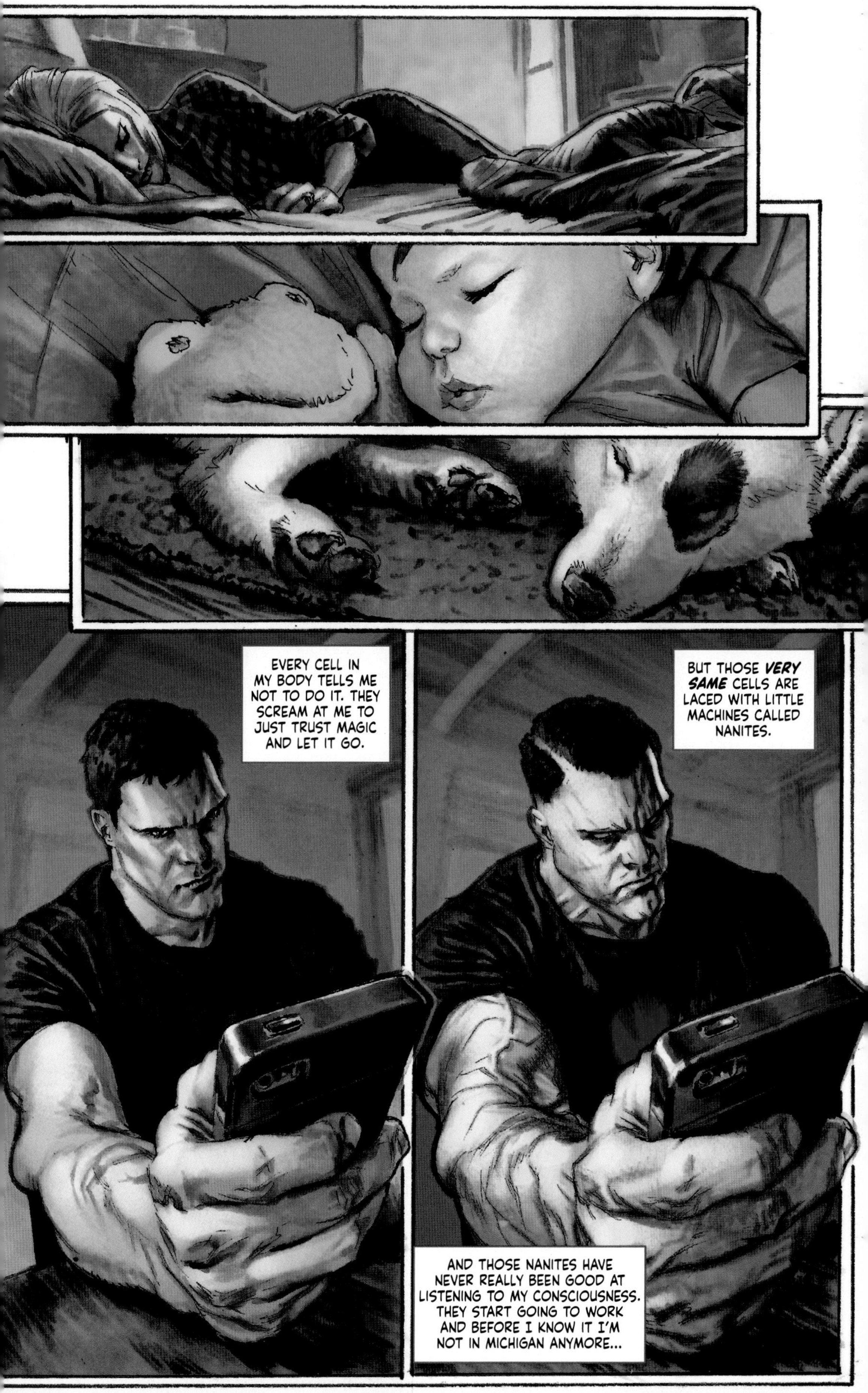
EVERY CELL IN MY BODY TELLS ME NOT TO DO IT. THEY SCREAM AT ME TO JUST TRUST MAGIC AND LET IT GO.
BUT THOSE **VERY SAME** CELLS ARE LACED WITH LITTLE MACHINES CALLED NANITES.
AND THOSE NANITES HAVE NEVER REALLY BEEN GOOD AT LISTENING TO MY CONSCIOUSNESS. THEY START GOING TO WORK AND BEFORE I KNOW IT I'M NOT IN MICHIGAN ANYMORE...

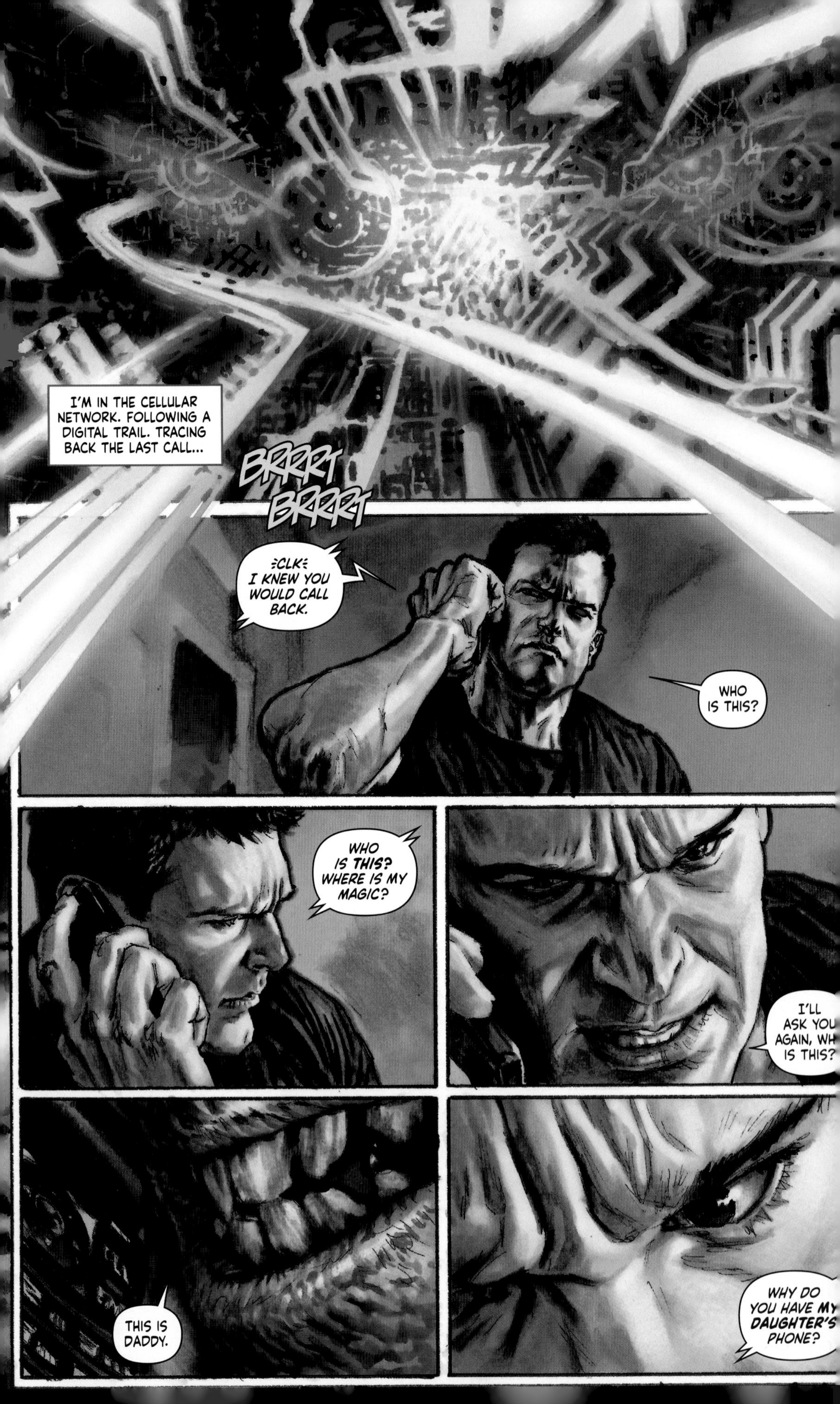
I'M IN THE CELLULAR NETWORK. FOLLOWING A DIGITAL TRAIL. TRACING BACK THE LAST CALL...
BRRRT BRRRT
CLK
I KNEW YOU WOULD CALL BACK.
WHO IS THIS?
WHO IS THIS? WHERE IS MY MAGIC?
I'LL ASK YOU AGAIN, WH IS THIS?
THIS IS DADDY.
WHY DO YOU HAVE MY DAUGHTER'S PHONE?

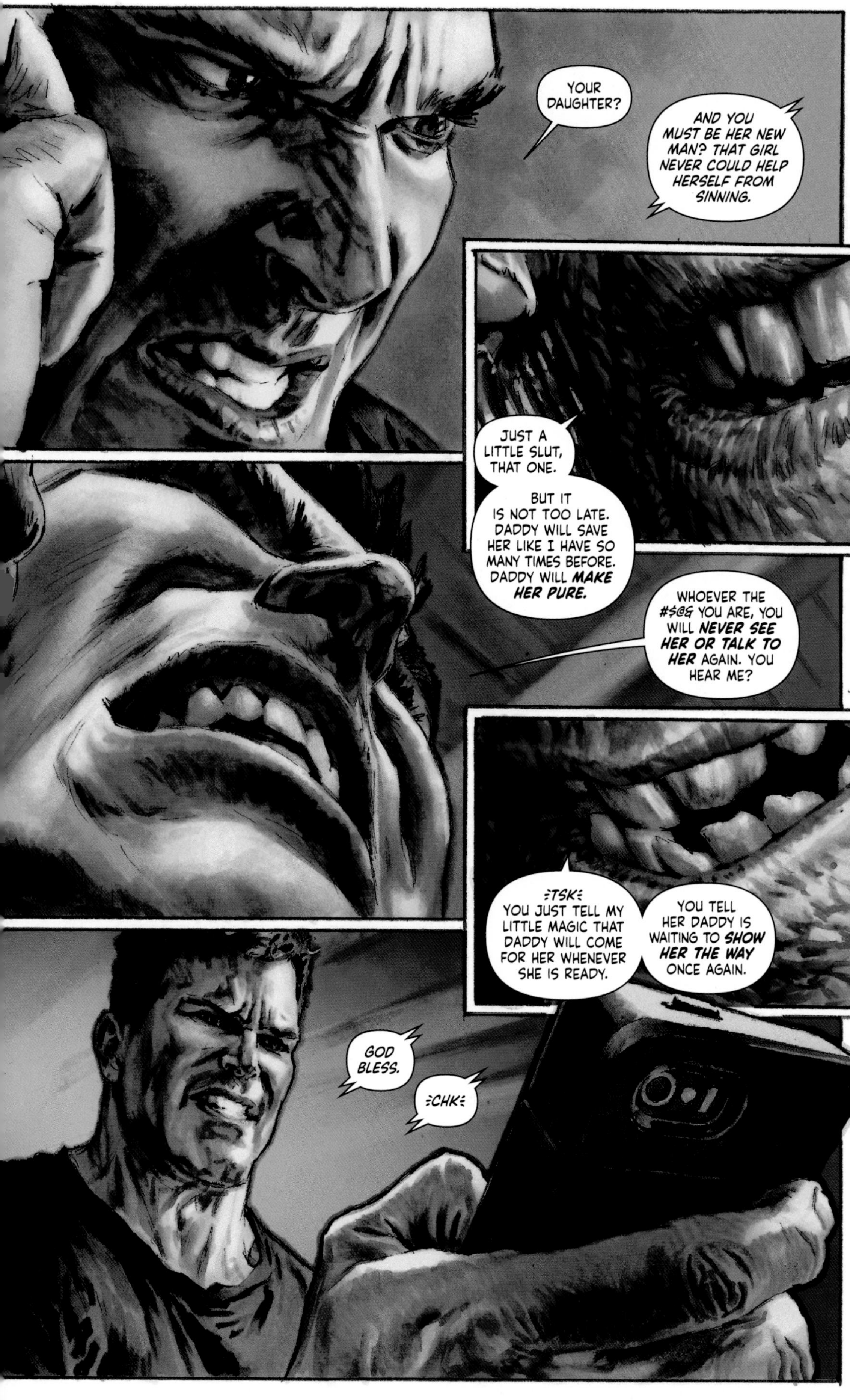
YOUR DAUGHTER?
AND YOU MUST BE HER NEW MAN? THAT GIRL NEVER COULD HELP HERSELF FROM SINNING.
JUST A LITTLE SLUT, THAT ONE.
BUT IT IS NOT TOO LATE. DADDY WILL SAVE HER LIKE I HAVE SO MANY TIMES BEFORE. DADDY WILL MAKE HER PURE.
WHOEVER THE #$@& YOU ARE, YOU WILL NEVER SEE HER OR TALK TO HER AGAIN. YOU HEAR ME?
TSK
YOU JUST TELL MY LITTLE MAGIC THAT DADDY WILL COME FOR HER WHENEVER SHE IS READY.
YOU TELL HER DADDY IS WAITING TO SHOW HER THE WAY ONCE AGAIN.
GOD BLESS.
CHK

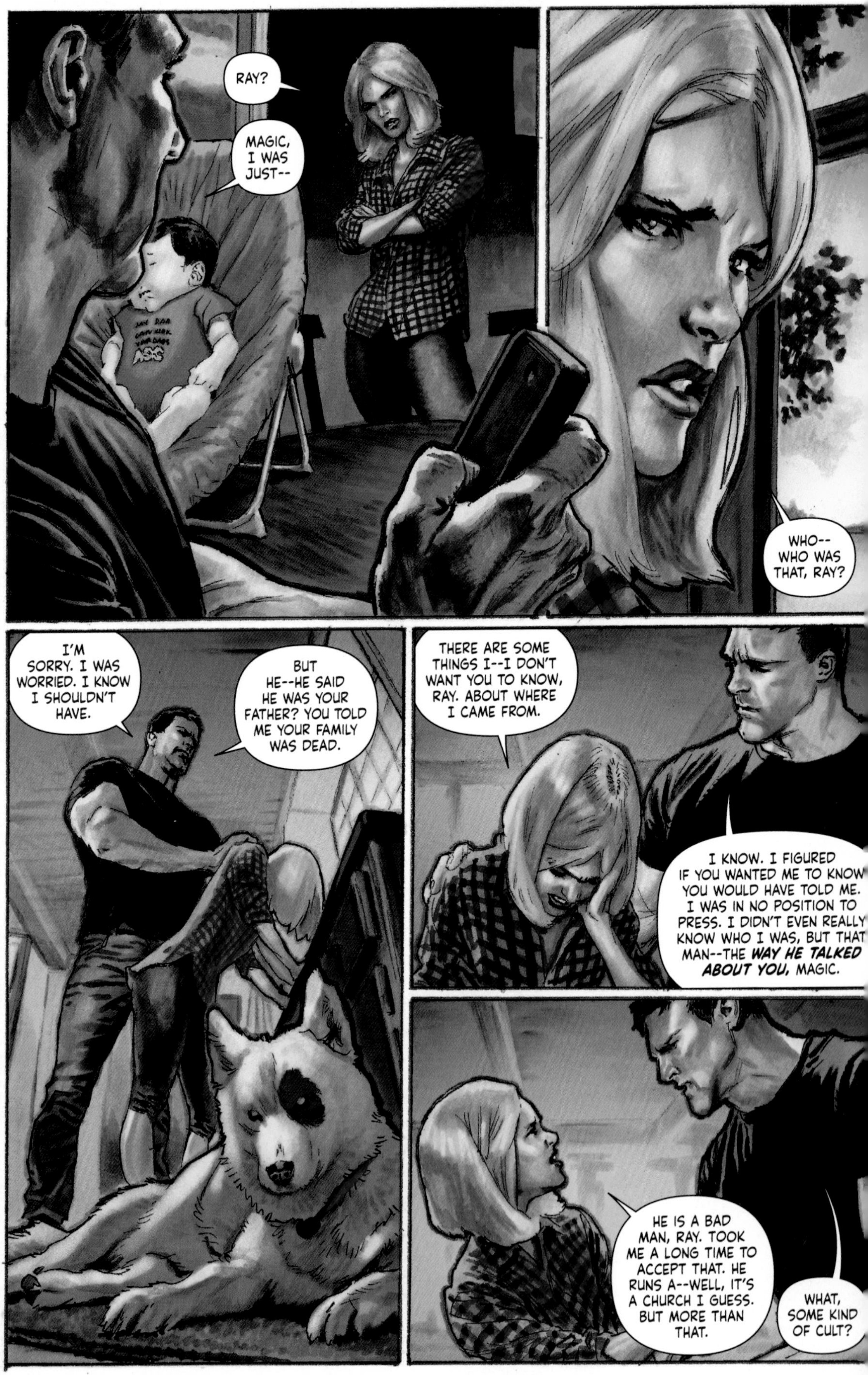
RAY?
MAGIC, I WAS JUST--
WHO-- WHO WAS THAT, RAY?
I'M SORRY. I WAS WORRIED. I KNOW I SHOULDN'T HAVE.
BUT HE--HE SAID HE WAS YOUR FATHER? YOU TOLD ME YOUR FAMILY WAS DEAD.
THERE ARE SOME THINGS I--I DON'T WANT YOU TO KNOW, RAY. ABOUT WHERE I CAME FROM.
I KNOW. I FIGURED IF YOU WANTED ME TO KNOW YOU WOULD HAVE TOLD ME. I WAS IN NO POSITION TO PRESS. I DIDN'T EVEN REALLY KNOW WHO I WAS, BUT THAT MAN--THE WAY HE TALKED ABOUT YOU, MAGIC.
HE IS A BAD MAN, RAY. TOOK ME A LONG TIME TO ACCEPT THAT. HE RUNS A--WELL, IT'S A CHURCH I GUESS. BUT MORE THAN THAT.
WHAT, SOME KIND OF CULT?

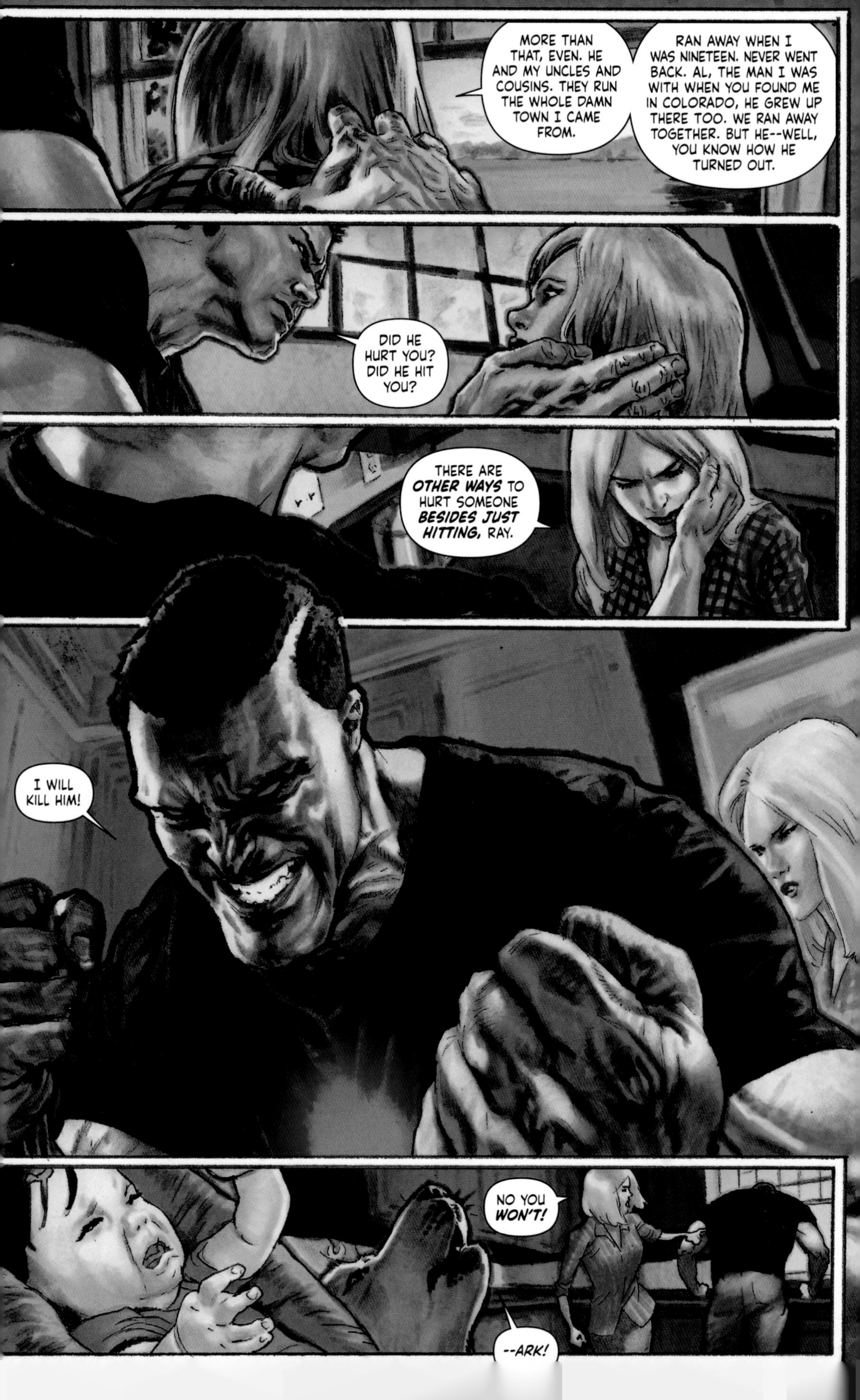

MORE THAN THAT, EVEN. HE AND MY UNCLES AND COUSINS. THEY RUN THE WHOLE DAMN TOWN I CAME FROM.
RAN AWAY WHEN I WAS NINETEEN. NEVER WENT BACK. AL, THE MAN I WAS WITH WHEN YOU FOUND ME IN COLORADO, HE GREW UP THERE TOO. WE RAN AWAY TOGETHER. BUT HE--WELL, YOU KNOW HOW HE TURNED OUT.
DID HE HURT YOU? DID HE HIT YOU?
THERE ARE OTHER WAYS TO HURT SOMEONE BESIDES JUST HITTING, RAY.
I WILL KILL HIM!
NO YOU WON'T!
--ARK!

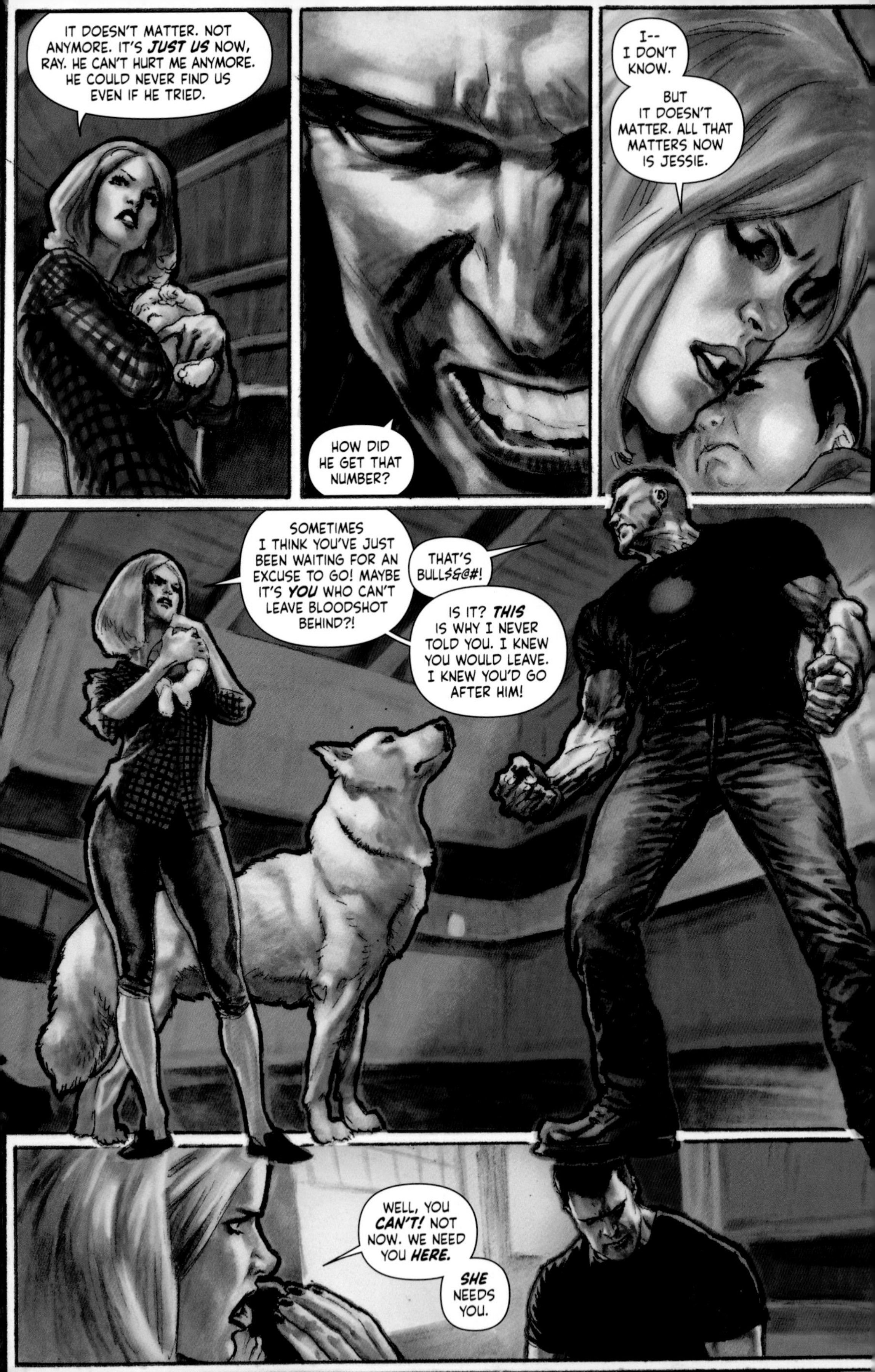
IT DOESN'T MATTER. NOT ANYMORE. IT'S JUST US NOW, RAY. HE CAN'T HURT ME ANYMORE. HE COULD NEVER FIND US EVEN IF HE TRIED.
HOW DID HE GET THAT NUMBER?
I-- I DON'T KNOW.
BUT IT DOESN'T MATTER. ALL THAT MATTERS NOW IS JESSIE.
SOMETIMES I THINK YOU'VE JUST BEEN WAITING FOR AN EXCUSE TO GO! MAYBE IT'S YOU WHO CAN'T LEAVE BLOODSHOT BEHIND?!
THAT'S BULL$&@#!
IS IT? THIS IS WHY I NEVER TOLD YOU. I KNEW YOU WOULD LEAVE. I KNEW YOU'D GO AFTER HIM!
WELL, YOU CAN'T! NOT NOW. WE NEED YOU HERE.
SHE NEEDS YOU.

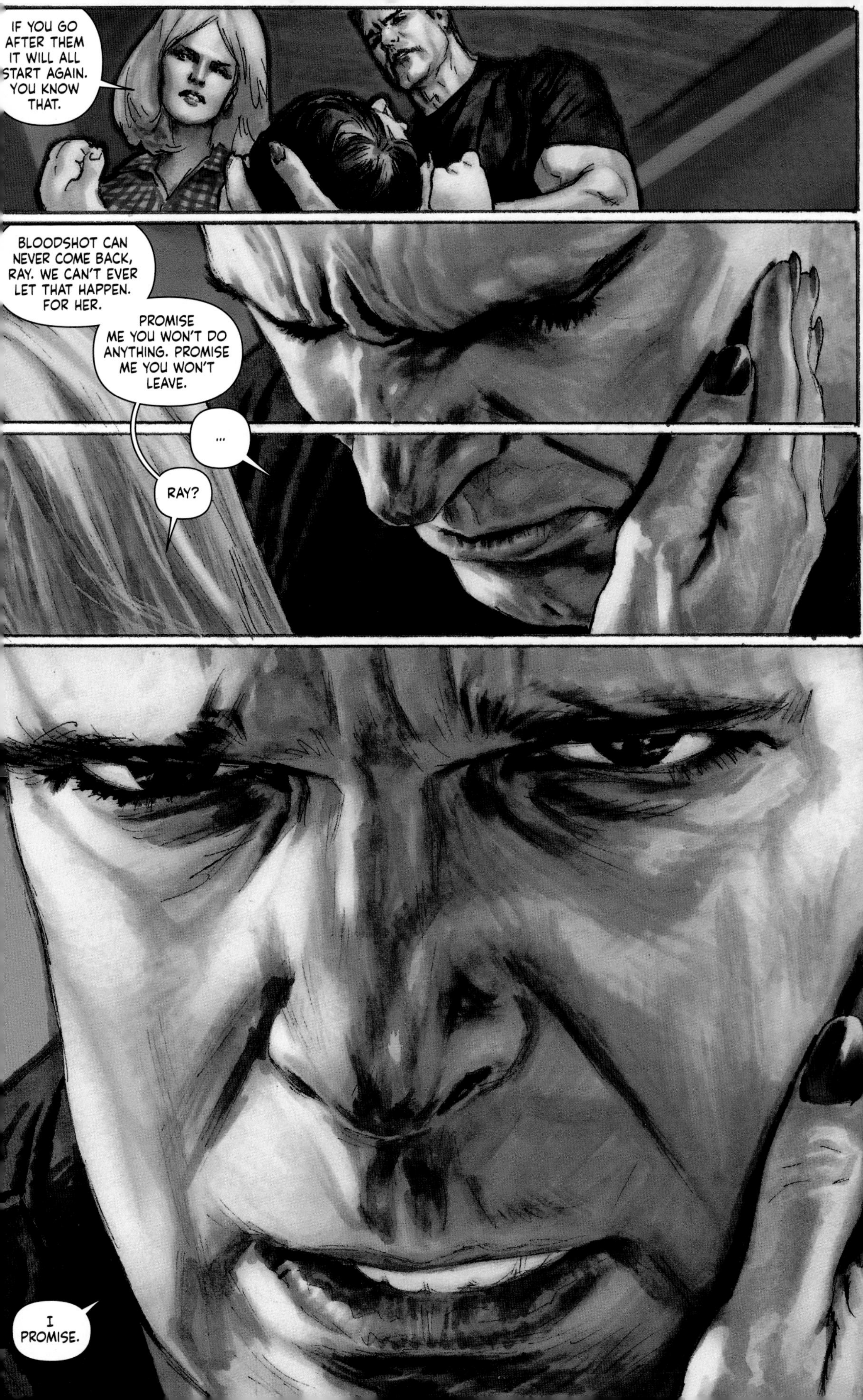
IF YOU GO AFTER THEM IT WILL ALL START AGAIN. YOU KNOW THAT.
BLOODSHOT CAN NEVER COME BACK, RAY. WE CAN'T EVER LET THAT HAPPEN. FOR HER.
PROMISE ME YOU WON'T DO ANYTHING. PROMISE ME YOU WON'T LEAVE.
...
RAY?
I PROMISE.

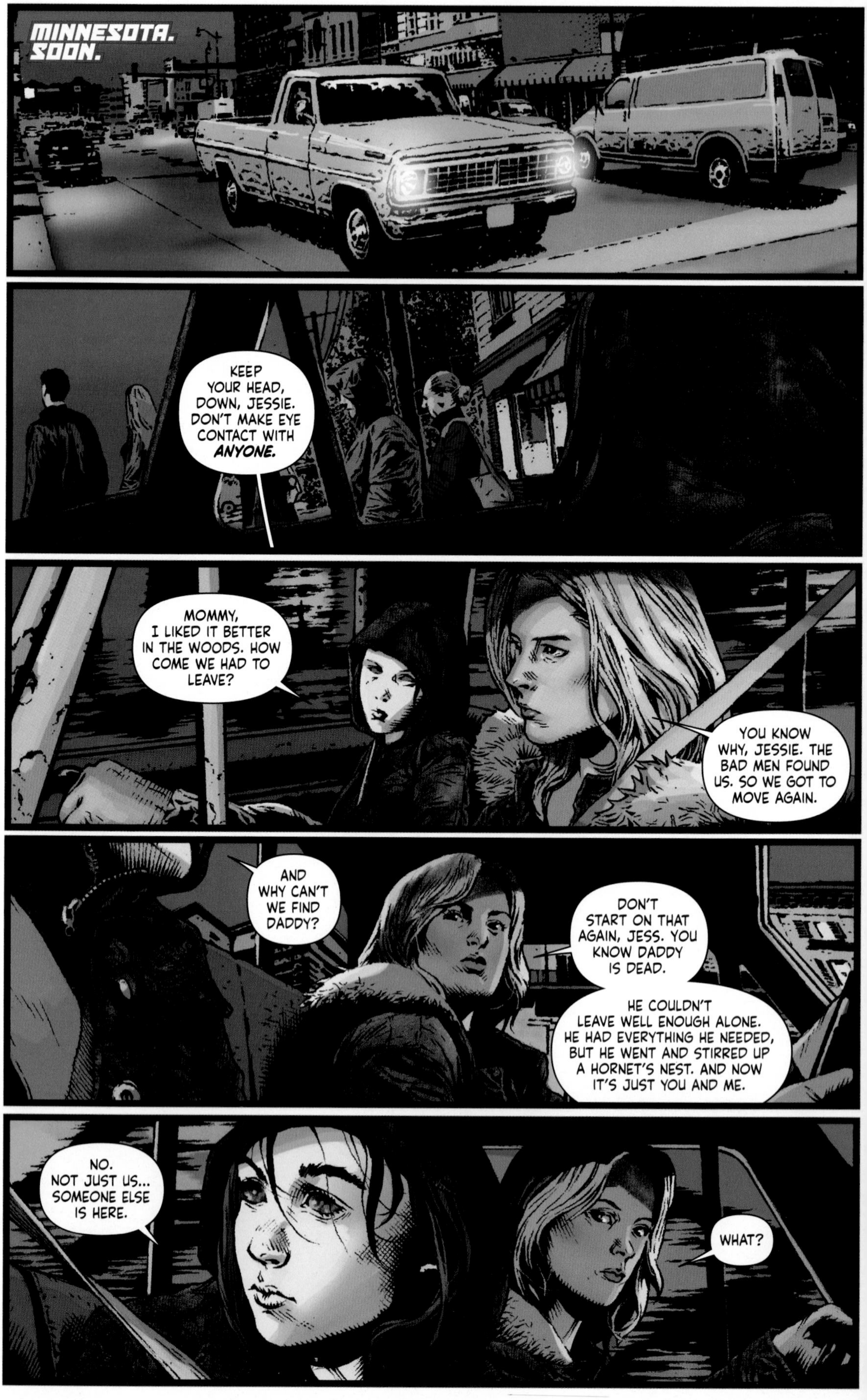
MINNESOTA. SOON.
KEEP YOUR HEAD, DOWN, JESSIE. DON'T MAKE EYE CONTACT WITH ANYONE.
MOMMY, I LIKED IT BETTER IN THE WOODS. HOW COME WE HAD TO LEAVE?
YOU KNOW WHY, JESSIE. THE BAD MEN FOUND US. SO WE GOT TO MOVE AGAIN.
AND WHY CAN'T WE FIND DADDY?
DON'T START ON THAT AGAIN, JESS. YOU KNOW DADDY IS DEAD.
HE COULDN'T LEAVE WELL ENOUGH ALONE. HE HAD EVERYTHING HE NEEDED, BUT HE WENT AND STIRRED UP A HORNET'S NEST. AND NOW IT'S JUST YOU AND ME.
NO. NOT JUST US... SOMEONE ELSE IS HERE.
WHAT?

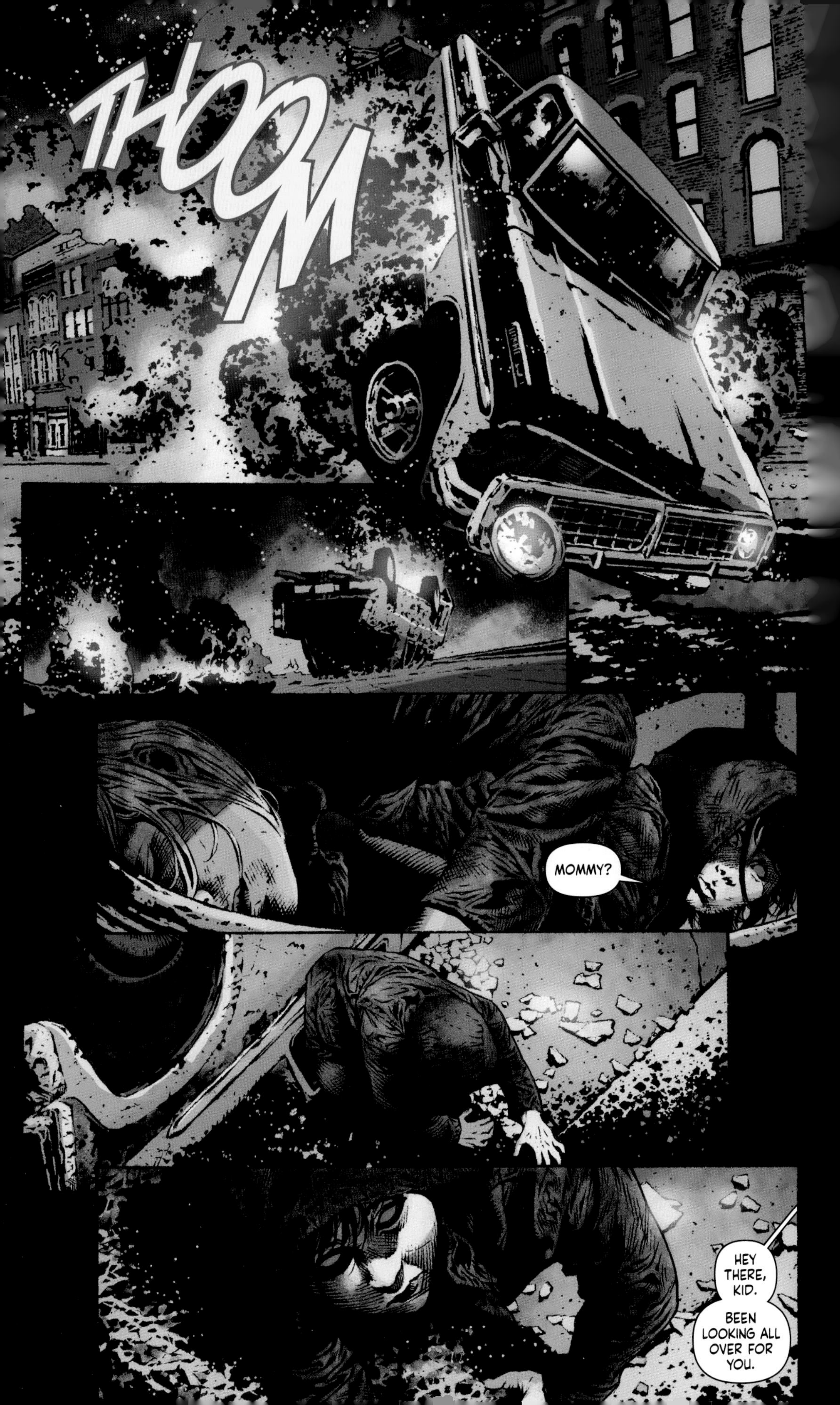
THOOM
MOMMY?
HEY THERE, KID.
BEEN LOOKING ALL OVER FOR YOU.

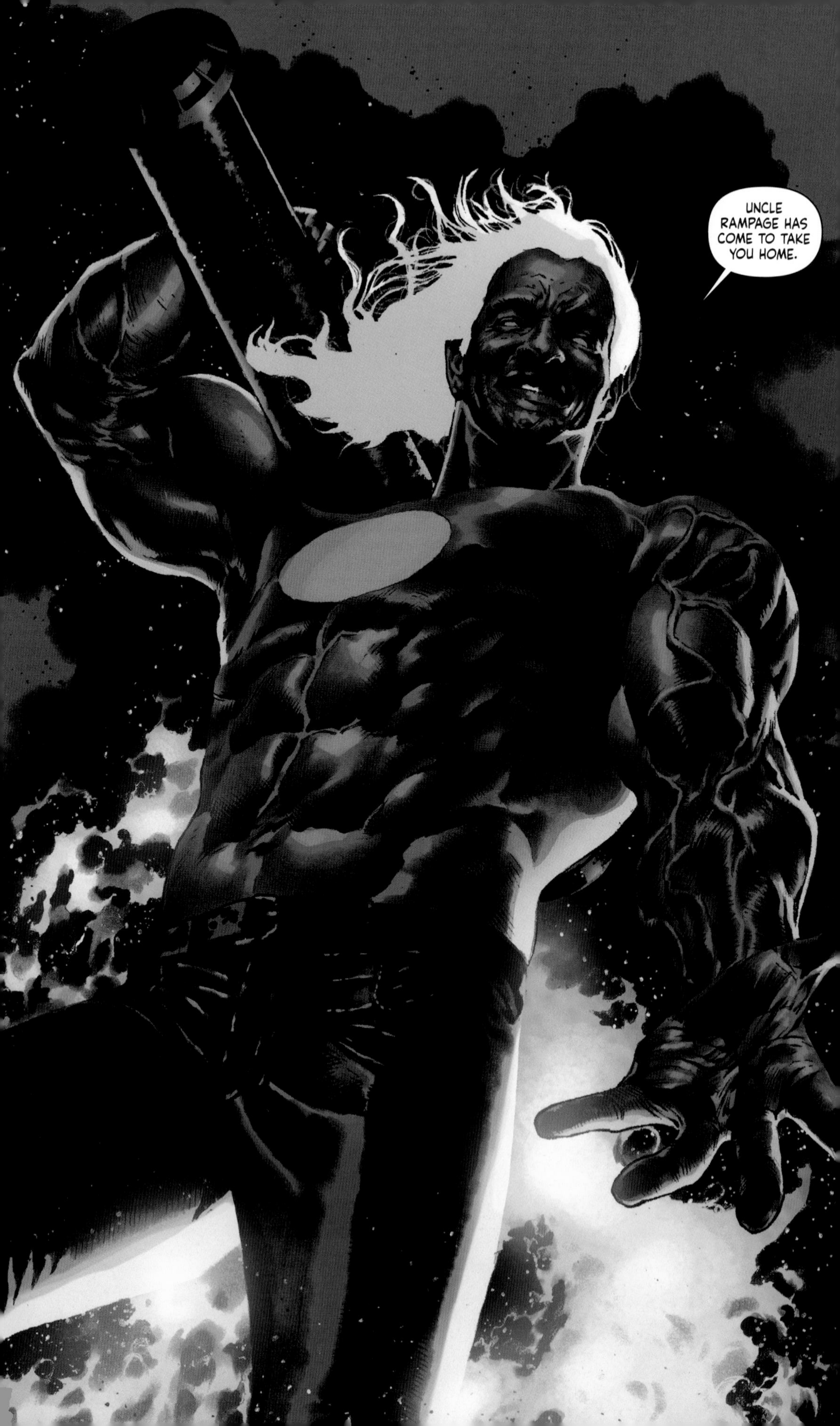
UNCLE RAMPAGE HAS COME TO TAKE YOU HOME.

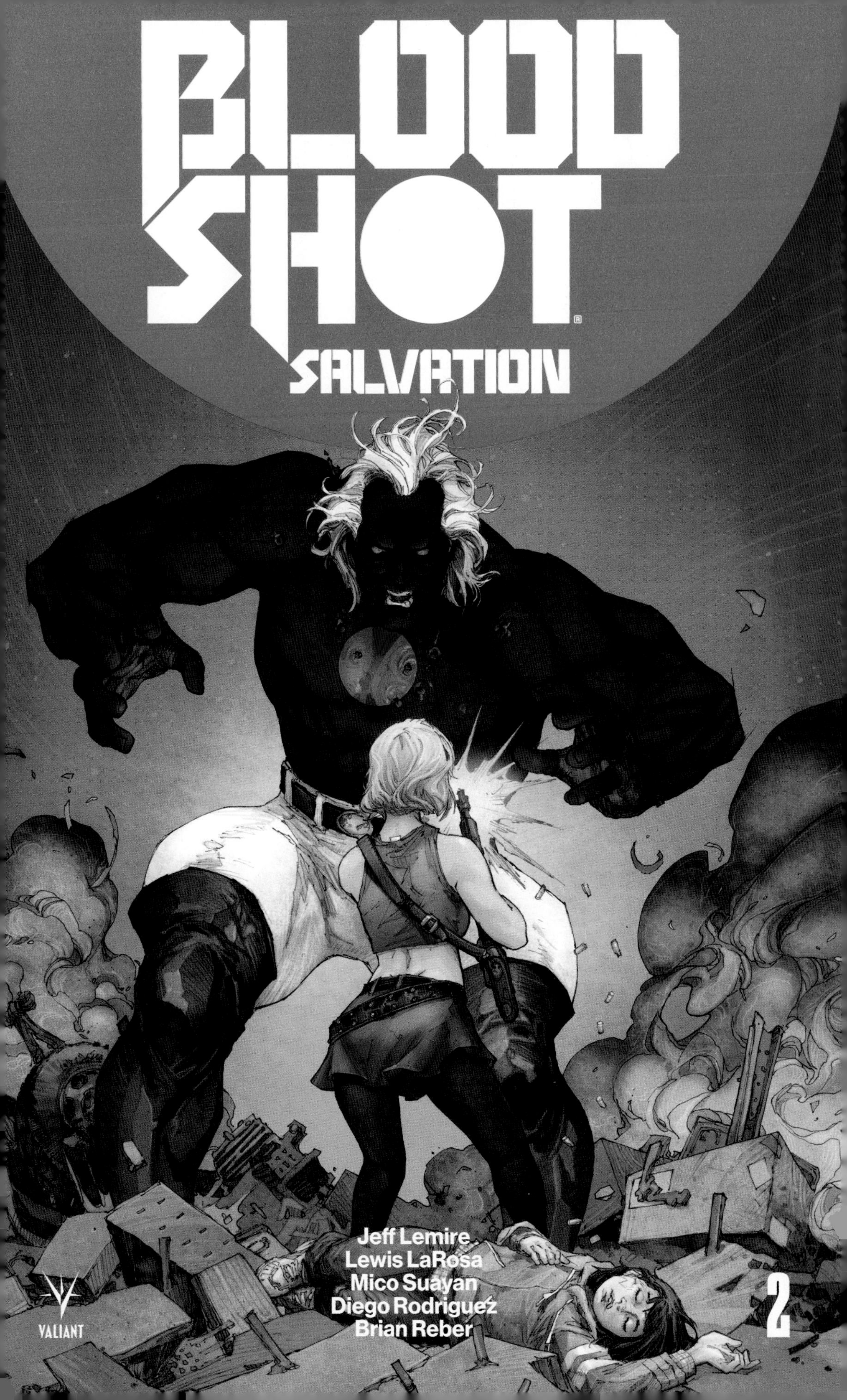
BLOOD SHOT®
SALVATION
Jeff Lemire
Lewis LaRosa
Mico Suayan
Diego Rodriguez
Brian Reber
VALIANT
2

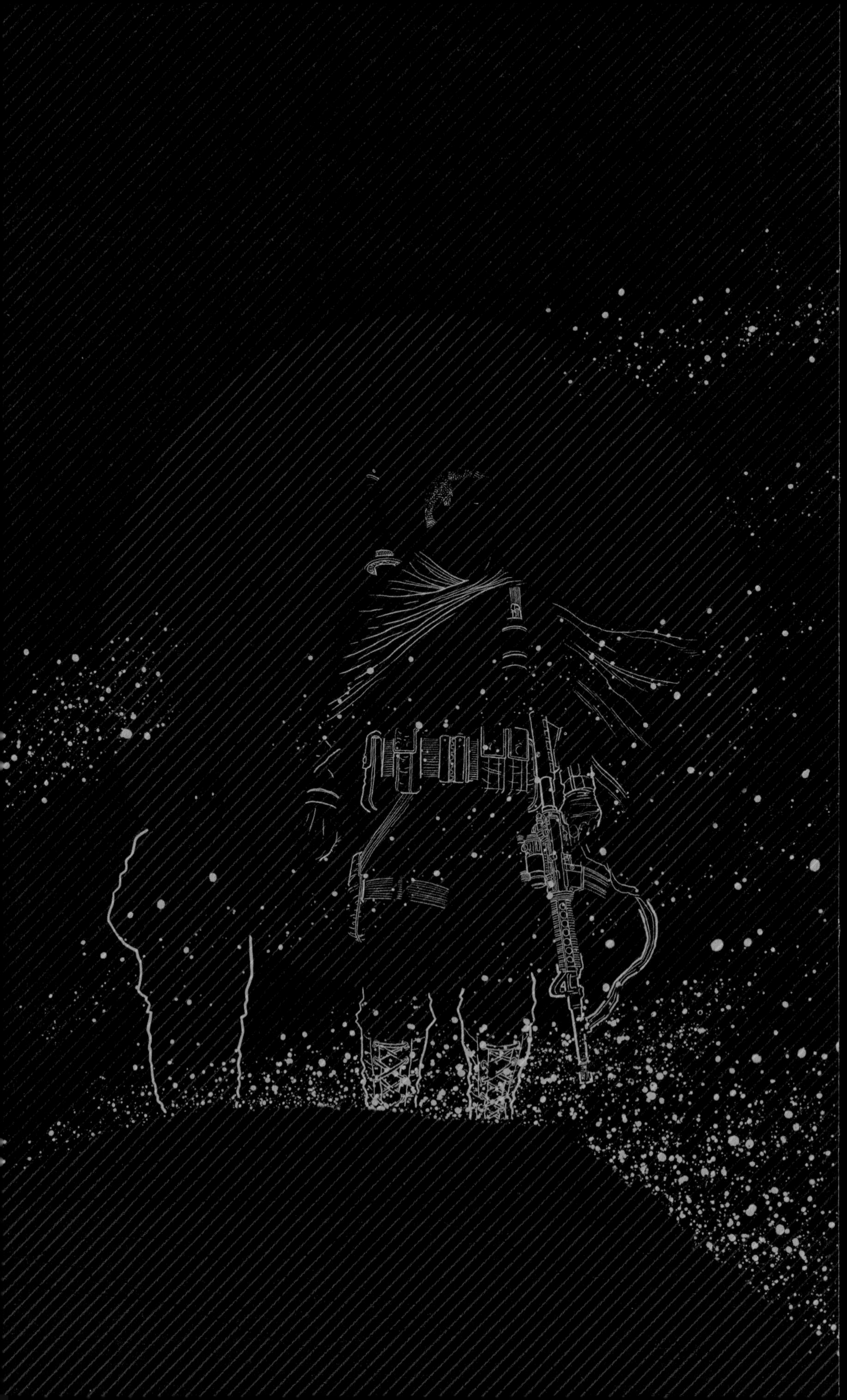

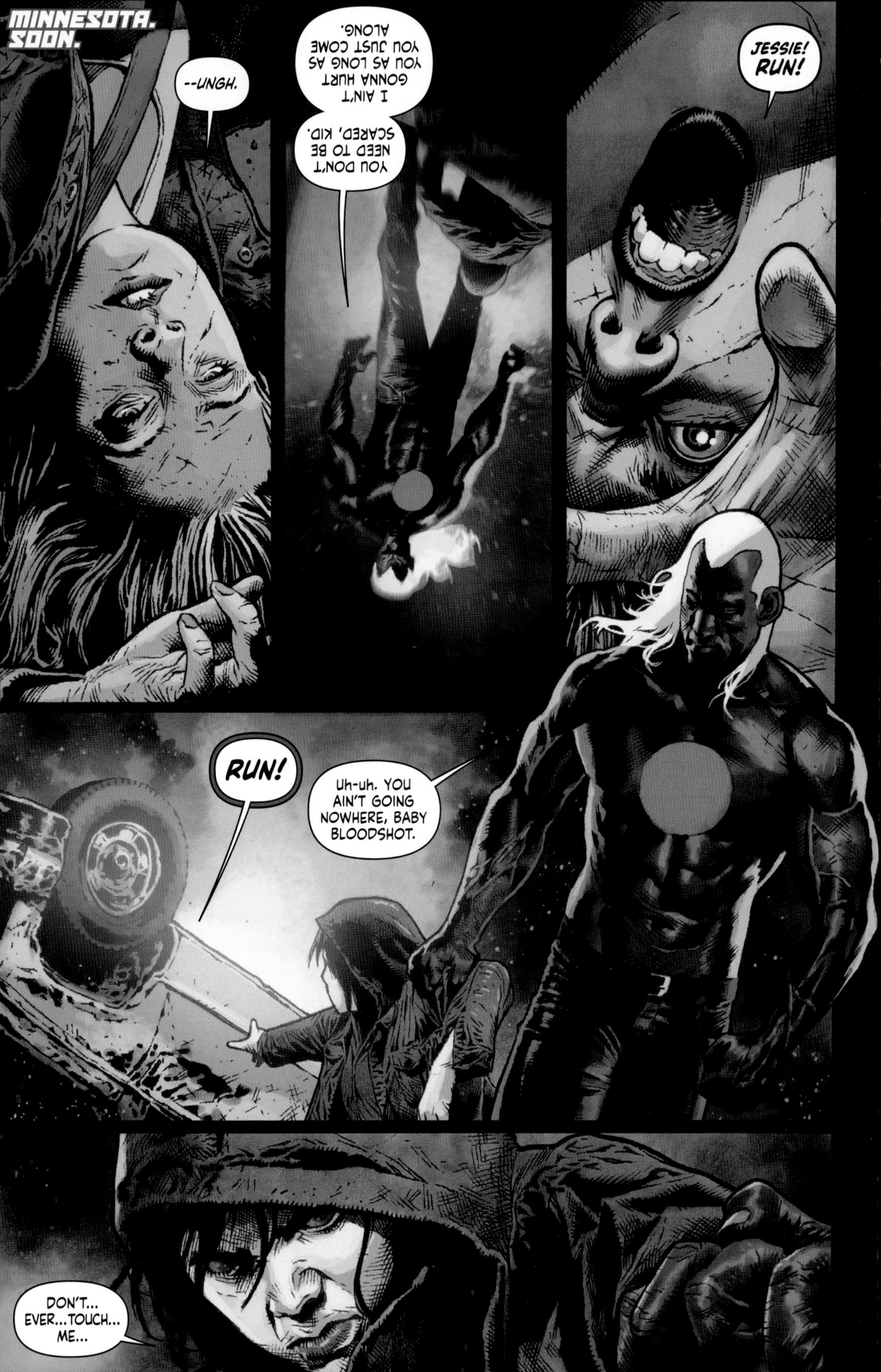
MINNESOTA. SOON.
--UNGH.
YOU DON'T NEED TO BE SCARED, KID. I AIN'T GONNA HURT YOU AS LONG AS YOU JUST COME ALONG.
JESSIE! RUN!
RUN!
Uh-uh. YOU AIN'T GOING NOWHERE, BABY BLOODSHOT.
DON'T... EVER...TOUCH... ME...

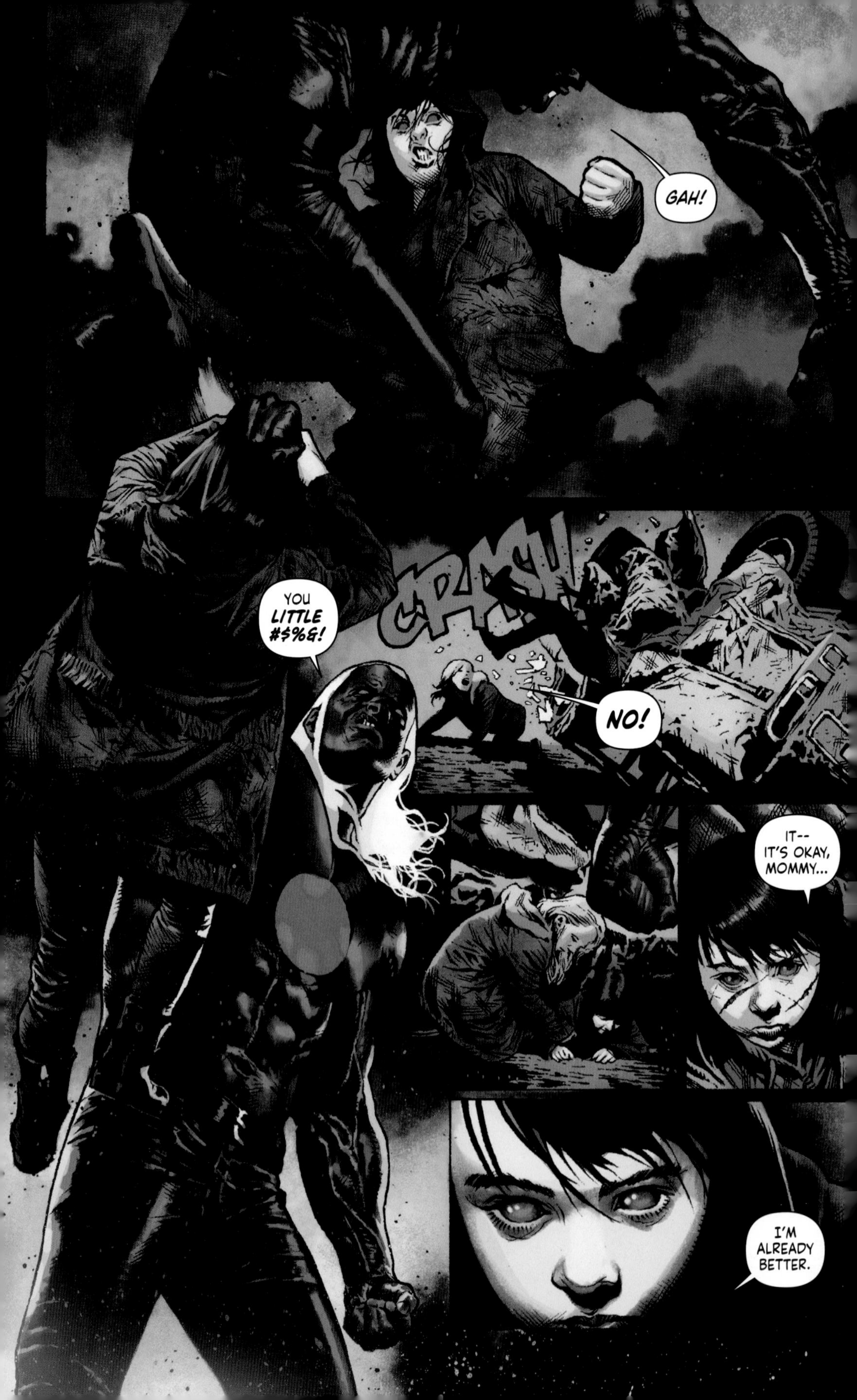
GAH!
CRASH
YOU LITTLE #$%&!
NO!
IT-- IT'S OKAY, MOMMY...
I'M ALREADY BETTER.

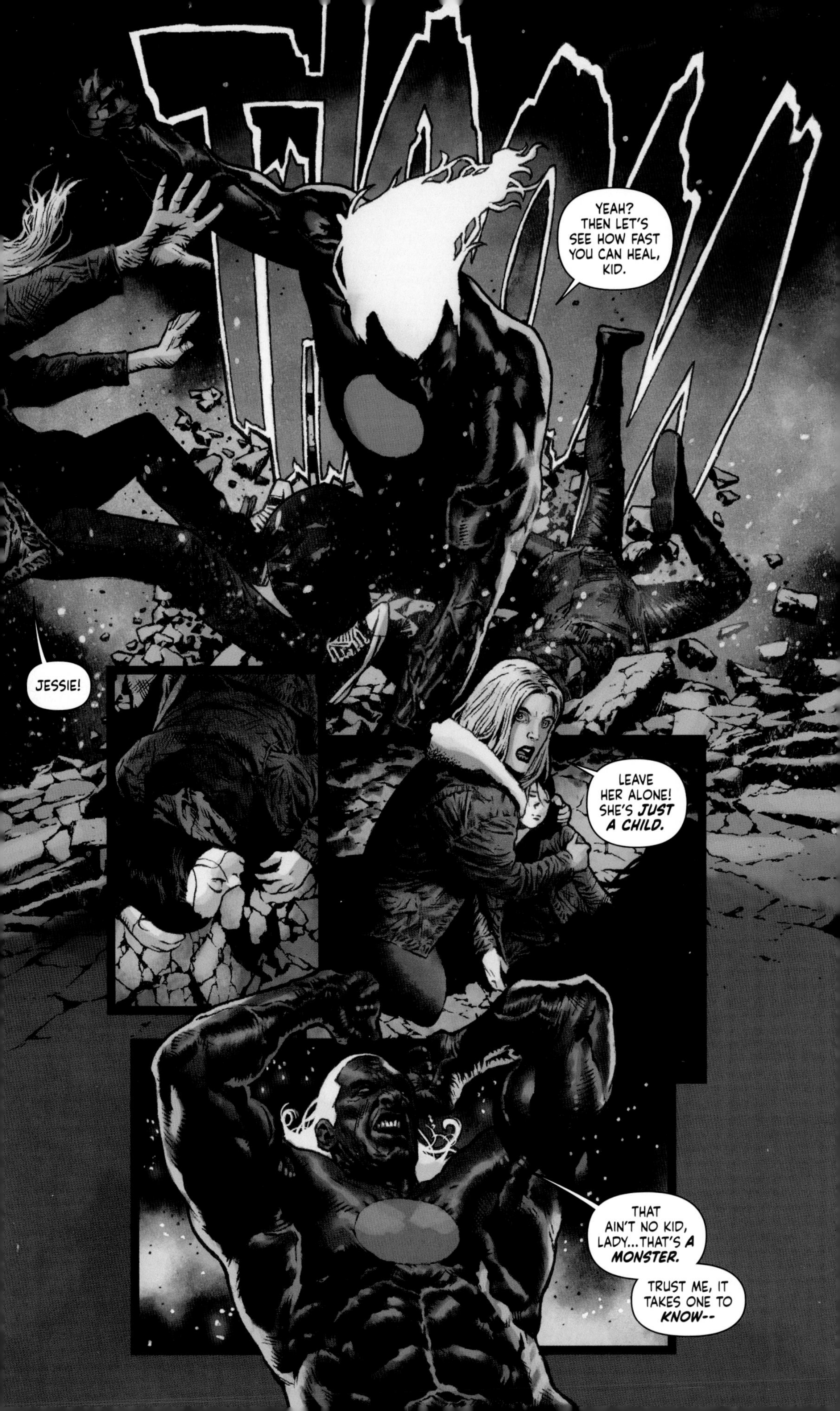
THOOM
YEAH? THEN LET'S SEE HOW FAST YOU CAN HEAL, KID.
JESSIE!
LEAVE HER ALONE! SHE'S JUST A CHILD.
THAT AIN'T NO KID, LADY...THAT'S A MONSTER.
TRUST ME, IT TAKES ONE TO KNOW--

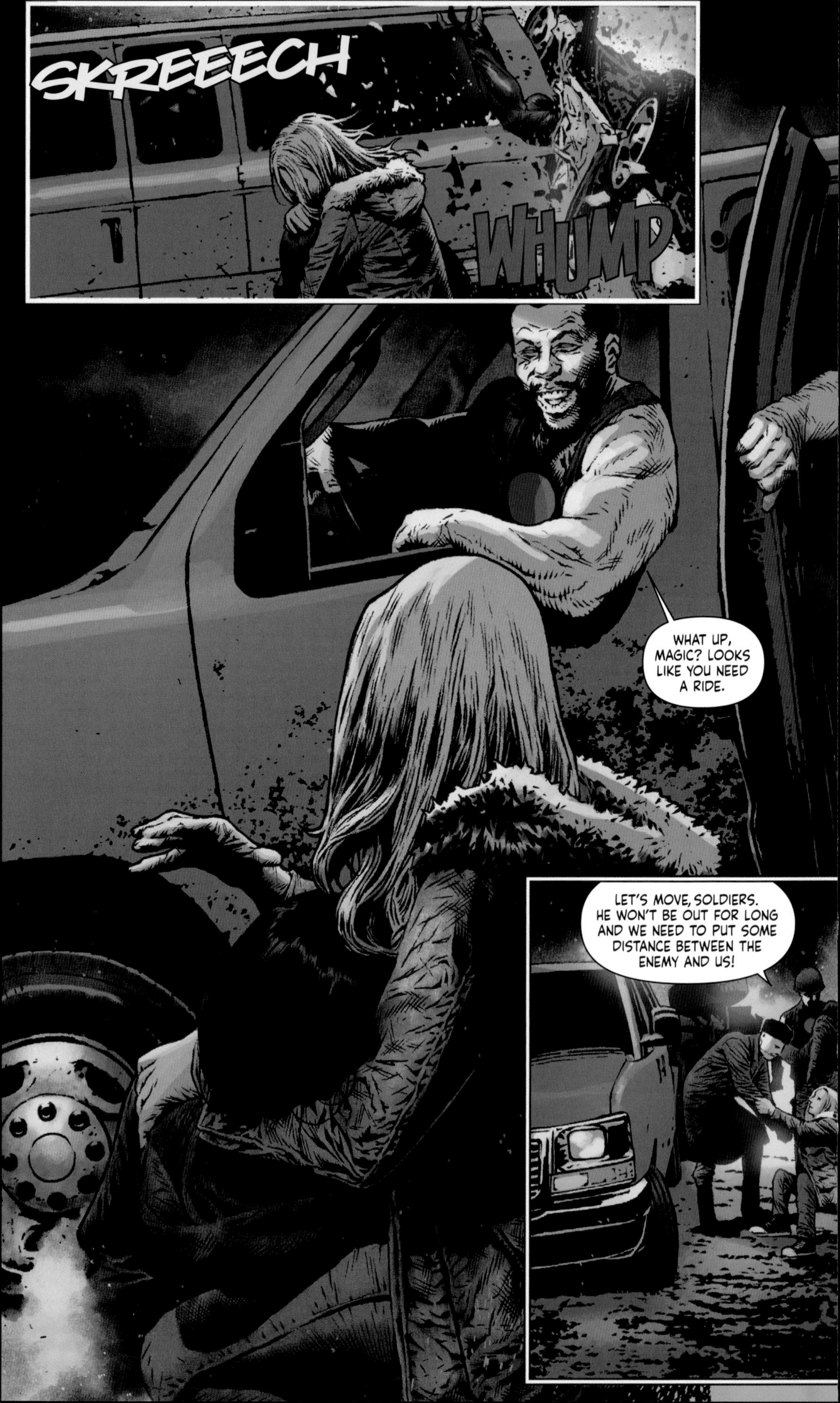
SKREEECH
WHUMP
WHAT UP, MAGIC? LOOKS LIKE YOU NEED A RIDE.
LET'S MOVE, SOLDIERS. HE WON'T BE OUT FOR LONG AND WE NEED TO PUT SOME DISTANCE BETWEEN THE ENEMY AND US!

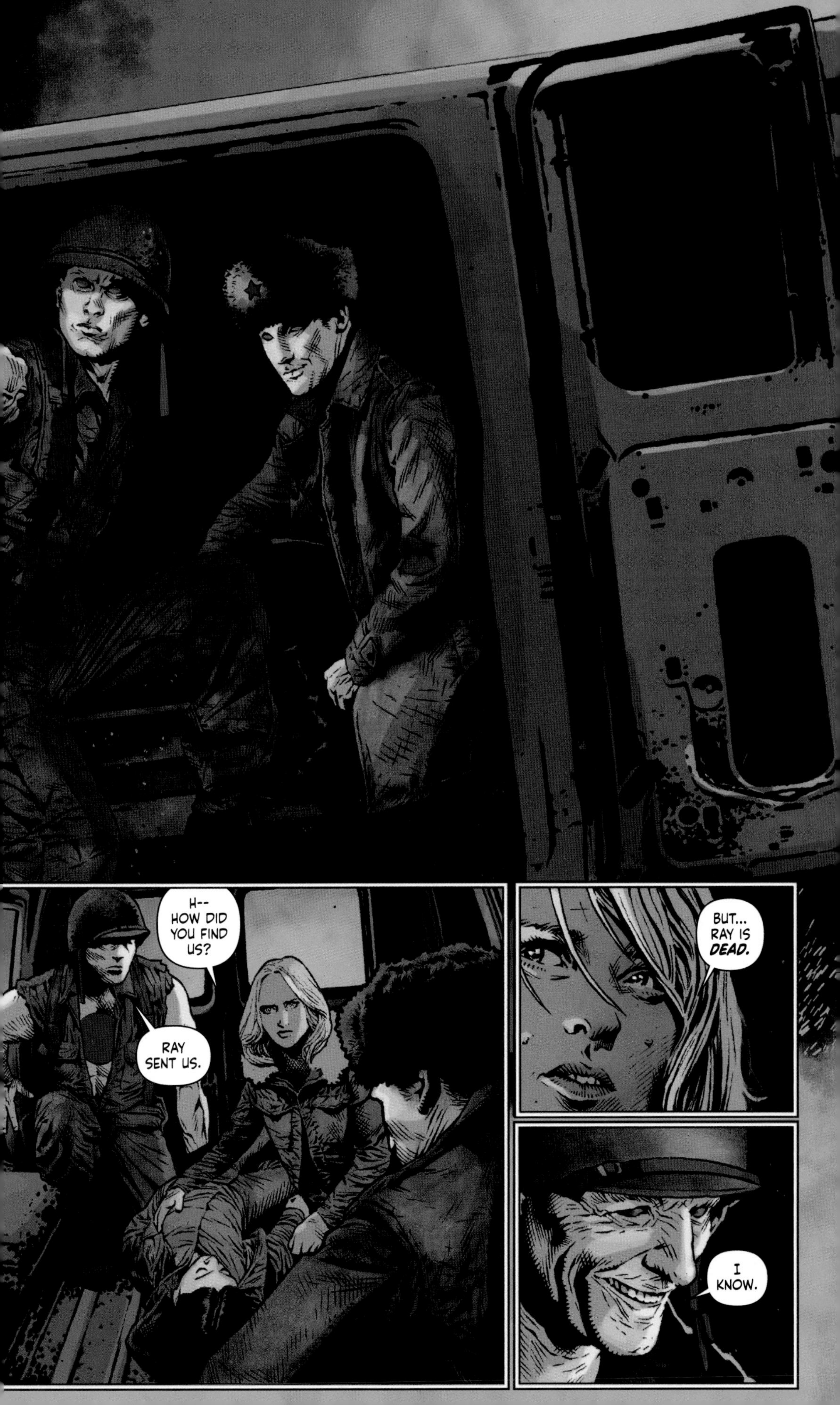
H-- HOW DID YOU FIND US?
RAY SENT US.
BUT... RAY IS *DEAD.*
I KNOW.

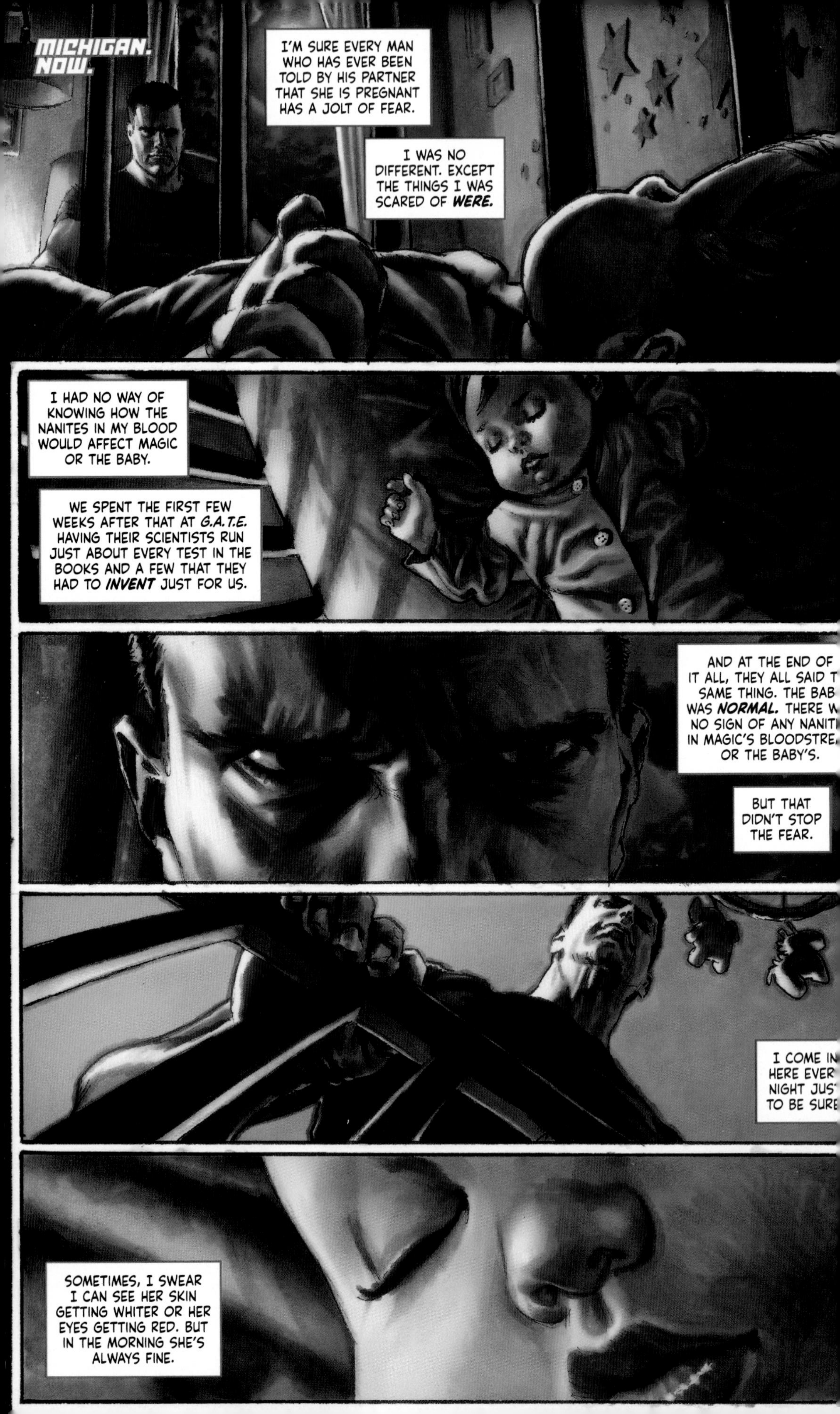
MICHIGAN. NOW.
I'M SURE EVERY MAN WHO HAS EVER BEEN TOLD BY HIS PARTNER THAT SHE IS PREGNANT HAS A JOLT OF FEAR.
I WAS NO DIFFERENT. EXCEPT THE THINGS I WAS SCARED OF ***WERE.***
I HAD NO WAY OF KNOWING HOW THE NANITES IN MY BLOOD WOULD AFFECT MAGIC OR THE BABY.
WE SPENT THE FIRST FEW WEEKS AFTER THAT AT *G.A.T.E.* HAVING THEIR SCIENTISTS RUN JUST ABOUT EVERY TEST IN THE BOOKS AND A FEW THAT THEY HAD TO ***INVENT*** JUST FOR US.
AND AT THE END OF IT ALL, THEY ALL SAID T SAME THING. THE BAB WAS ***NORMAL.*** THERE W NO SIGN OF ANY NANIT IN MAGIC'S BLOODSTRE OR THE BABY'S.
BUT THAT DIDN'T STOP THE FEAR.
I COME IN HERE EVER NIGHT JUST TO BE SURE
SOMETIMES, I SWEAR I CAN SEE HER SKIN GETTING WHITER OR HER EYES GETTING RED. BUT IN THE MORNING SHE'S ALWAYS FINE.

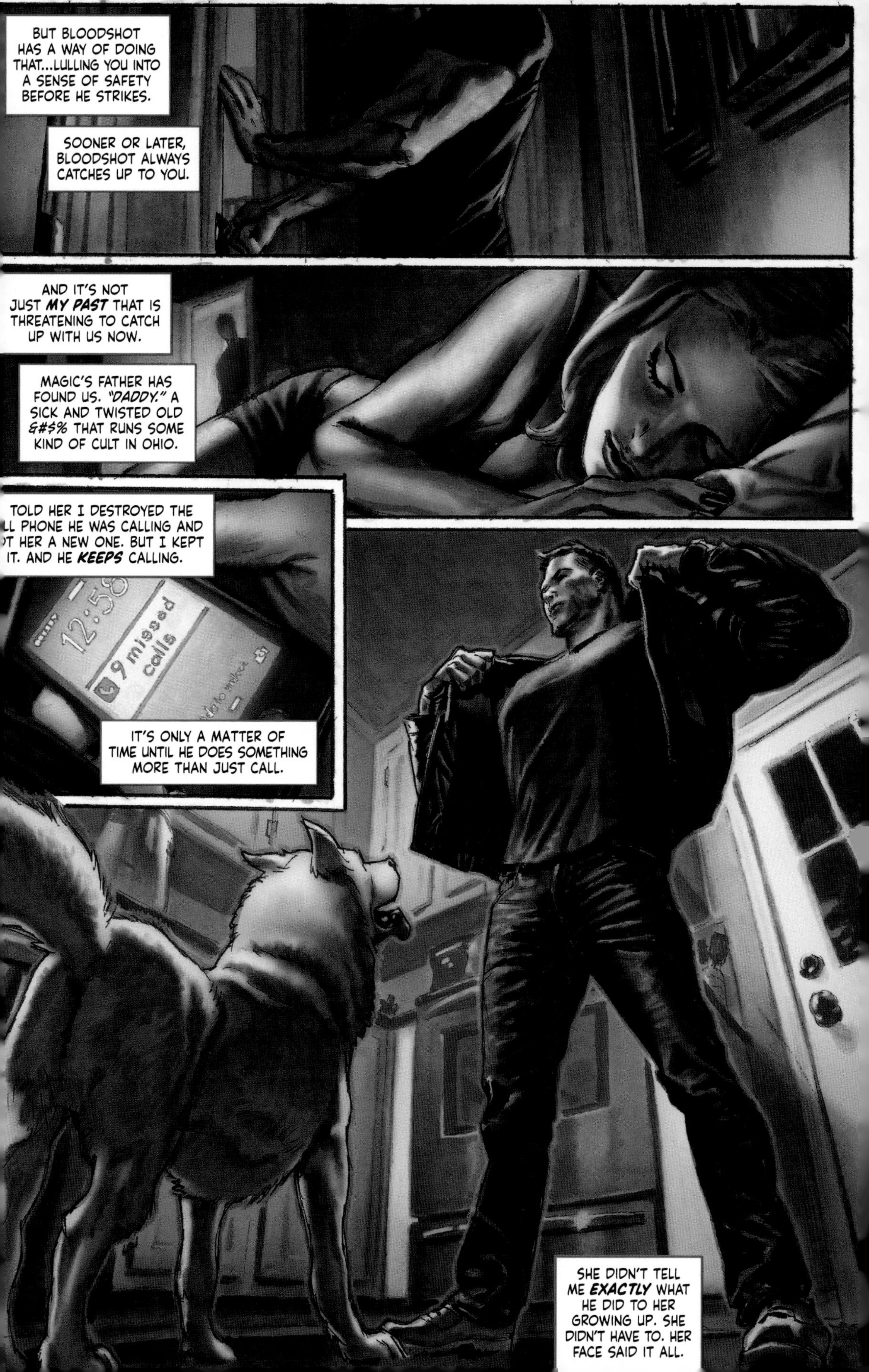
BUT BLOODSHOT HAS A WAY OF DOING THAT...LULLING YOU INTO A SENSE OF SAFETY BEFORE HE STRIKES.
SOONER OR LATER, BLOODSHOT ALWAYS CATCHES UP TO YOU.
AND IT'S NOT JUST MY PAST THAT IS THREATENING TO CATCH UP WITH US NOW.
MAGIC'S FATHER HAS FOUND US. "DADDY." A SICK AND TWISTED OLD &#$% THAT RUNS SOME KIND OF CULT IN OHIO.
TOLD HER I DESTROYED THE LL PHONE HE WAS CALLING AND T HER A NEW ONE. BUT I KEPT IT. AND HE KEEPS CALLING.
12:58
9 missed calls
IT'S ONLY A MATTER OF TIME UNTIL HE DOES SOMETHING MORE THAN JUST CALL.
SHE DIDN'T TELL ME EXACTLY WHAT HE DID TO HER GROWING UP. SHE DIDN'T HAVE TO. HER FACE SAID IT ALL.

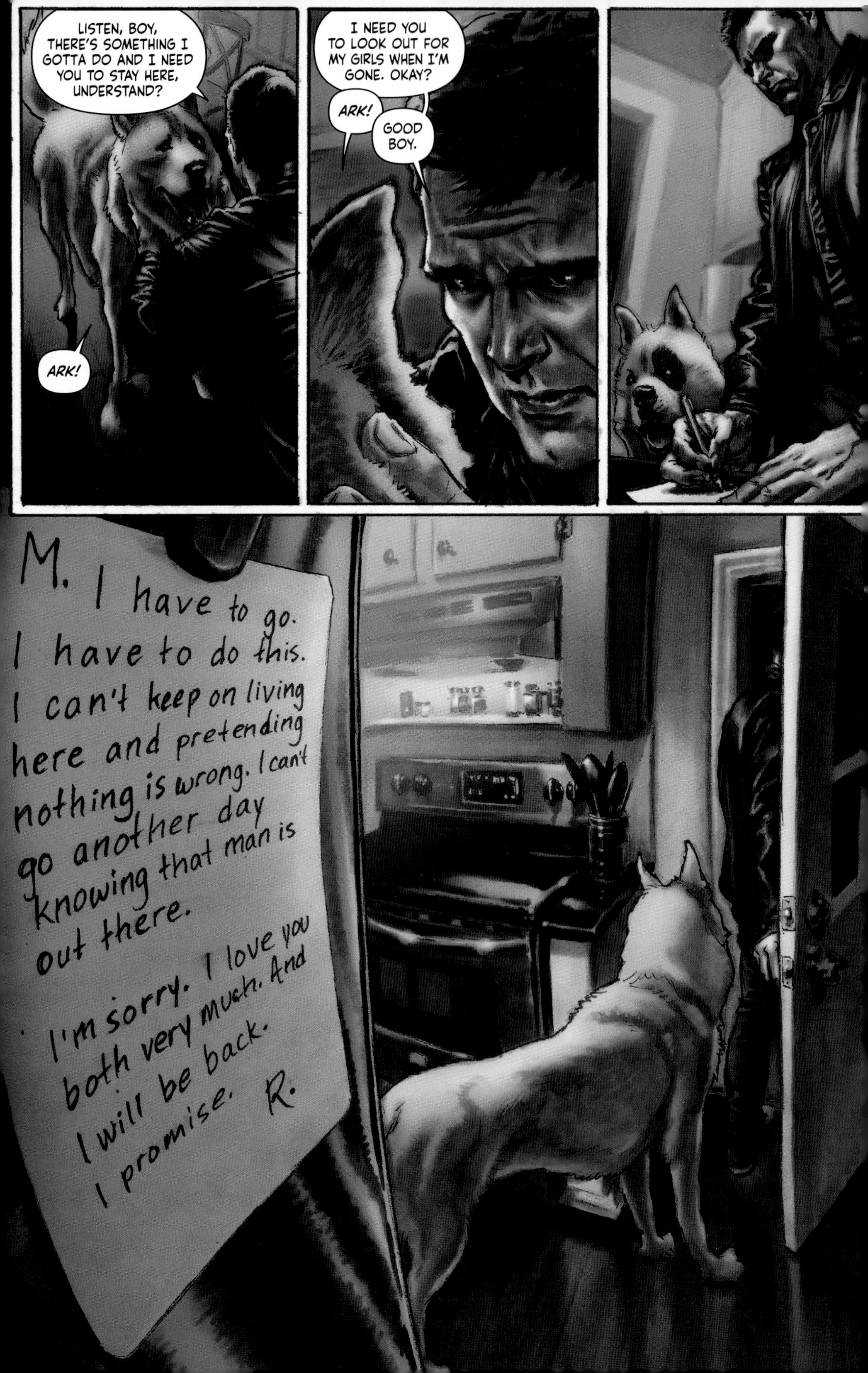
LISTEN, BOY, THERE'S SOMETHING I GOTTA DO AND I NEED YOU TO STAY HERE, UNDERSTAND?
ARK!
I NEED YOU TO LOOK OUT FOR MY GIRLS WHEN I'M GONE. OKAY?
ARK!
GOOD BOY.
M. I have to go. I have to do this. I can't keep on living here and pretending nothing is wrong. I can't go another day knowing that man is out there.
I'm sorry. I love you both very much. And I will be back. I promise. R.

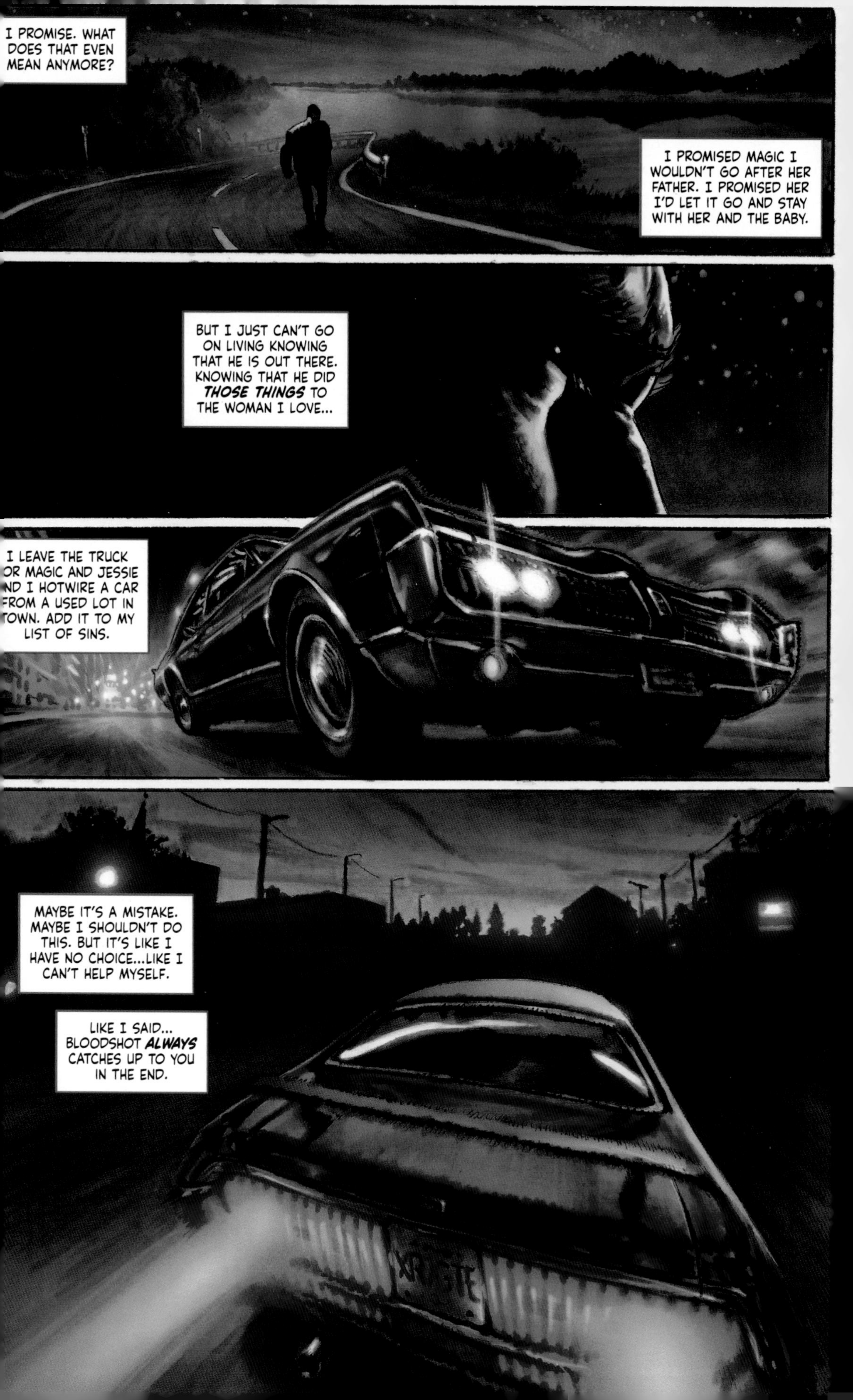
I PROMISE. WHAT DOES THAT EVEN MEAN ANYMORE?
I PROMISED MAGIC I WOULDN'T GO AFTER HER FATHER. I PROMISED HER I'D LET IT GO AND STAY WITH HER AND THE BABY.
BUT I JUST CAN'T GO ON LIVING KNOWING THAT HE IS OUT THERE. KNOWING THAT HE DID ***THOSE THINGS*** TO THE WOMAN I LOVE...
I LEAVE THE TRUCK OR MAGIC AND JESSIE ND I HOTWIRE A CAR FROM A USED LOT IN TOWN. ADD IT TO MY LIST OF SINS.
MAYBE IT'S A MISTAKE. MAYBE I SHOULDN'T DO THIS. BUT IT'S LIKE I HAVE NO CHOICE...LIKE I CAN'T HELP MYSELF.
LIKE I SAID... BLOODSHOT ***ALWAYS*** CATCHES UP TO YOU IN THE END.

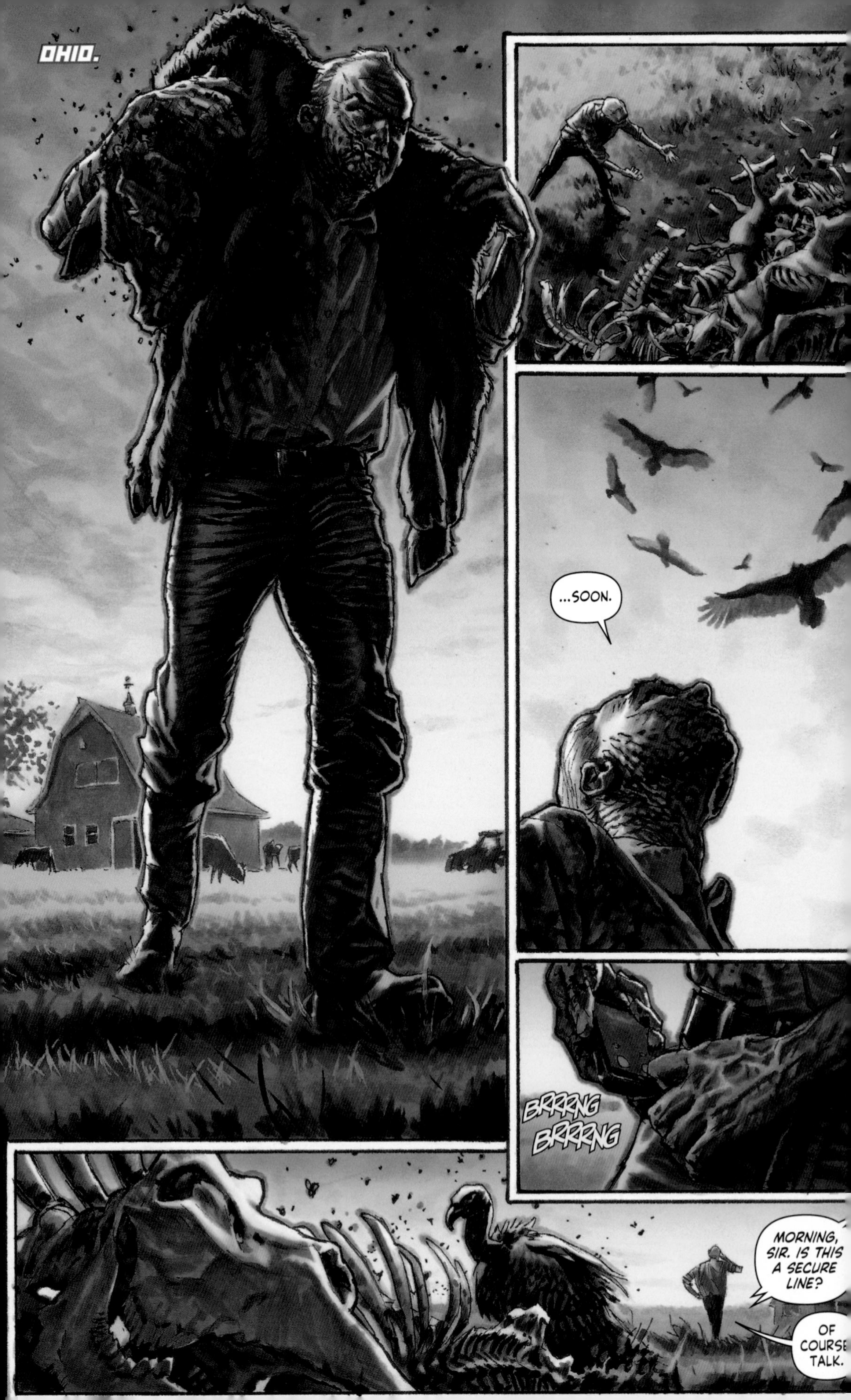
OHIO.
...SOON.
BRRRNG
BRRRNG
MORNING, SIR. IS THIS A SECURE LINE?
OF COURSE. TALK.

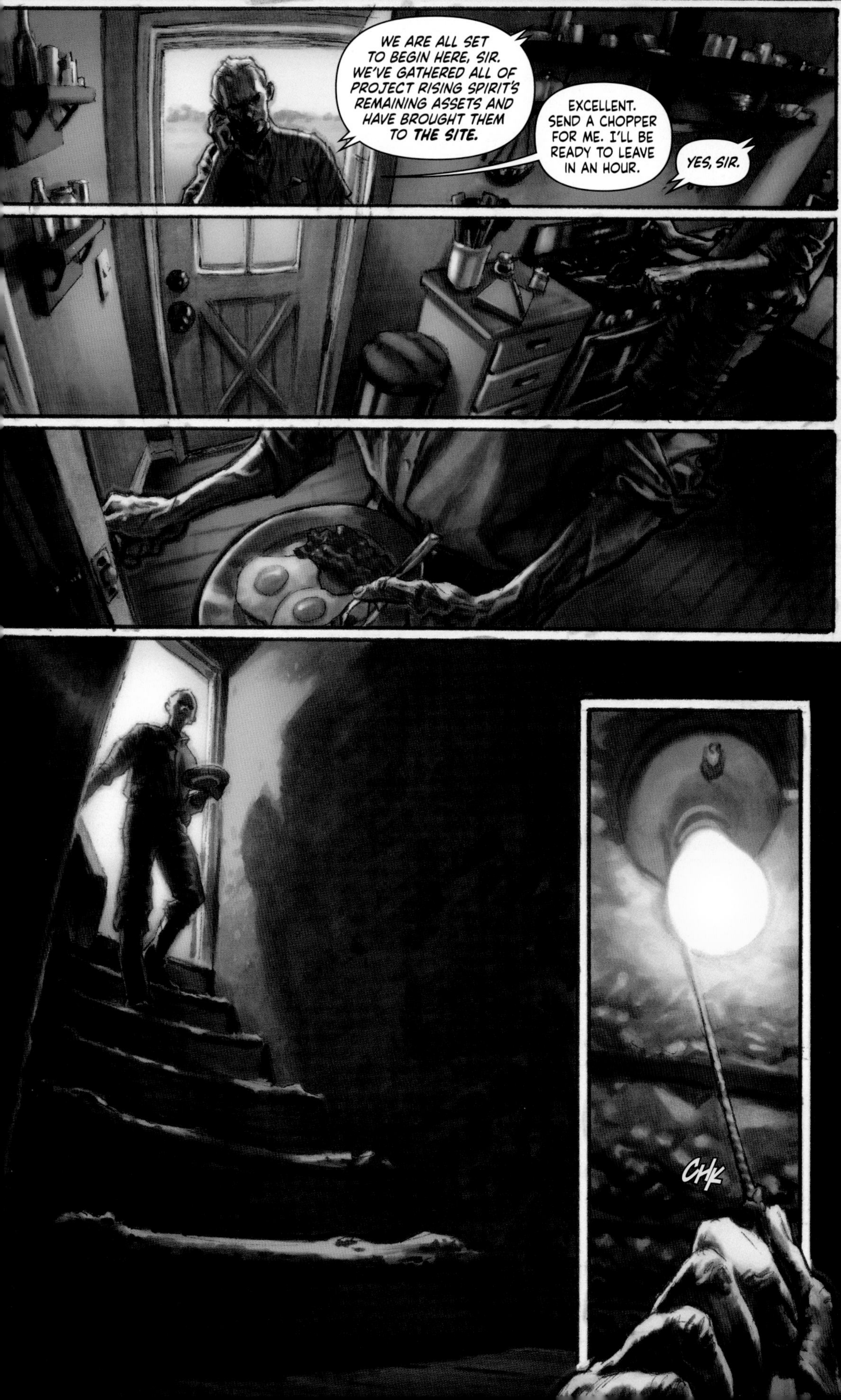

WE ARE ALL SET TO BEGIN HERE, SIR. WE'VE GATHERED ALL OF PROJECT RISING SPIRIT'S REMAINING ASSETS AND HAVE BROUGHT THEM TO **THE SITE.**
EXCELLENT. SEND A CHOPPER FOR ME. I'LL BE READY TO LEAVE IN AN HOUR.
YES, SIR.
CHK

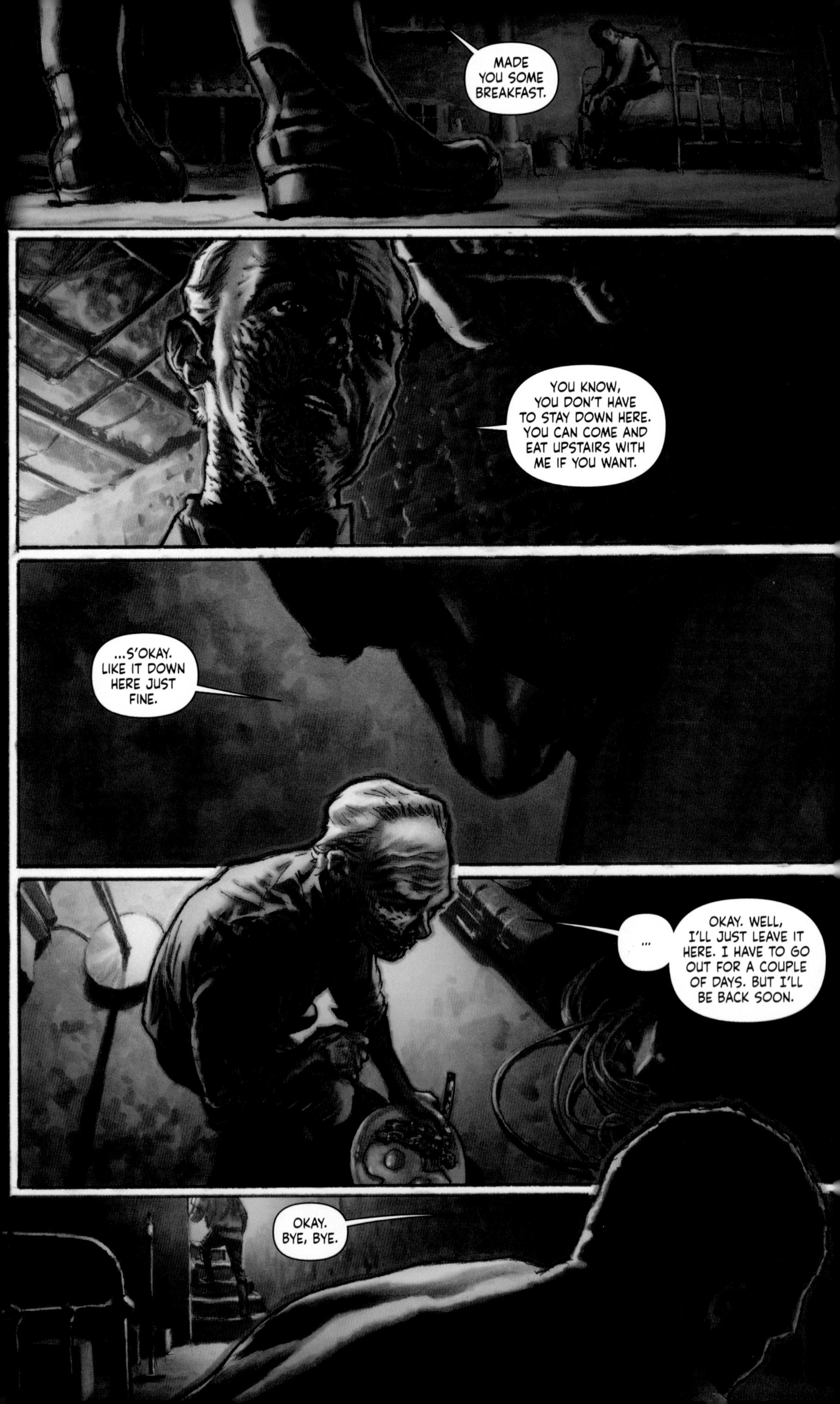
MADE YOU SOME BREAKFAST.
YOU KNOW, YOU DON'T HAVE TO STAY DOWN HERE. YOU CAN COME AND EAT UPSTAIRS WITH ME IF YOU WANT.
...S'OKAY. LIKE IT DOWN HERE JUST FINE.
...
OKAY. WELL, I'LL JUST LEAVE IT HERE. I HAVE TO GO OUT FOR A COUPLE OF DAYS. BUT I'LL BE BACK SOON.
OKAY. BYE, BYE.

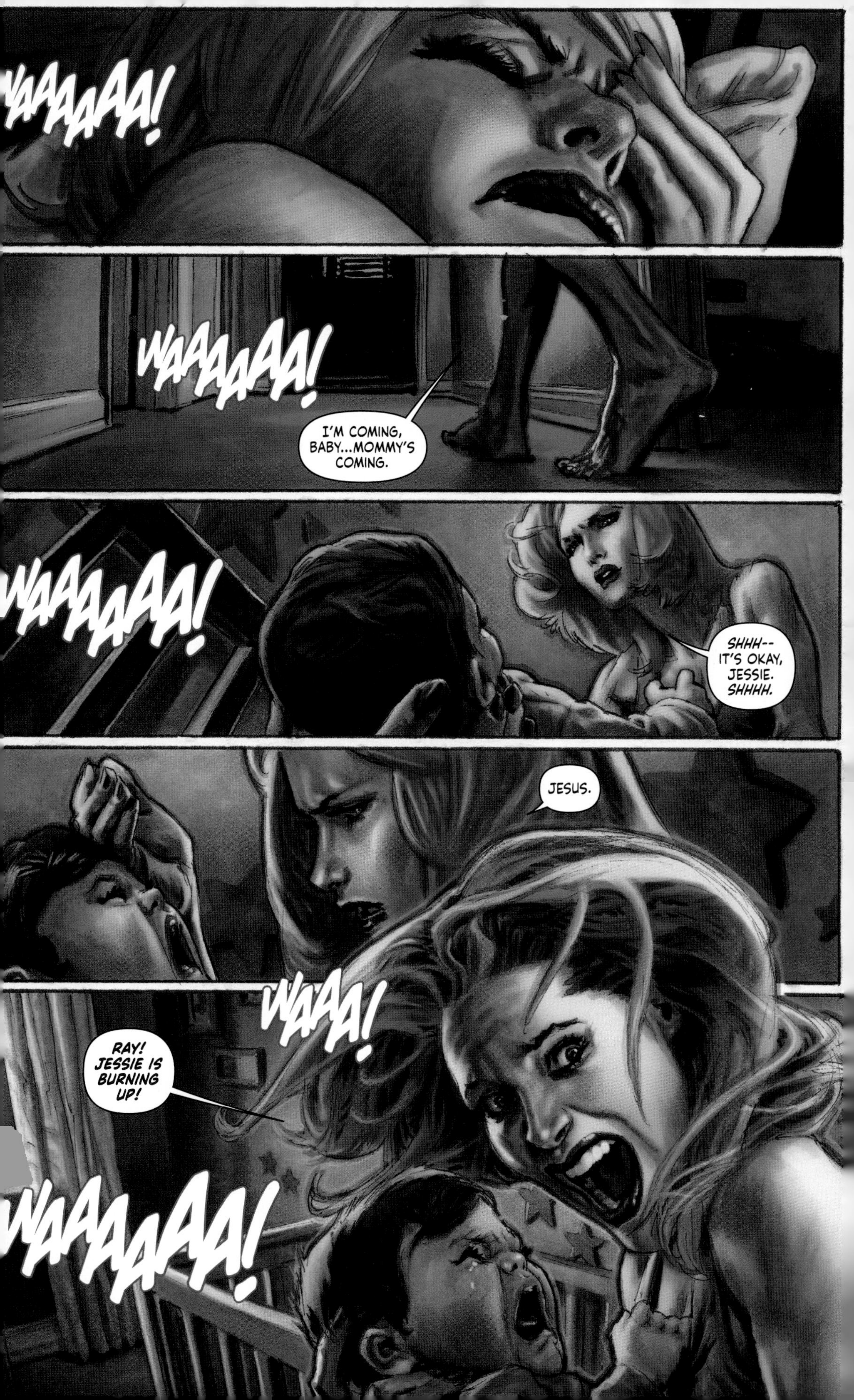
WAAAAAAA!
WAAAAAAA!
I'M COMING, BABY...MOMMY'S COMING.
WAAAAAAA!
SHHH-- IT'S OKAY, JESSIE. SHHHH.
JESUS.
WAAAA!
RAY! JESSIE IS BURNING UP!
WAAAAAAA!

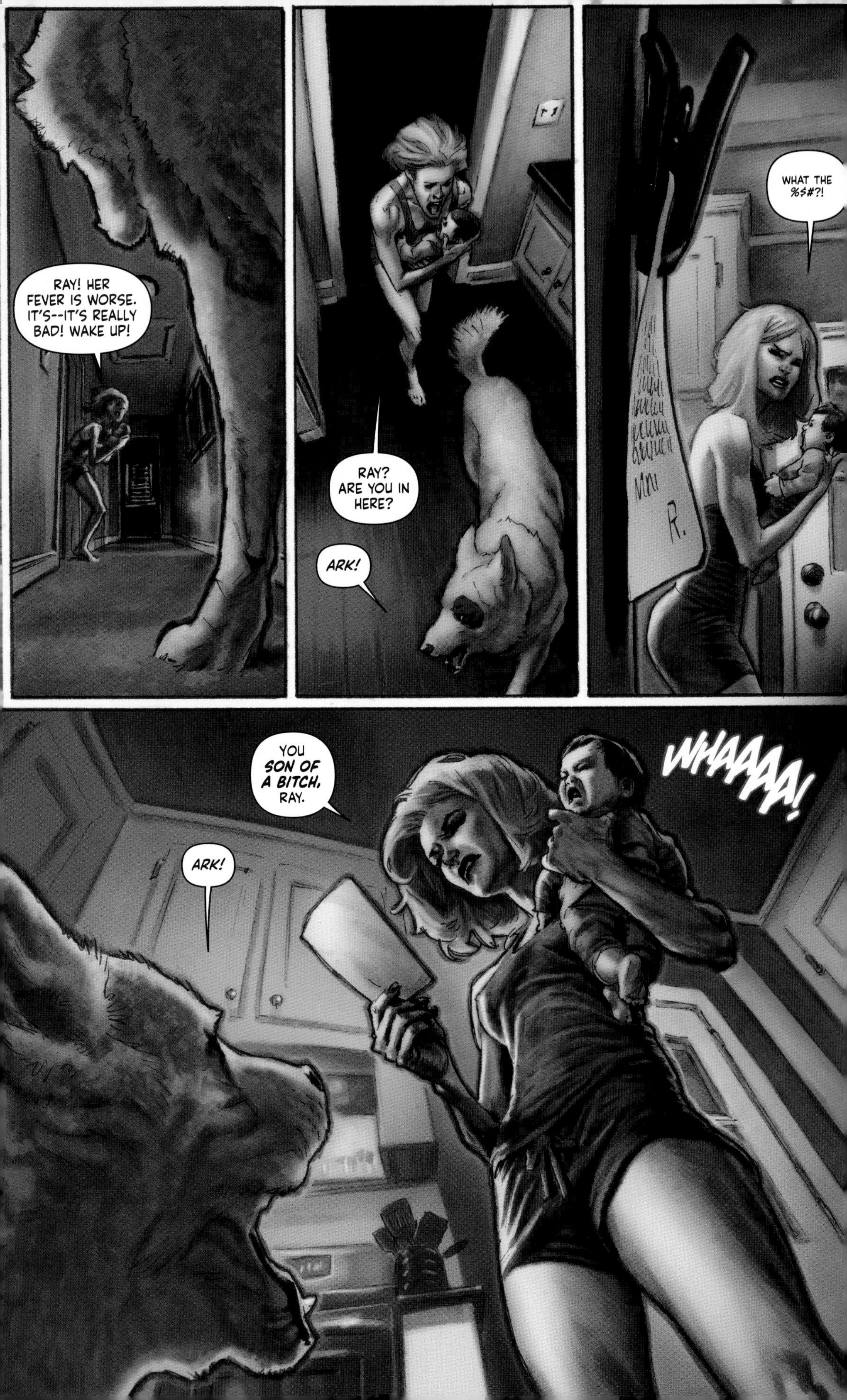
RAY! HER FEVER IS WORSE. IT'S--IT'S REALLY BAD! WAKE UP!
RAY? ARE YOU IN HERE?
ARK!
WHAT THE %$#?!
R.
YOU SON OF A BITCH, RAY.
ARK!
WHAAAAA!

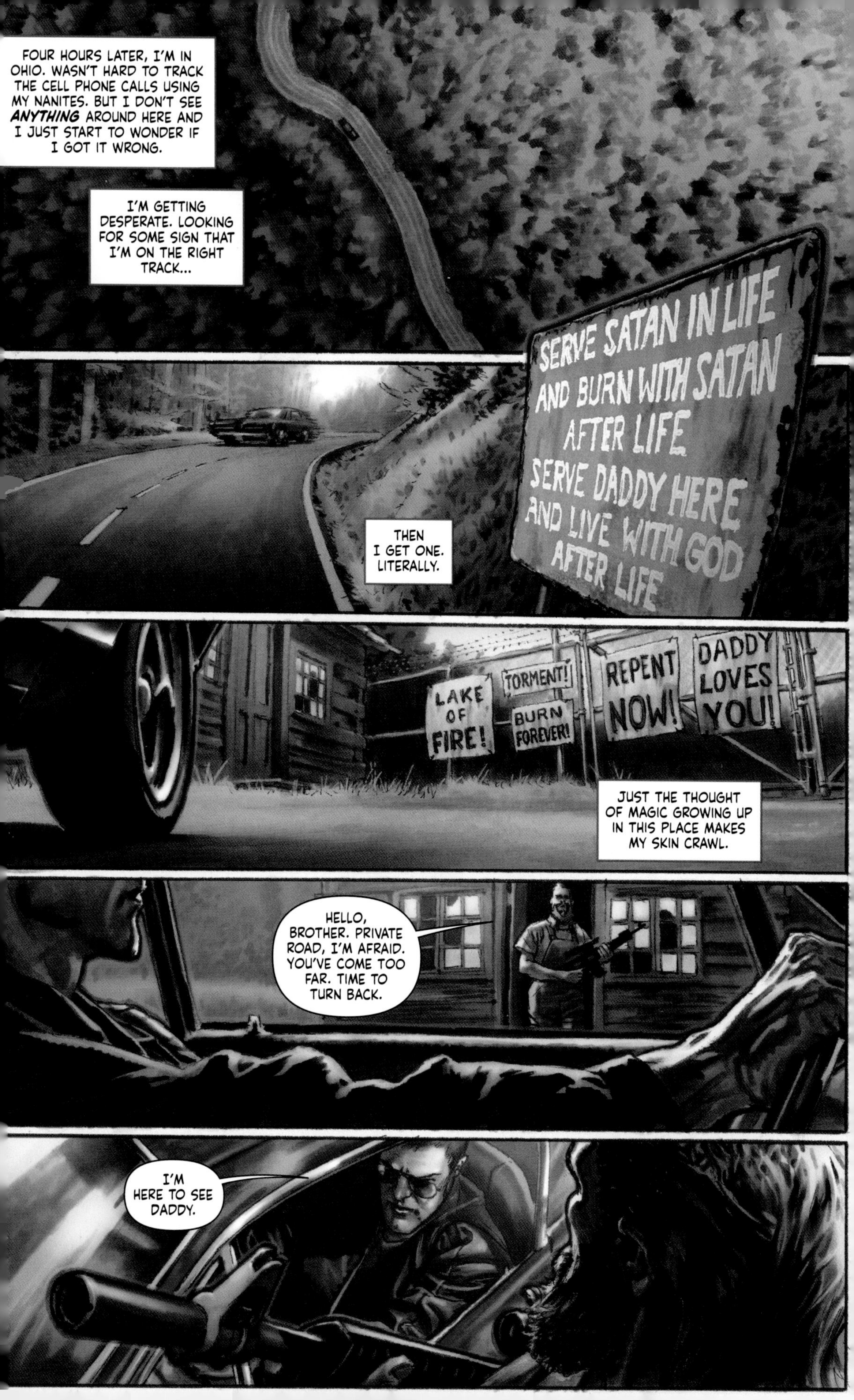
FOUR HOURS LATER, I'M IN OHIO. WASN'T HARD TO TRACK THE CELL PHONE CALLS USING MY NANITES. BUT I DON'T SEE *ANYTHING* AROUND HERE AND I JUST START TO WONDER IF I GOT IT WRONG.
I'M GETTING DESPERATE. LOOKING FOR SOME SIGN THAT I'M ON THE RIGHT TRACK...
SERVE SATAN IN LIFE AND BURN WITH SATAN AFTER LIFE SERVE DADDY HERE AND LIVE WITH GOD AFTER LIFE
THEN I GET ONE. LITERALLY.
LAKE OF FIRE!
TORMENT!
BURN FOREVER!
REPENT NOW!
DADDY LOVES YOU!
JUST THE THOUGHT OF MAGIC GROWING UP IN THIS PLACE MAKES MY SKIN CRAWL.
HELLO, BROTHER. PRIVATE ROAD, I'M AFRAID. YOU'VE COME TOO FAR. TIME TO TURN BACK.
I'M HERE TO SEE DADDY.

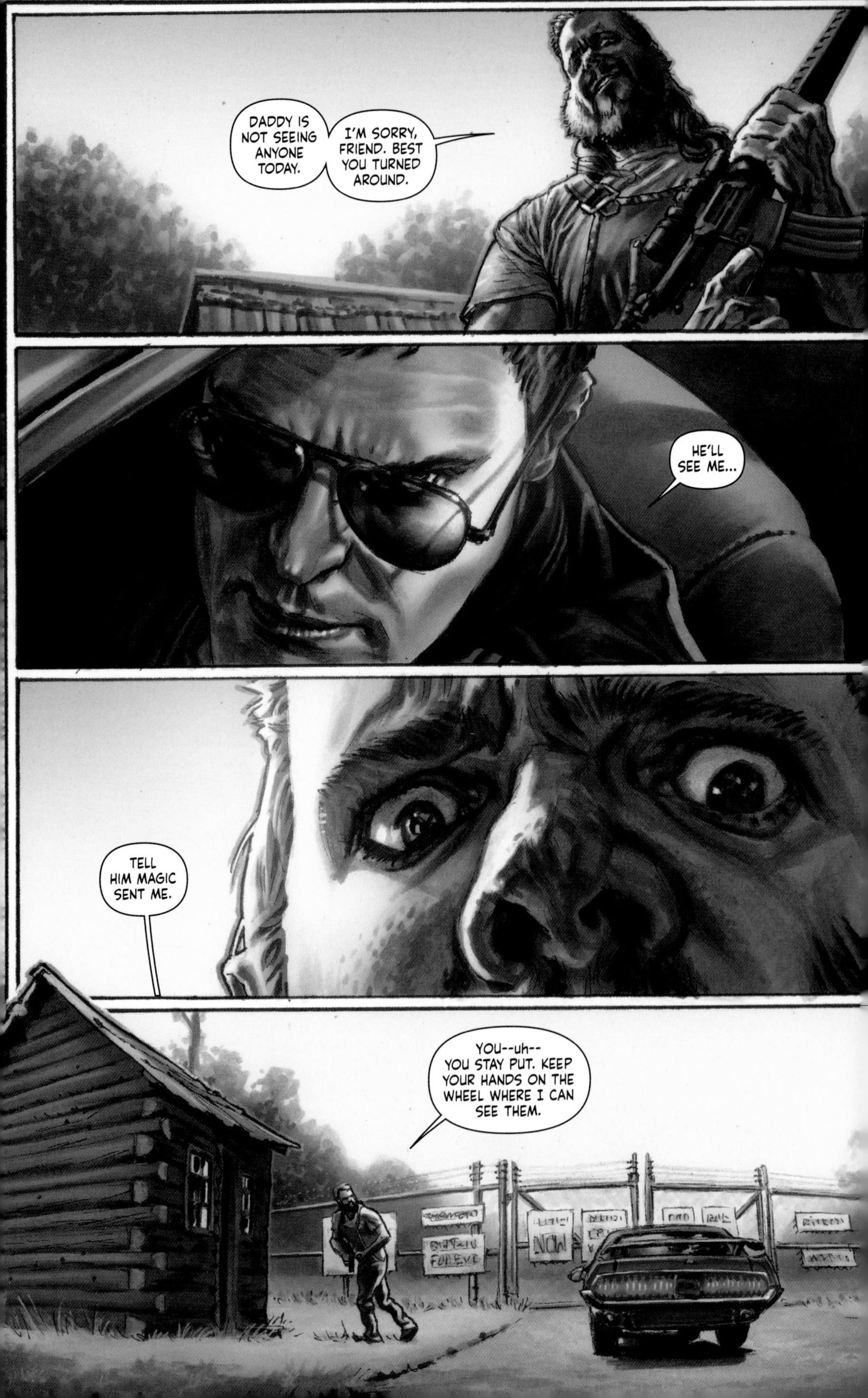
DADDY IS NOT SEEING ANYONE TODAY.
I'M SORRY, FRIEND. BEST YOU TURNED AROUND.
HE'LL SEE ME...
TELL HIM MAGIC SENT ME.
YOU--uh-- YOU STAY PUT. KEEP YOUR HANDS ON THE WHEEL WHERE I CAN SEE THEM.

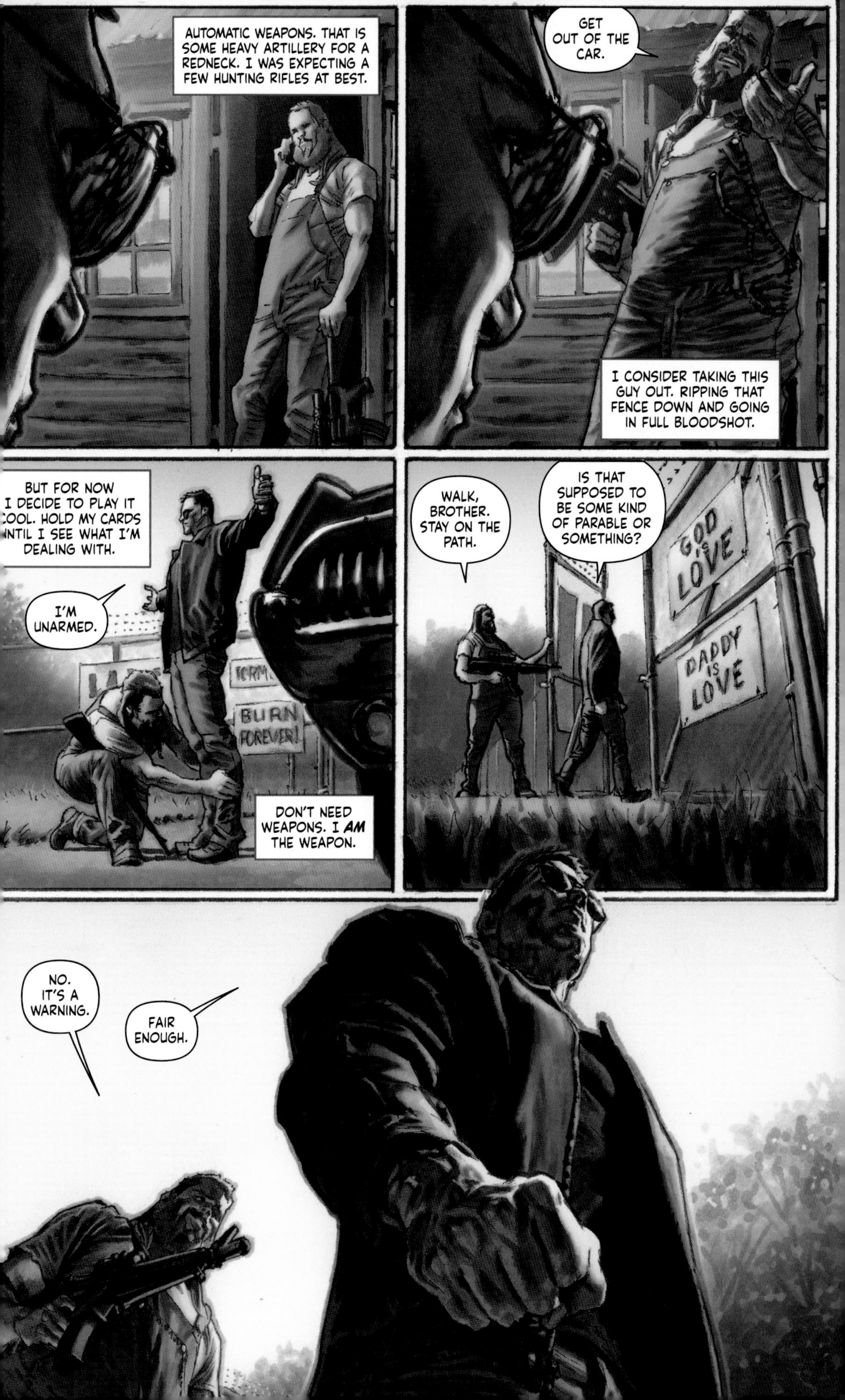
AUTOMATIC WEAPONS. THAT IS SOME HEAVY ARTILLERY FOR A REDNECK. I WAS EXPECTING A FEW HUNTING RIFLES AT BEST.
GET OUT OF THE CAR.
I CONSIDER TAKING THIS GUY OUT. RIPPING THAT FENCE DOWN AND GOING IN FULL BLOODSHOT.
BUT FOR NOW I DECIDE TO PLAY IT COOL. HOLD MY CARDS UNTIL I SEE WHAT I'M DEALING WITH.
I'M UNARMED.
BURN FOREVER!
DON'T NEED WEAPONS. I *AM* THE WEAPON.
WALK, BROTHER. STAY ON THE PATH.
IS THAT SUPPOSED TO BE SOME KIND OF PARABLE OR SOMETHING?
GOD IS LOVE
DADDY IS LOVE
NO. IT'S A WARNING.
FAIR ENOUGH.

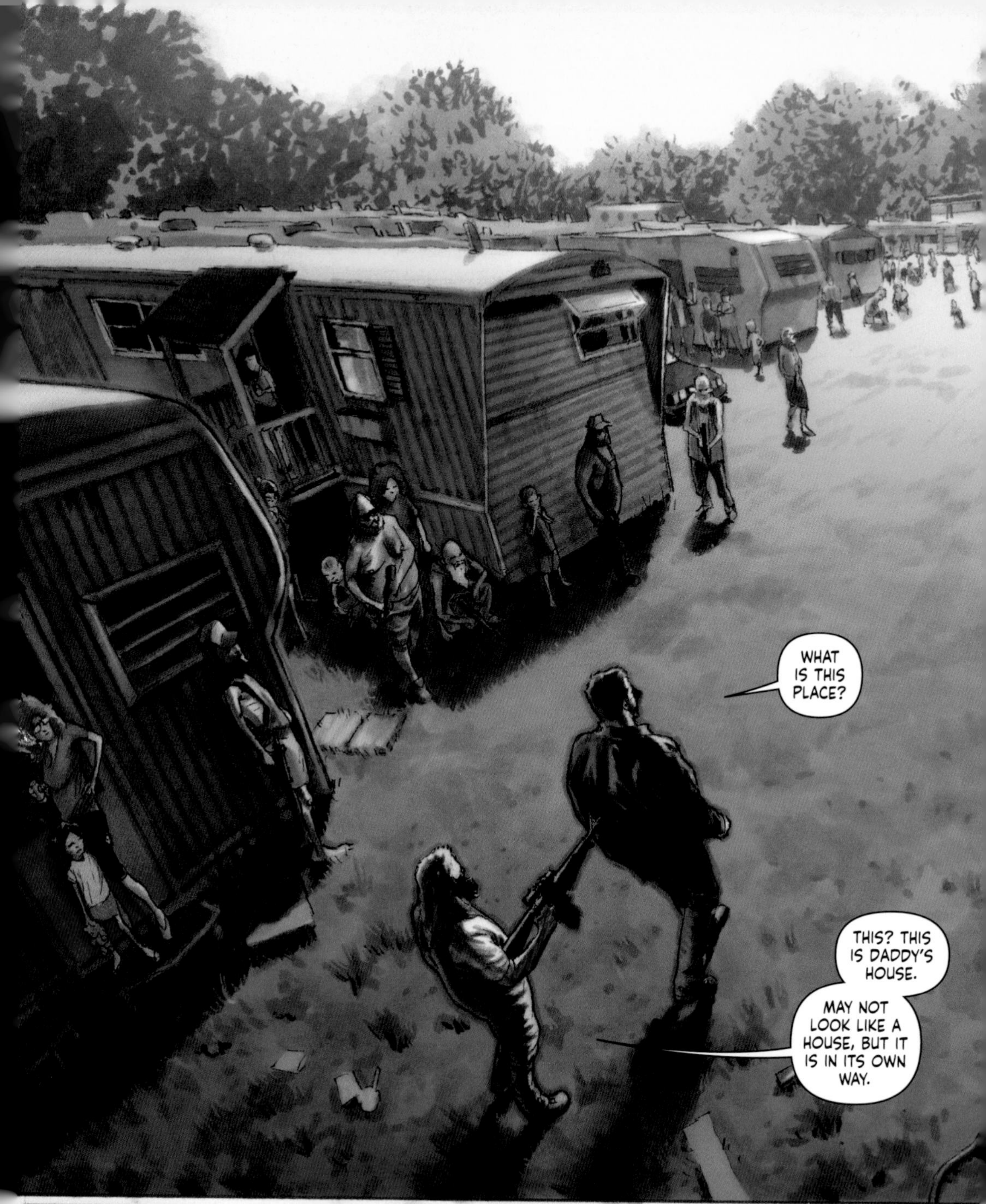
WHAT IS THIS PLACE?
THIS? THIS IS DADDY'S HOUSE.
MAY NOT LOOK LIKE A HOUSE, BUT IT IS IN ITS OWN WAY.

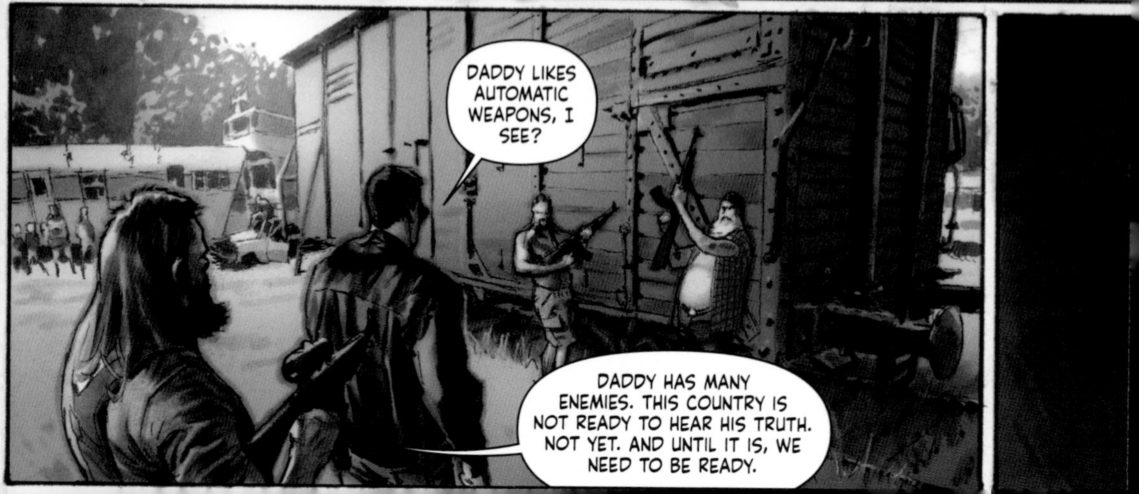
DADDY LIKES AUTOMATIC WEAPONS, I SEE?
DADDY HAS MANY ENEMIES. THIS COUNTRY IS NOT READY TO HEAR HIS TRUTH. NOT YET. AND UNTIL IT IS, WE NEED TO BE READY.

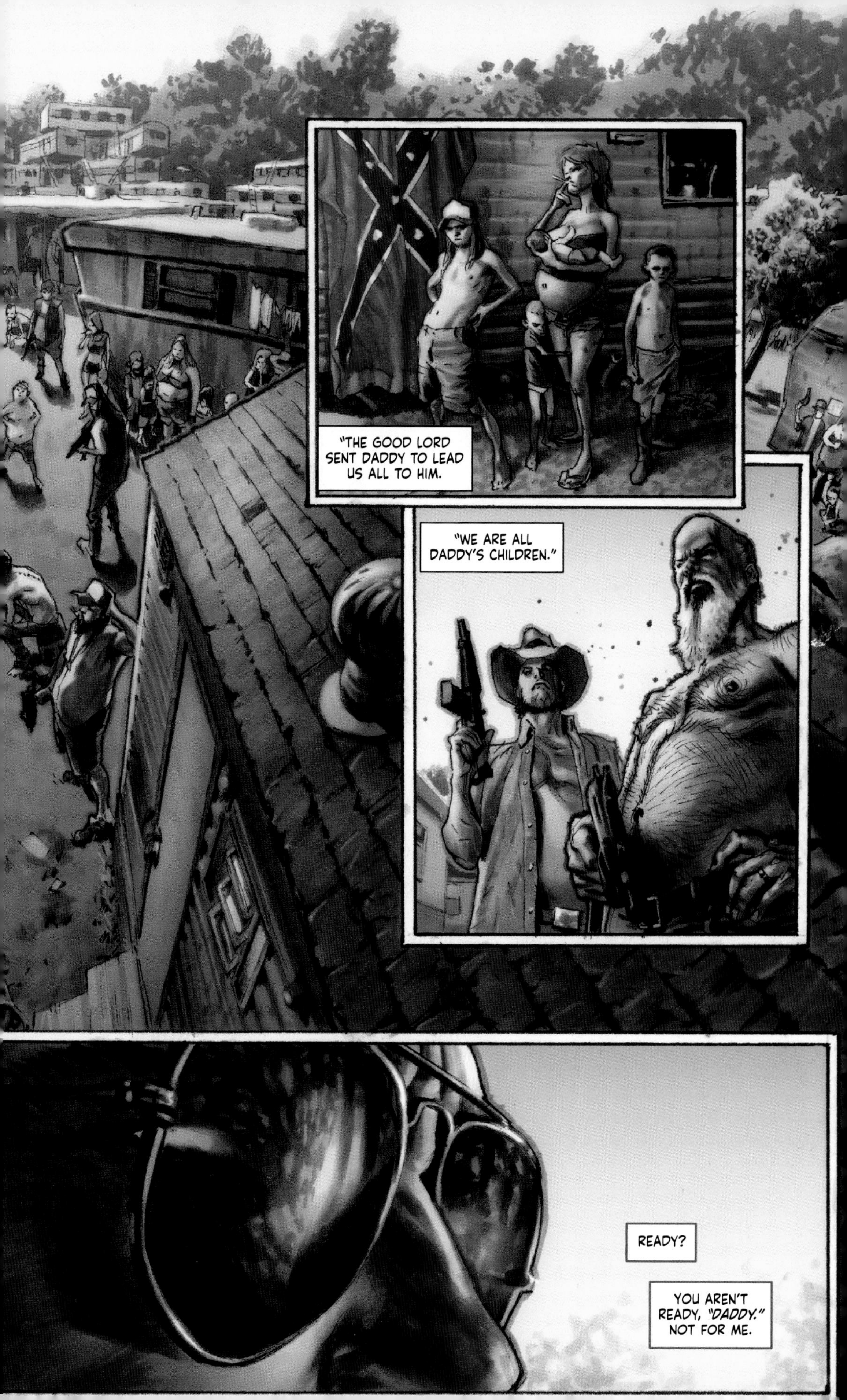
"THE GOOD LORD SENT DADDY TO LEAD US ALL TO HIM.
"WE ARE ALL DADDY'S CHILDREN."
READY?
YOU AREN'T READY, "DADDY." NOT FOR ME.

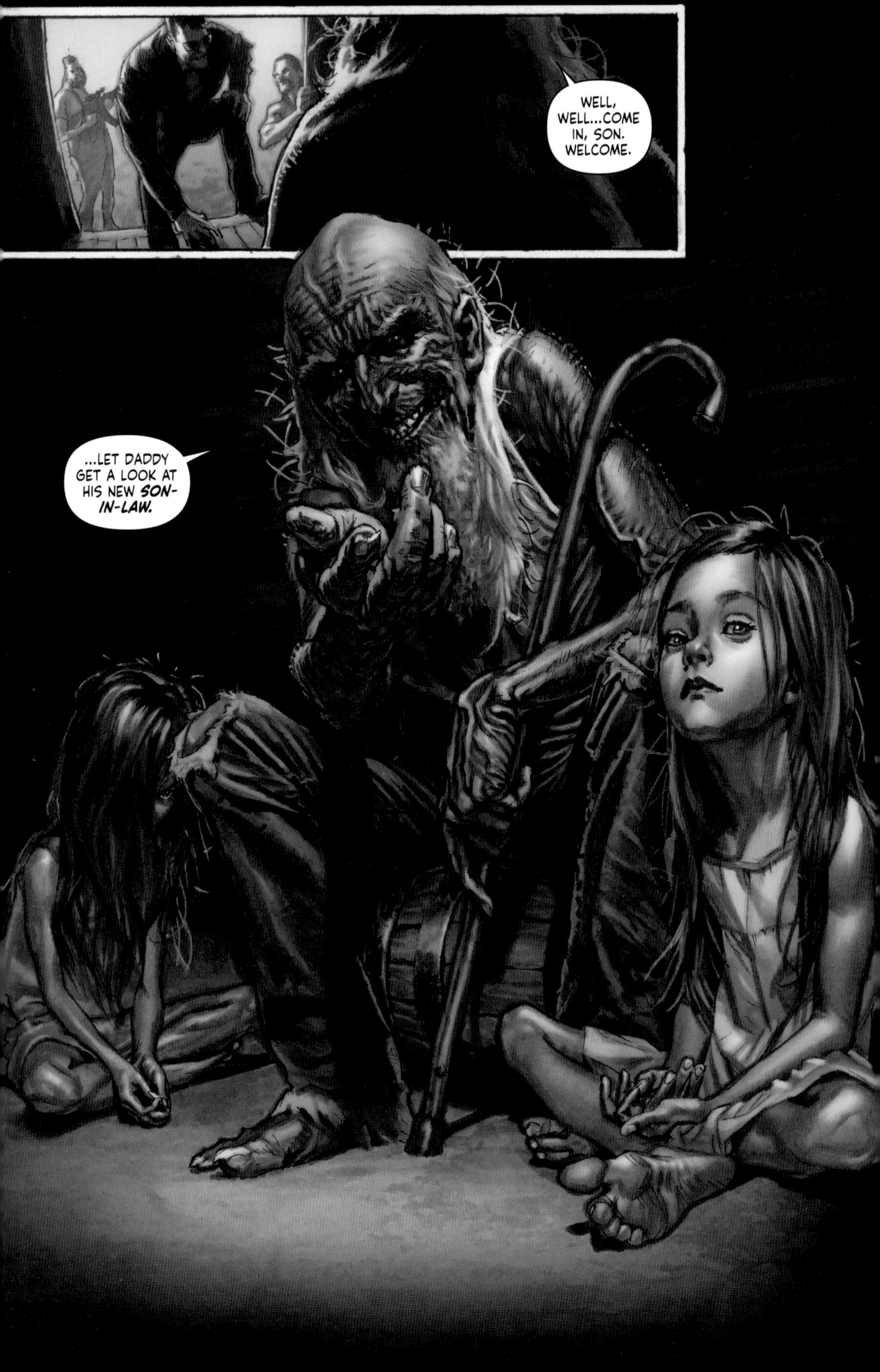
WELL, WELL...COME IN, SON. WELCOME.
...LET DADDY GET A LOOK AT HIS NEW *SON-IN-LAW.*

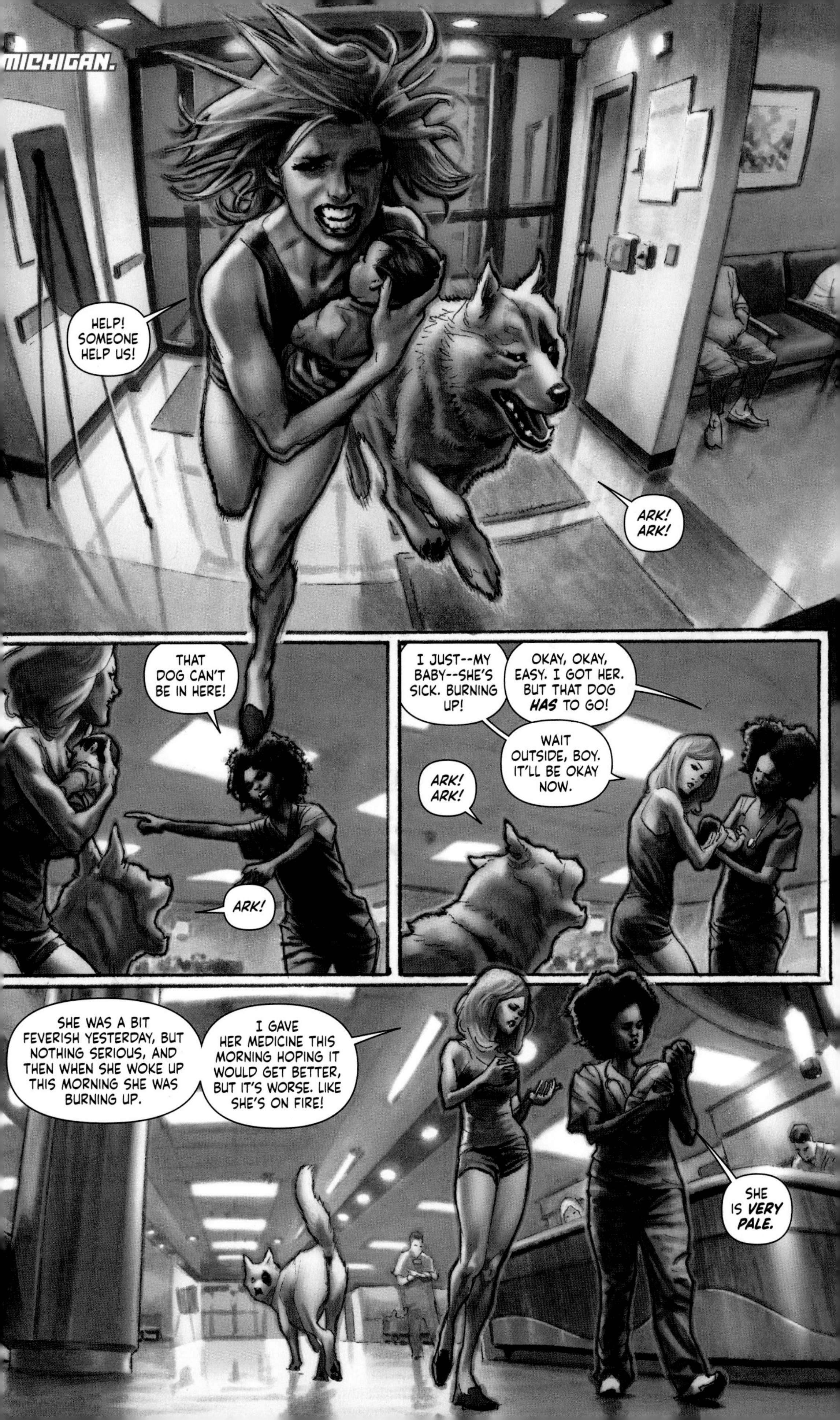
MICHIGAN.
HELP! SOMEONE HELP US!
ARK! ARK!
THAT DOG CAN'T BE IN HERE!
ARK!
I JUST--MY BABY--SHE'S SICK. BURNING UP!
OKAY, OKAY, EASY. I GOT HER. BUT THAT DOG HAS TO GO!
WAIT OUTSIDE, BOY. IT'LL BE OKAY NOW.
ARK! ARK!
SHE WAS A BIT FEVERISH YESTERDAY, BUT NOTHING SERIOUS, AND THEN WHEN SHE WOKE UP THIS MORNING SHE WAS BURNING UP.
I GAVE HER MEDICINE THIS MORNING HOPING IT WOULD GET BETTER, BUT IT'S WORSE. LIKE SHE'S ON FIRE!
SHE IS VERY PALE.

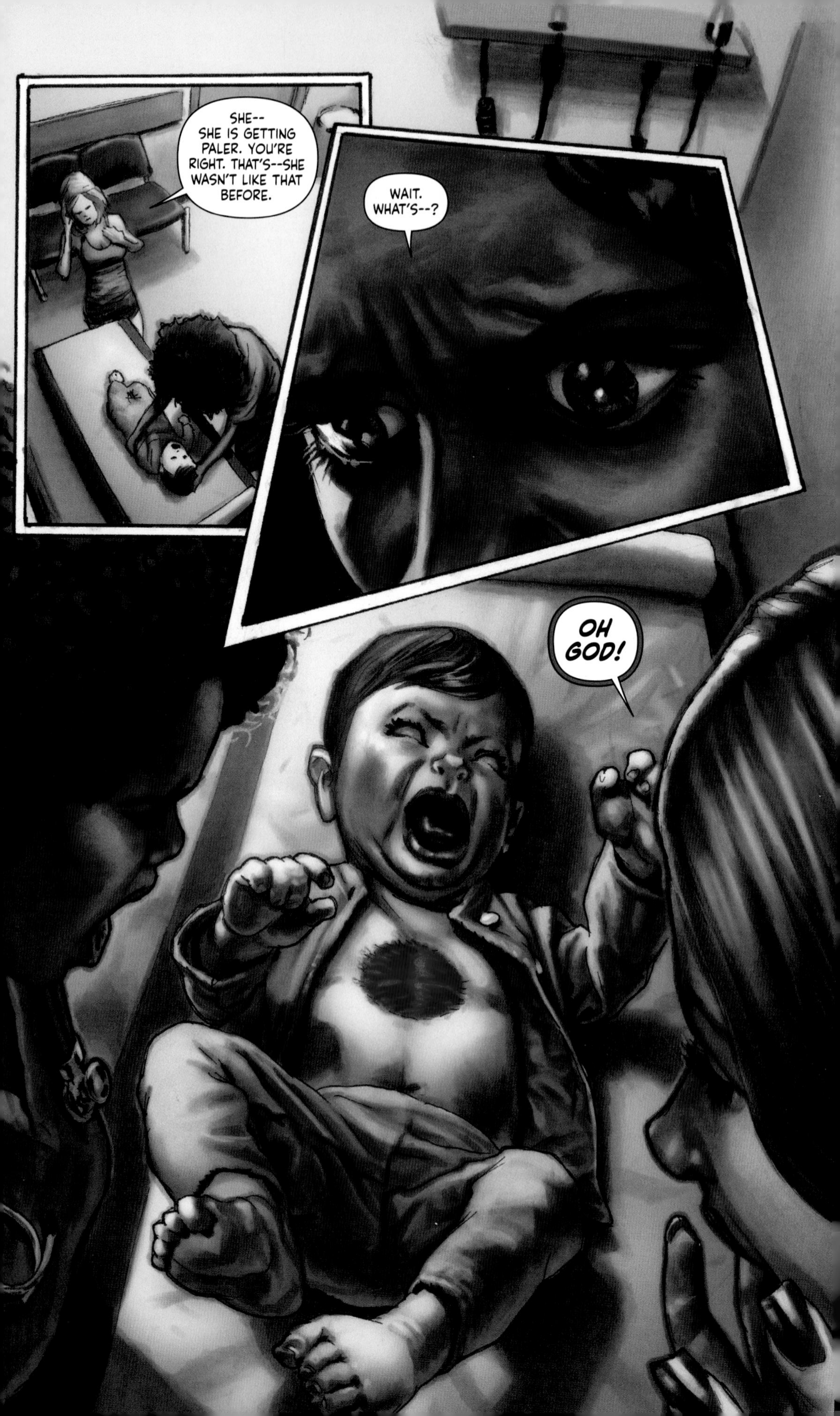
SHE--
SHE IS GETTING PALER. YOU'RE RIGHT. THAT'S--SHE WASN'T LIKE THAT BEFORE.
WAIT. WHAT'S--?
OH GOD!

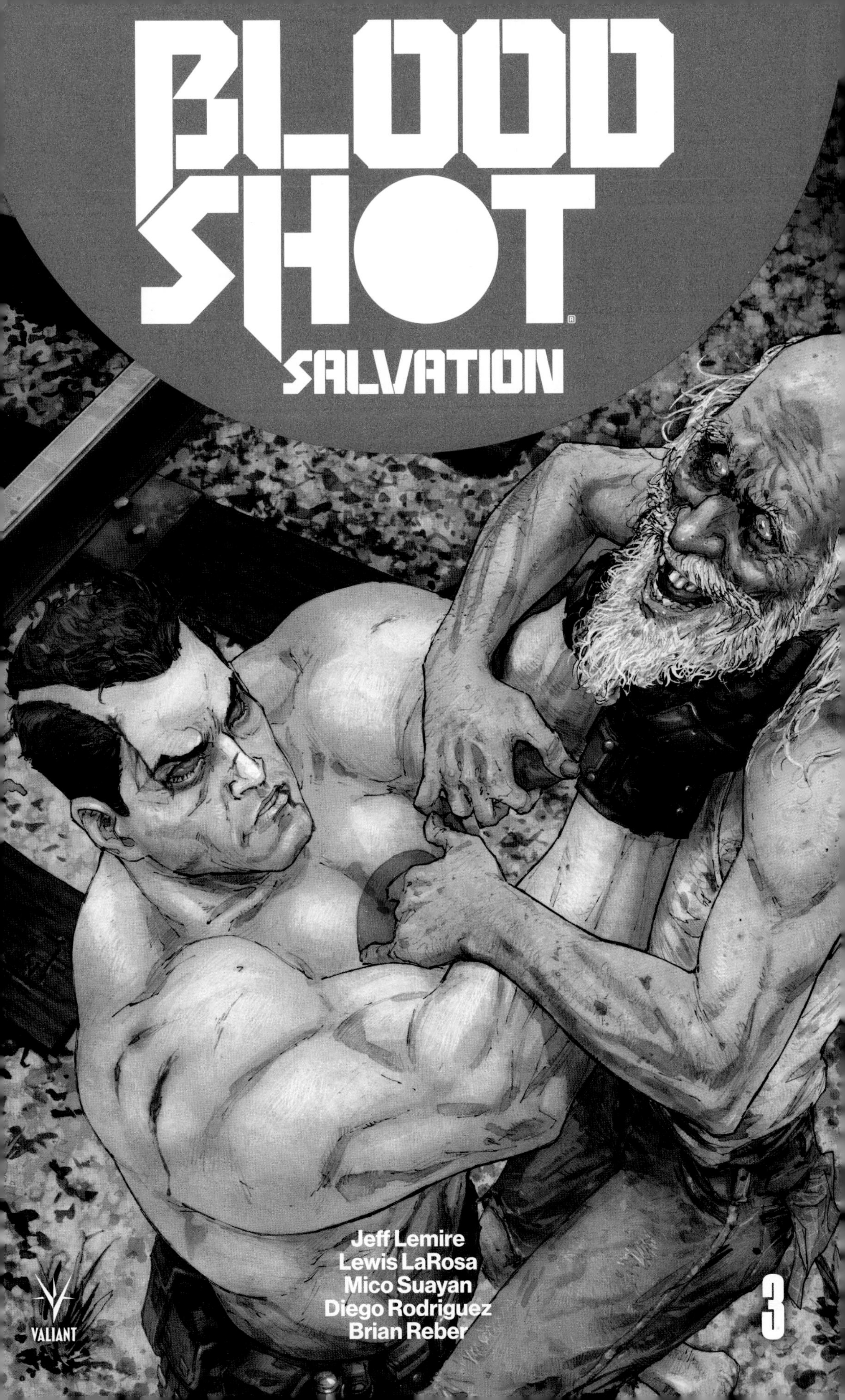
BLOODSHOT
SALVATION
Jeff Lemire
Lewis LaRosa
Mico Suayan
Diego Rodriguez
Brian Reber
VALIANT
3

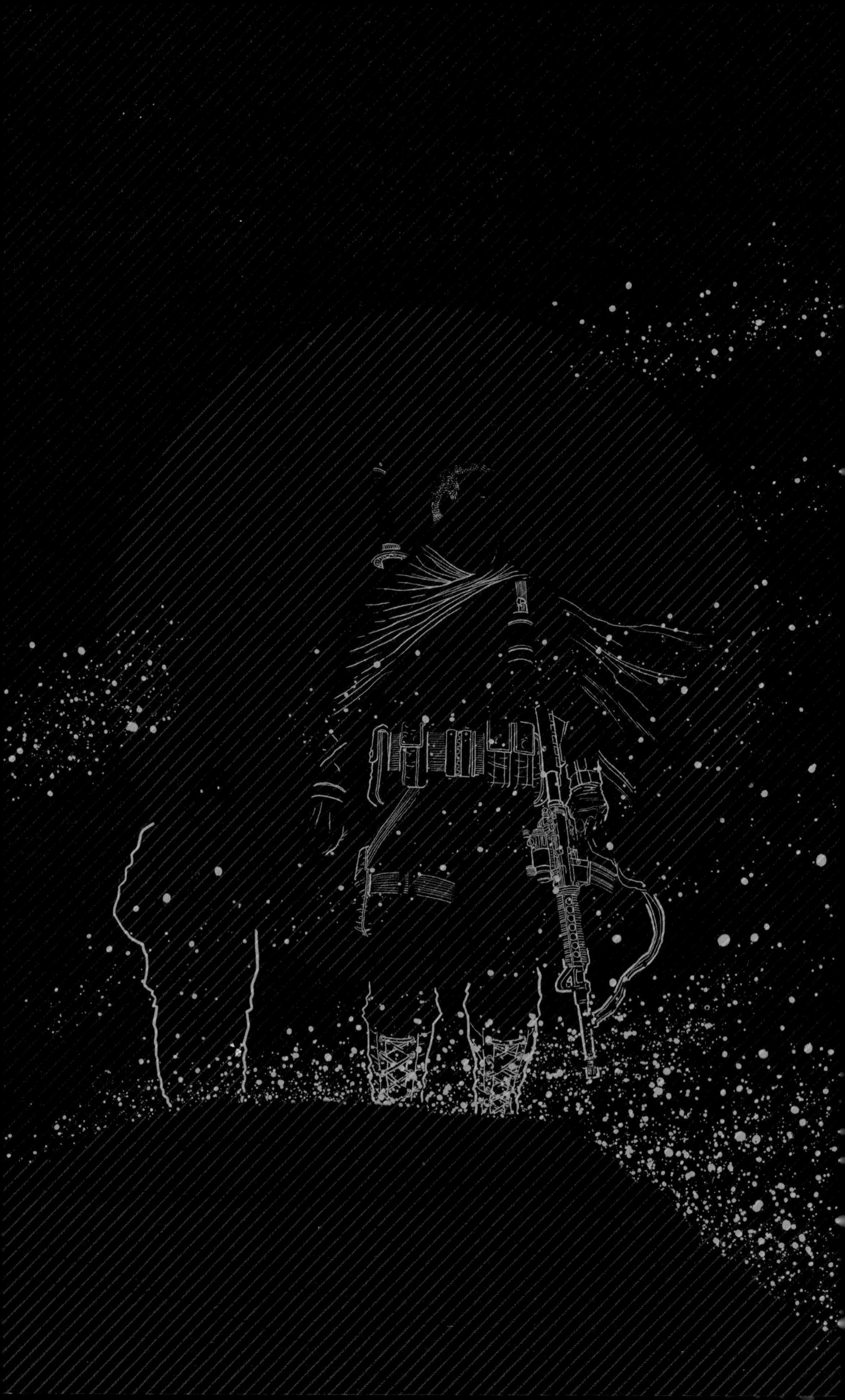

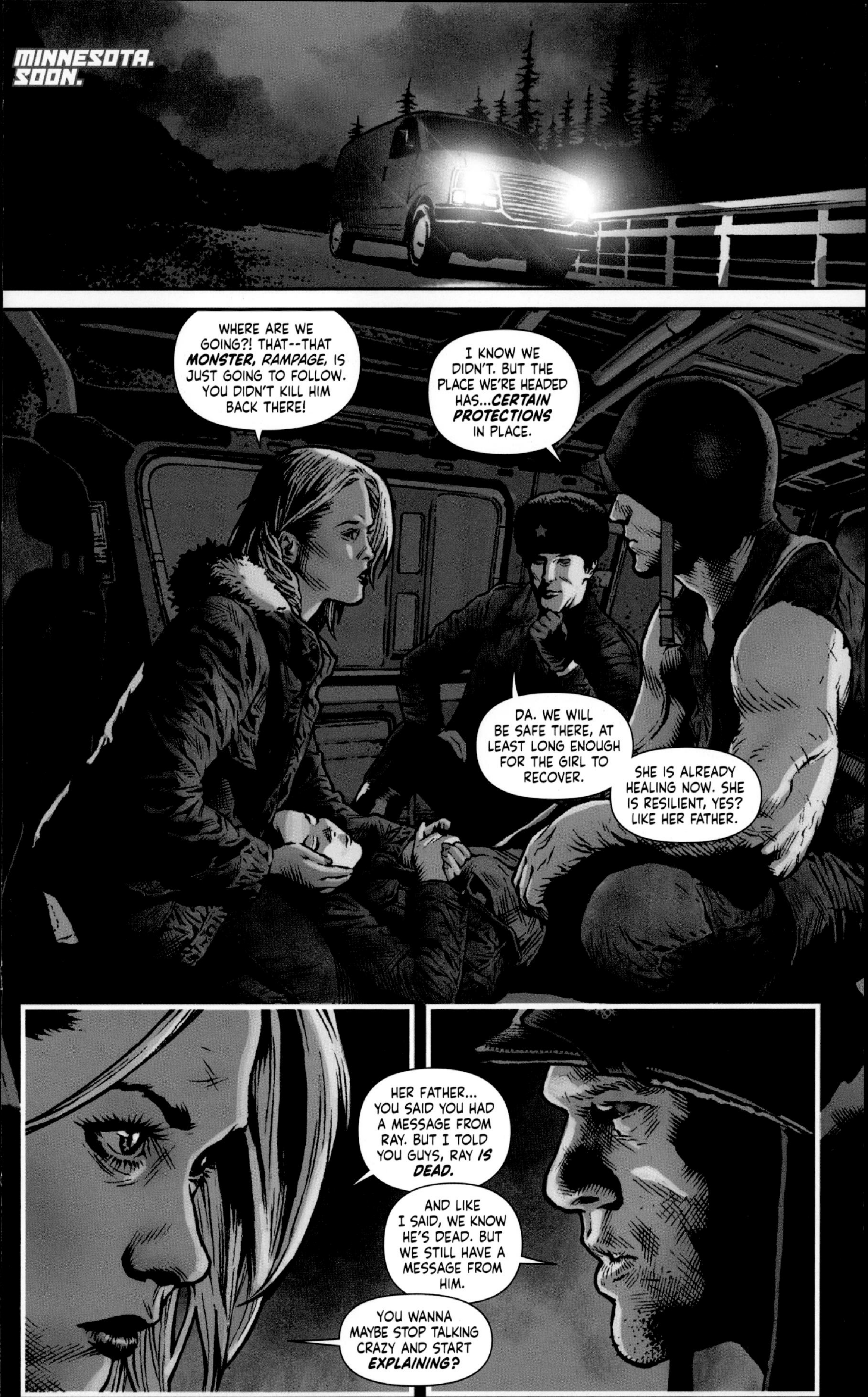
MINNESOTA. SOON.
WHERE ARE WE GOING?! THAT--THAT MONSTER, RAMPAGE, IS JUST GOING TO FOLLOW. YOU DIDN'T KILL HIM BACK THERE!
I KNOW WE DIDN'T. BUT THE PLACE WE'RE HEADED HAS...CERTAIN PROTECTIONS IN PLACE.
DA. WE WILL BE SAFE THERE, AT LEAST LONG ENOUGH FOR THE GIRL TO RECOVER.
SHE IS ALREADY HEALING NOW. SHE IS RESILIENT, YES? LIKE HER FATHER.
HER FATHER... YOU SAID YOU HAD A MESSAGE FROM RAY. BUT I TOLD YOU GUYS, RAY IS DEAD.
AND LIKE I SAID, WE KNOW HE'S DEAD. BUT WE STILL HAVE A MESSAGE FROM HIM.
YOU WANNA MAYBE STOP TALKING CRAZY AND START EXPLAINING?

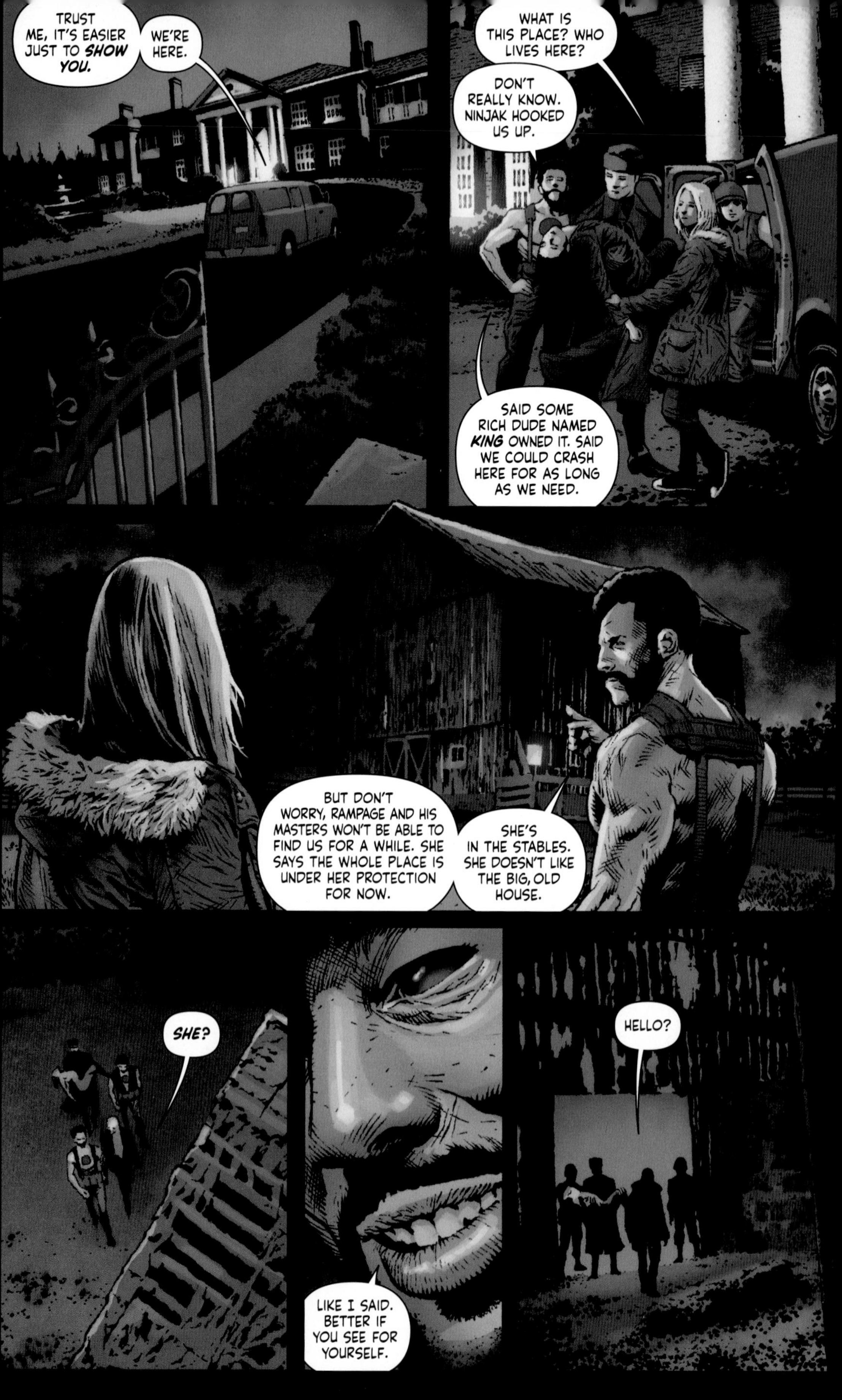
TRUST ME, IT'S EASIER JUST TO **SHOW YOU.**
WE'RE HERE.
WHAT IS THIS PLACE? WHO LIVES HERE?
DON'T REALLY KNOW. NINJAK HOOKED US UP.
SAID SOME RICH DUDE NAMED **KING** OWNED IT. SAID WE COULD CRASH HERE FOR AS LONG AS WE NEED.
BUT DON'T WORRY, RAMPAGE AND HIS MASTERS WON'T BE ABLE TO FIND US FOR A WHILE. SHE SAYS THE WHOLE PLACE IS UNDER HER PROTECTION FOR NOW.
SHE'S IN THE STABLES. SHE DOESN'T LIKE THE BIG, OLD HOUSE.
**SHE?**
LIKE I SAID. BETTER IF YOU SEE FOR YOURSELF.
HELLO?

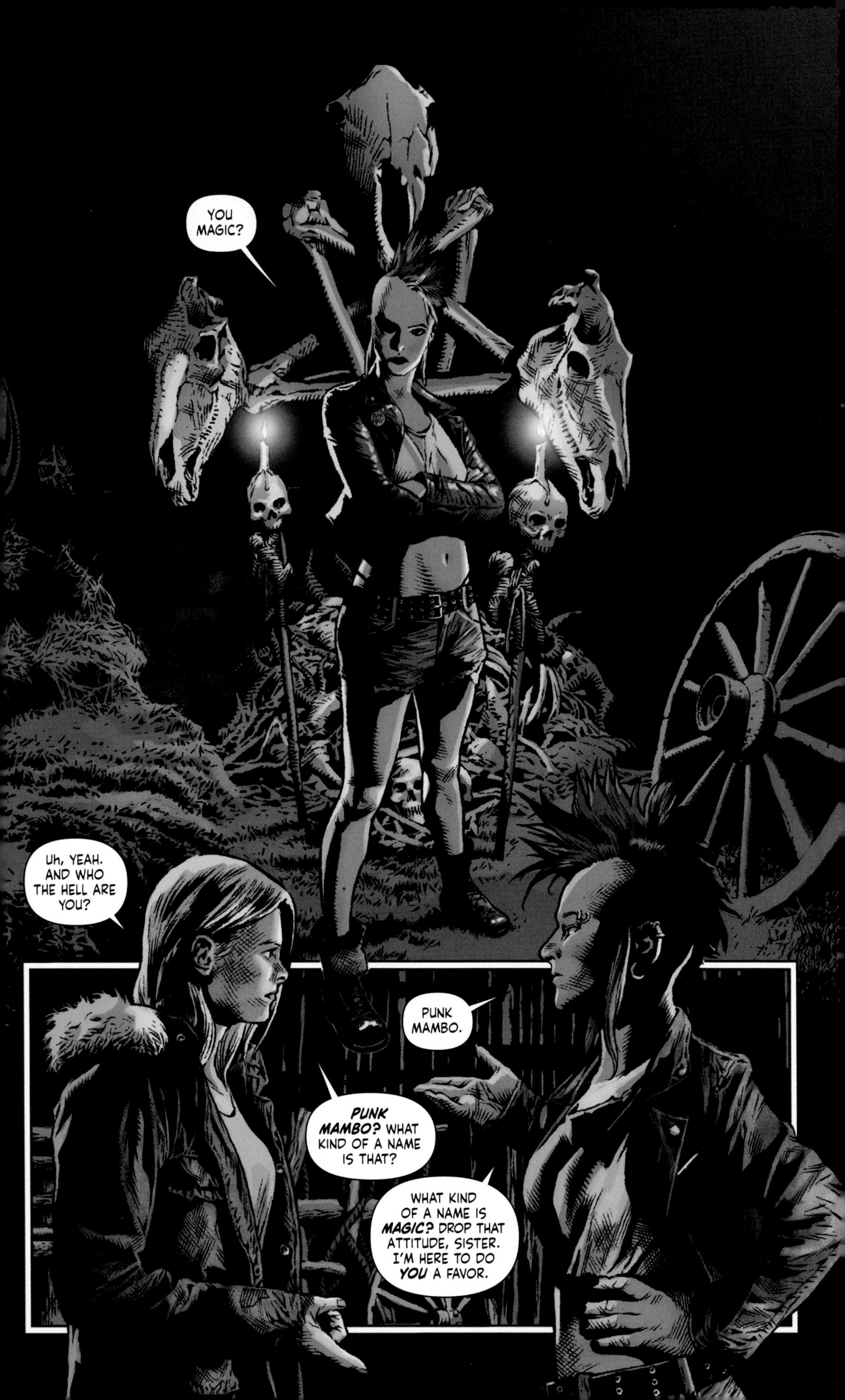
YOU MAGIC?
Uh, YEAH. AND WHO THE HELL ARE YOU?
PUNK MAMBO.
PUNK MAMBO? WHAT KIND OF A NAME IS THAT?
WHAT KIND OF A NAME IS MAGIC? DROP THAT ATTITUDE, SISTER. I'M HERE TO DO YOU A FAVOR.

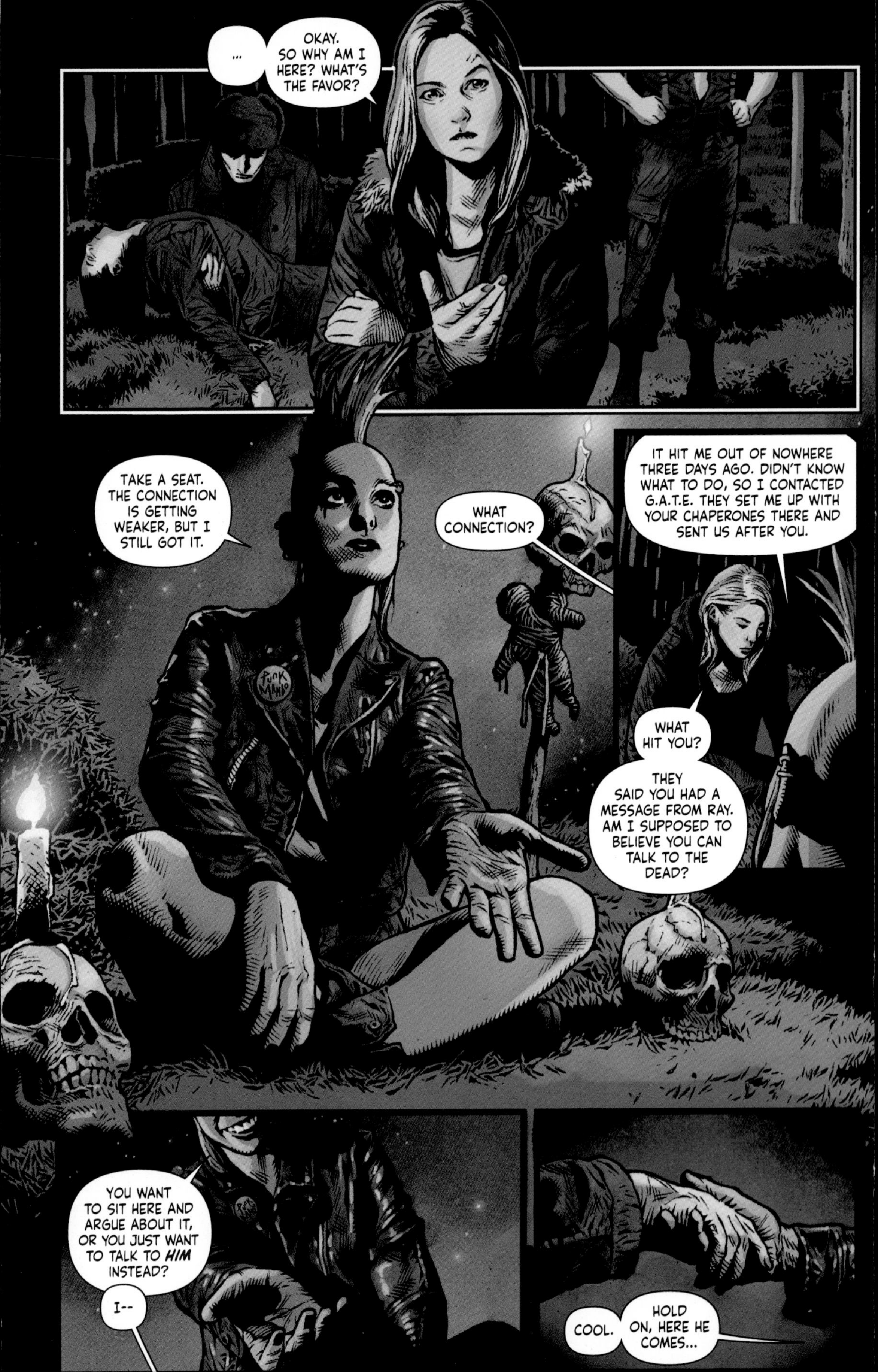
...
OKAY. SO WHY AM I HERE? WHAT'S THE FAVOR?
TAKE A SEAT. THE CONNECTION IS GETTING WEAKER, BUT I STILL GOT IT.
WHAT CONNECTION?
IT HIT ME OUT OF NOWHERE THREE DAYS AGO. DIDN'T KNOW WHAT TO DO, SO I CONTACTED G.A.T.E. THEY SET ME UP WITH YOUR CHAPERONES THERE AND SENT US AFTER YOU.
WHAT HIT YOU?
THEY SAID YOU HAD A MESSAGE FROM RAY. AM I SUPPOSED TO BELIEVE YOU CAN TALK TO THE DEAD?
PUNK MAMBO
YOU WANT TO SIT HERE AND ARGUE ABOUT IT, OR YOU JUST WANT TO TALK TO *HIM* INSTEAD?
I--
COOL.
HOLD ON, HERE HE COMES...

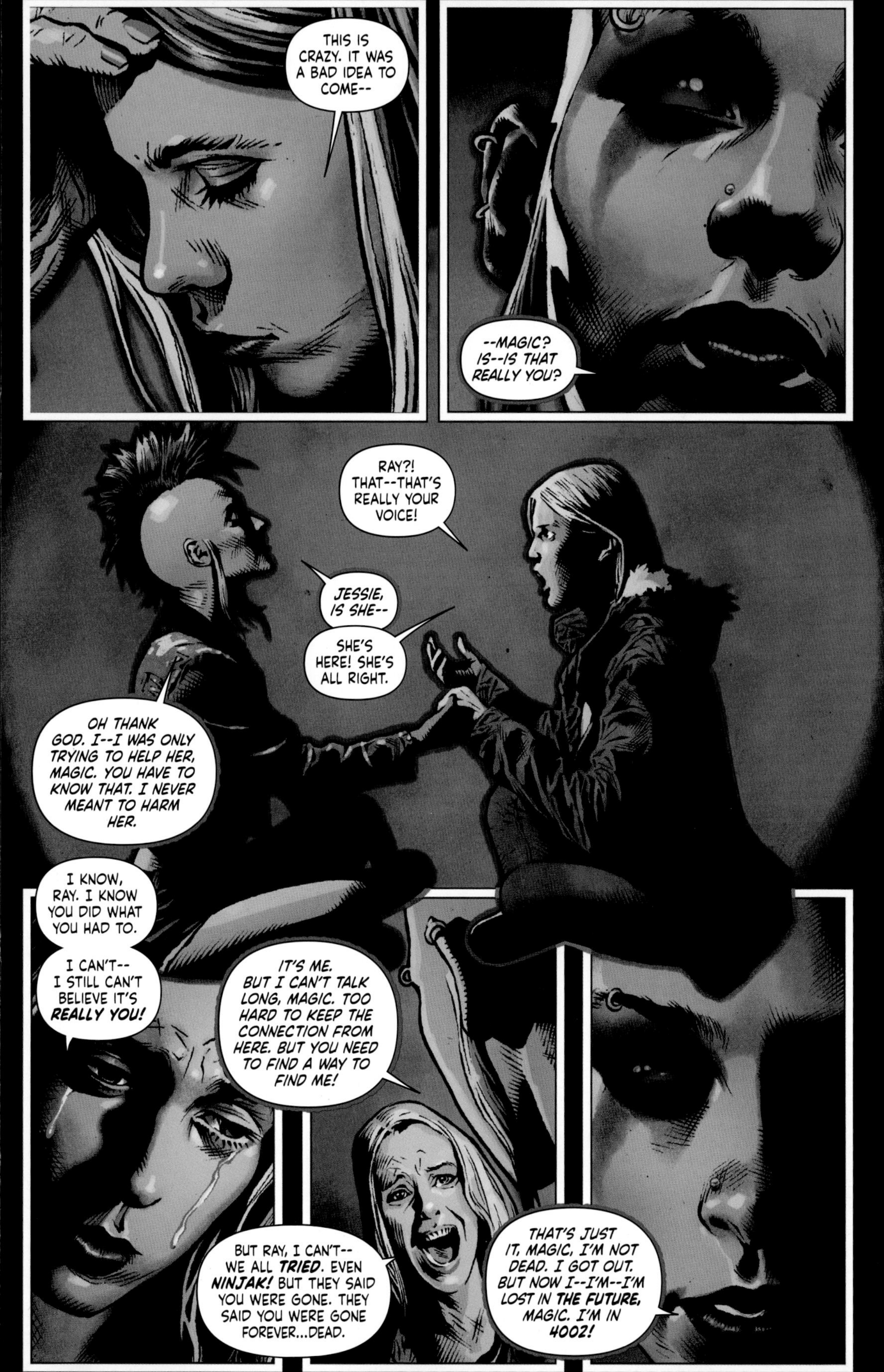

THIS IS CRAZY. IT WAS A BAD IDEA TO COME--
--MAGIC? IS--IS THAT REALLY YOU?
RAY?! THAT--THAT'S REALLY YOUR VOICE!
JESSIE, IS SHE--
SHE'S HERE! SHE'S ALL RIGHT.
OH THANK GOD. I--I WAS ONLY TRYING TO HELP HER, MAGIC. YOU HAVE TO KNOW THAT. I NEVER MEANT TO HARM HER.
I KNOW, RAY. I KNOW YOU DID WHAT YOU HAD TO.
I CAN'T-- I STILL CAN'T BELIEVE IT'S REALLY YOU!
IT'S ME. BUT I CAN'T TALK LONG, MAGIC. TOO HARD TO KEEP THE CONNECTION FROM HERE. BUT YOU NEED TO FIND A WAY TO FIND ME!
BUT RAY, I CAN'T-- WE ALL TRIED. EVEN NINJAK! BUT THEY SAID YOU WERE GONE. THEY SAID YOU WERE GONE FOREVER...DEAD.
THAT'S JUST IT, MAGIC, I'M NOT DEAD. I GOT OUT. BUT NOW I--I'M--I'M LOST IN THE FUTURE, MAGIC. I'M IN 4002!

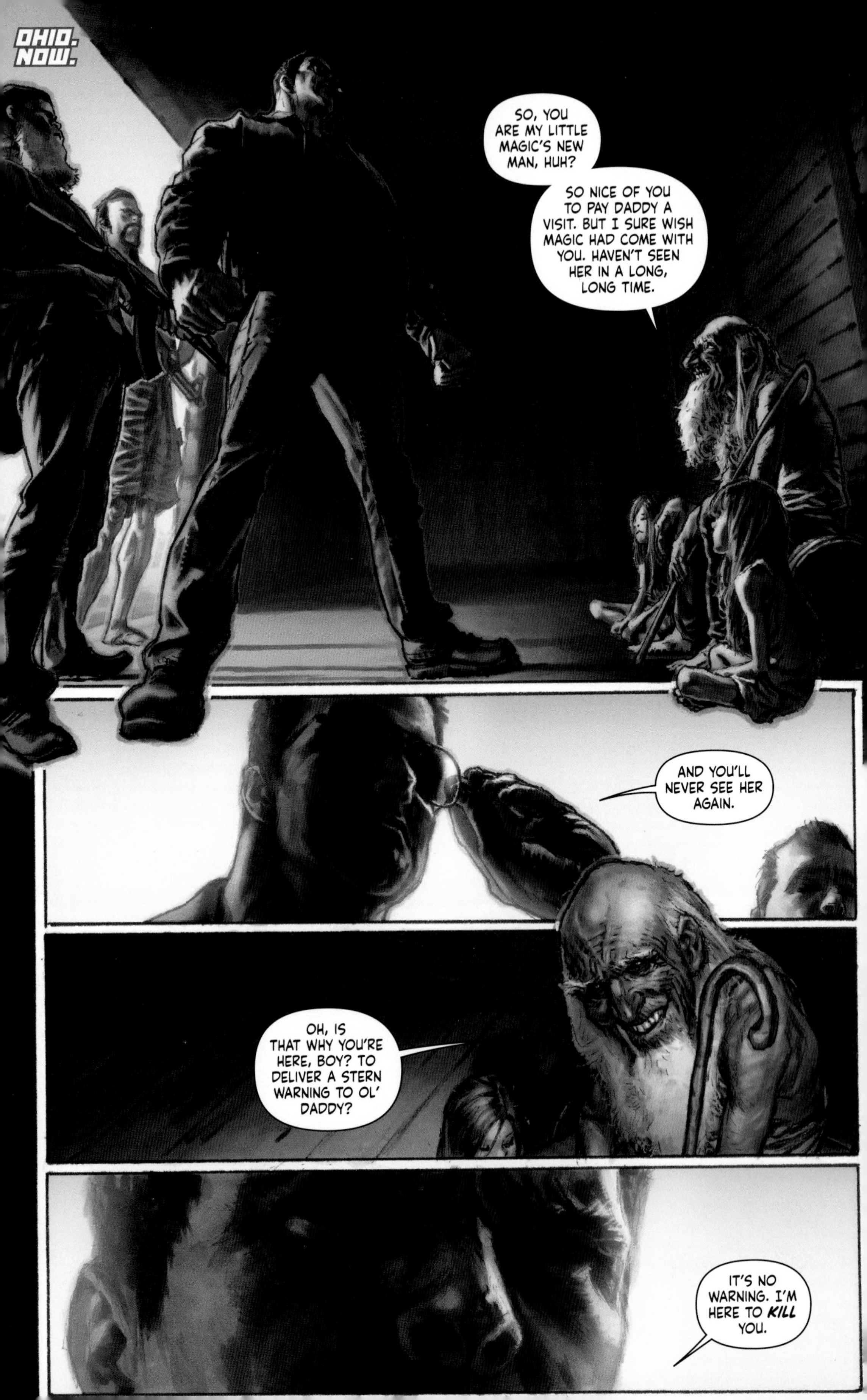
OHIO. NOW.
SO, YOU ARE MY LITTLE MAGIC'S NEW MAN, HUH?
SO NICE OF YOU TO PAY DADDY A VISIT. BUT I SURE WISH MAGIC HAD COME WITH YOU. HAVEN'T SEEN HER IN A LONG, LONG TIME.
AND YOU'LL NEVER SEE HER AGAIN.
OH, IS THAT WHY YOU'RE HERE, BOY? TO DELIVER A STERN WARNING TO OL' DADDY?
IT'S NO WARNING. I'M HERE TO KILL YOU.

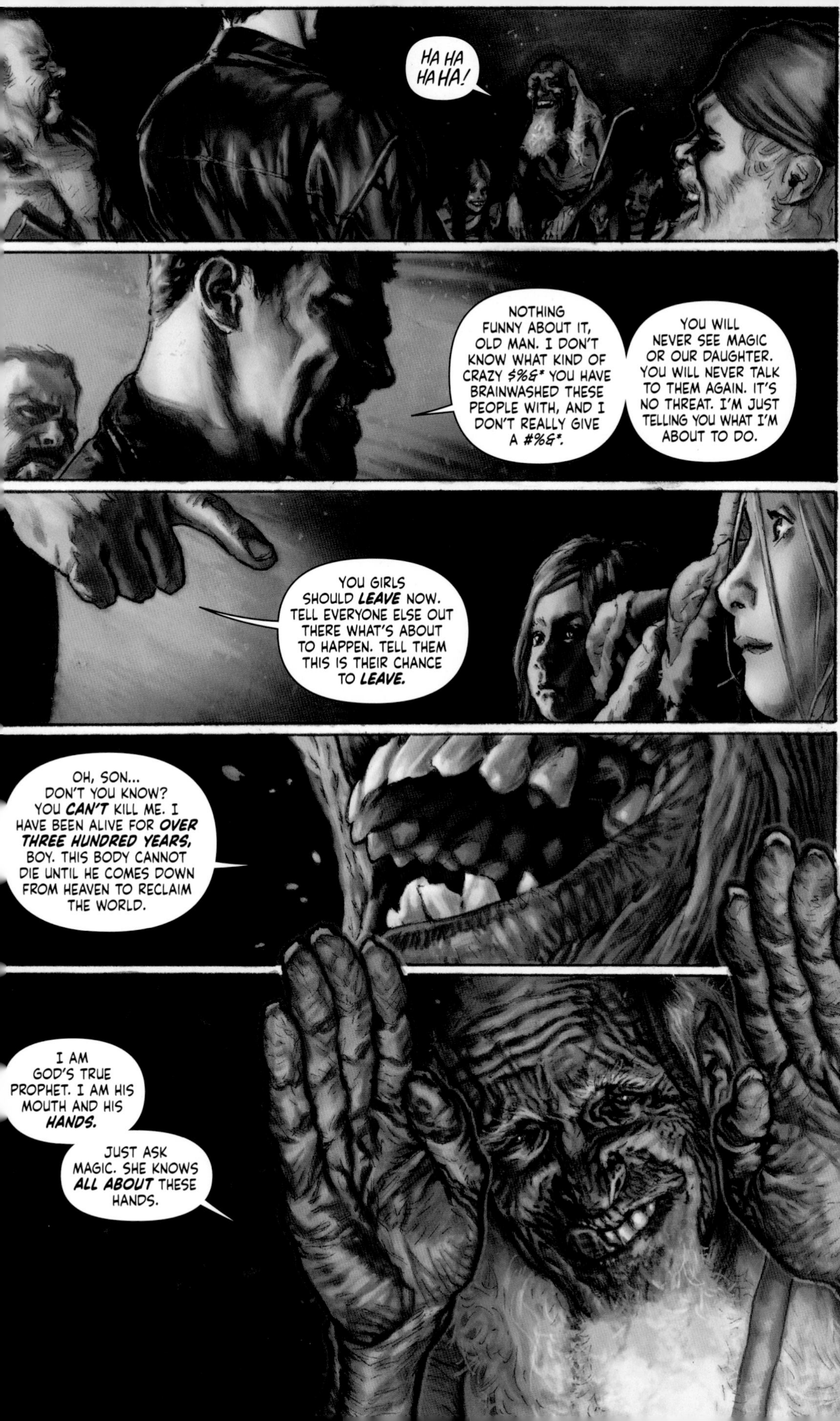
HA HA HA HA!
NOTHING FUNNY ABOUT IT, OLD MAN. I DON'T KNOW WHAT KIND OF CRAZY $%&* YOU HAVE BRAINWASHED THESE PEOPLE WITH, AND I DON'T REALLY GIVE A #%&*.
YOU WILL NEVER SEE MAGIC OR OUR DAUGHTER. YOU WILL NEVER TALK TO THEM AGAIN. IT'S NO THREAT. I'M JUST TELLING YOU WHAT I'M ABOUT TO DO.
YOU GIRLS SHOULD **LEAVE** NOW. TELL EVERYONE ELSE OUT THERE WHAT'S ABOUT TO HAPPEN. TELL THEM THIS IS THEIR CHANCE TO **LEAVE.**
OH, SON... DON'T YOU KNOW? YOU **CAN'T** KILL ME. I HAVE BEEN ALIVE FOR **OVER THREE HUNDRED YEARS,** BOY. THIS BODY CANNOT DIE UNTIL HE COMES DOWN FROM HEAVEN TO RECLAIM THE WORLD.
I AM GOD'S TRUE PROPHET. I AM HIS MOUTH AND HIS **HANDS.**
JUST ASK MAGIC. SHE KNOWS **ALL ABOUT** THESE HANDS.

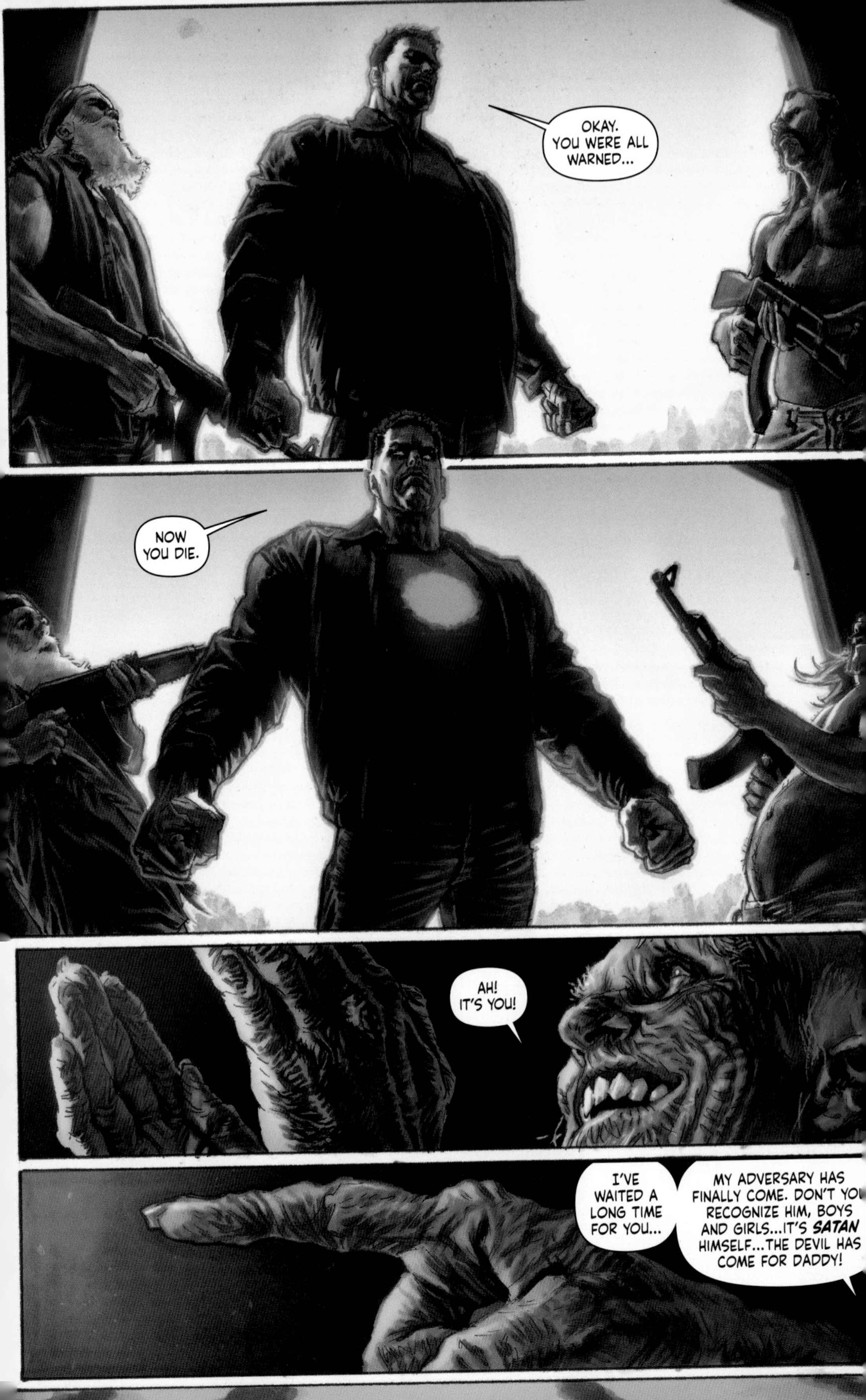
OKAY. YOU WERE ALL WARNED...
NOW YOU DIE.
AH! IT'S YOU!
I'VE WAITED A LONG TIME FOR YOU...
MY ADVERSARY HAS FINALLY COME. DON'T YOU RECOGNIZE HIM, BOYS AND GIRLS...IT'S *SATAN* HIMSELF...THE DEVIL HAS COME FOR DADDY!

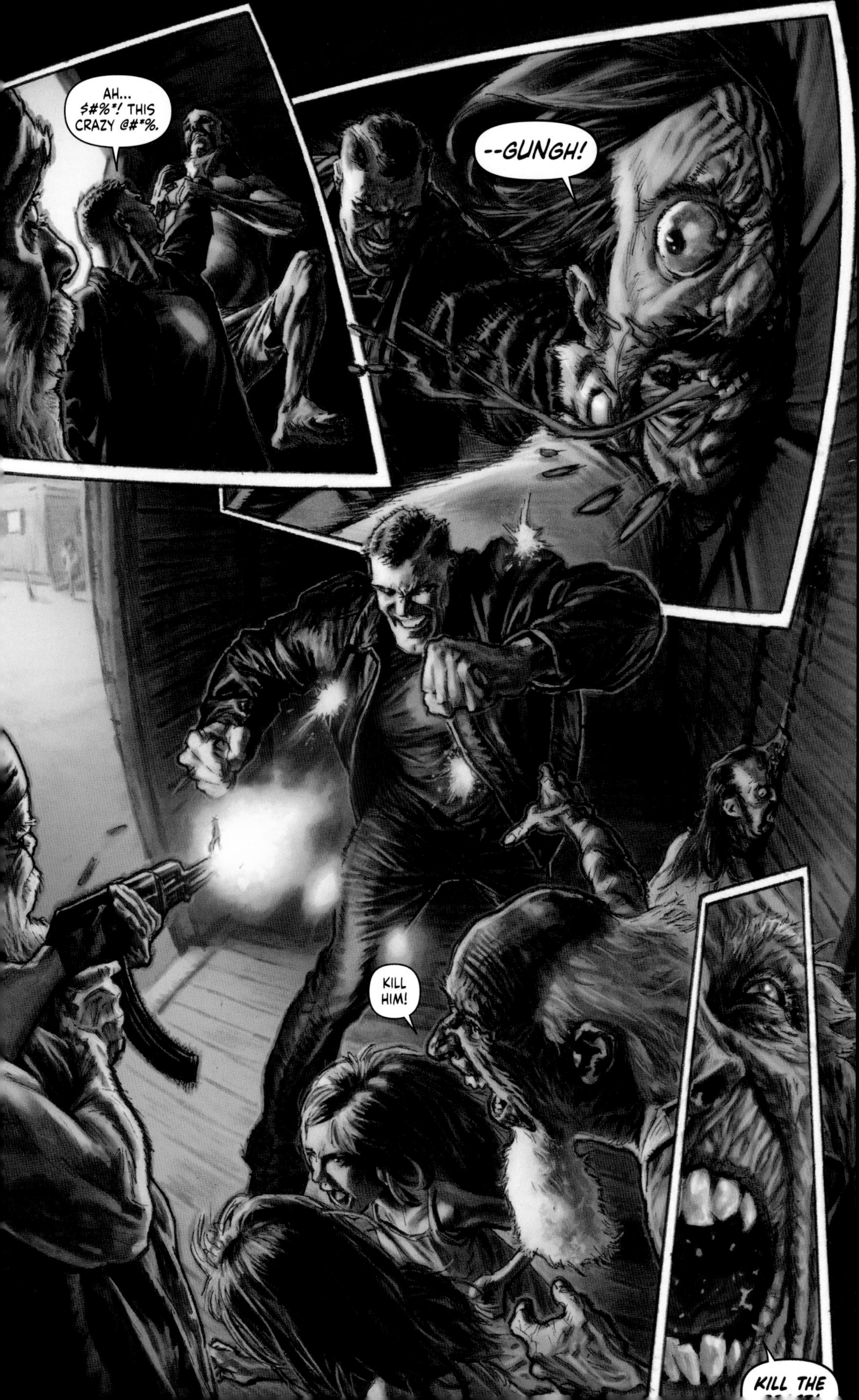
AH... $#%*! THIS CRAZY @#*%.
--GUNGH!
KILL HIM!
KILL THE

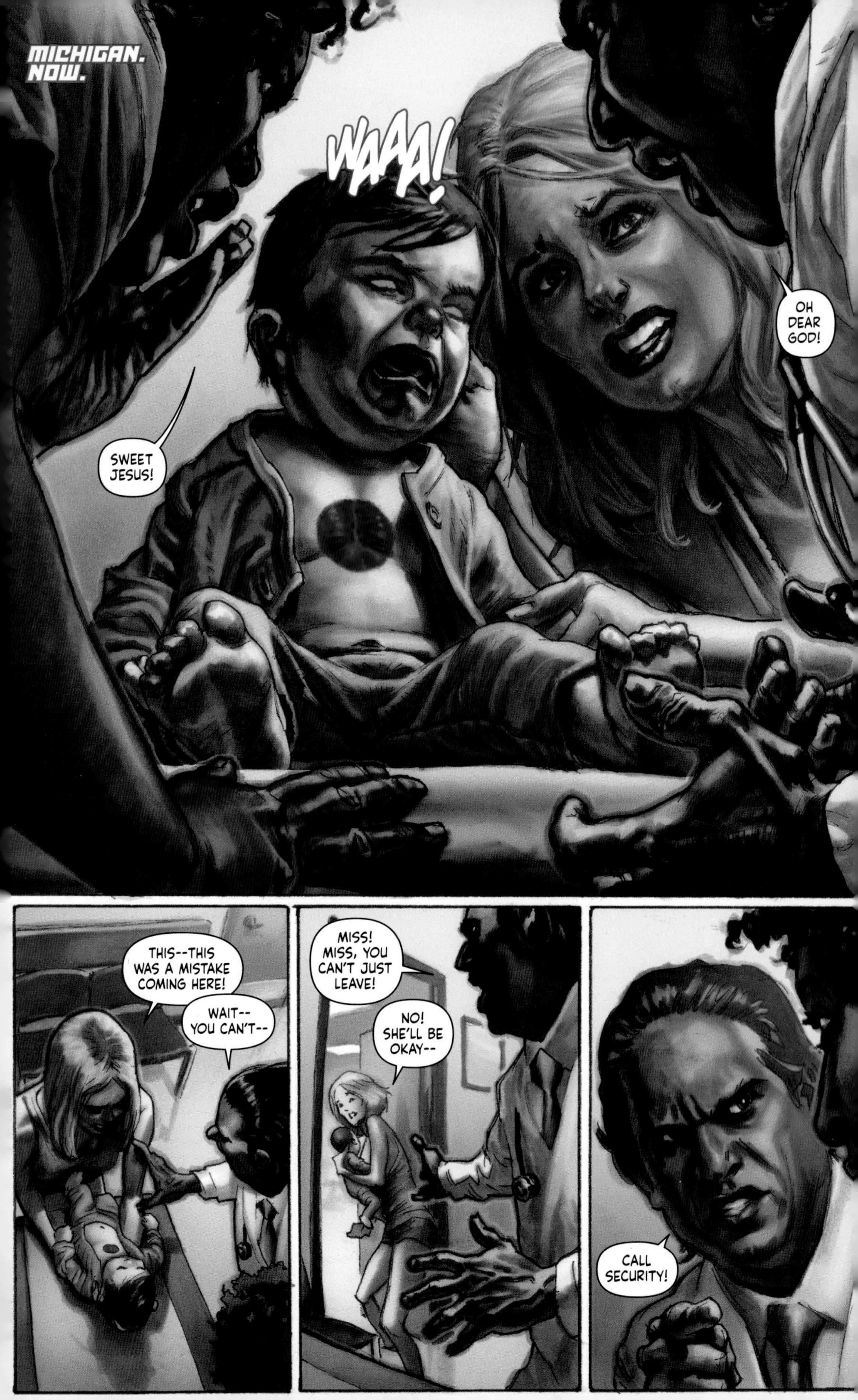
MICHIGAN. NOW.
WAAA!
OH DEAR GOD!
SWEET JESUS!
THIS--THIS WAS A MISTAKE COMING HERE!
WAIT-- YOU CAN'T--
MISS! MISS, YOU CAN'T JUST LEAVE!
NO! SHE'LL BE OKAY--
CALL SECURITY!

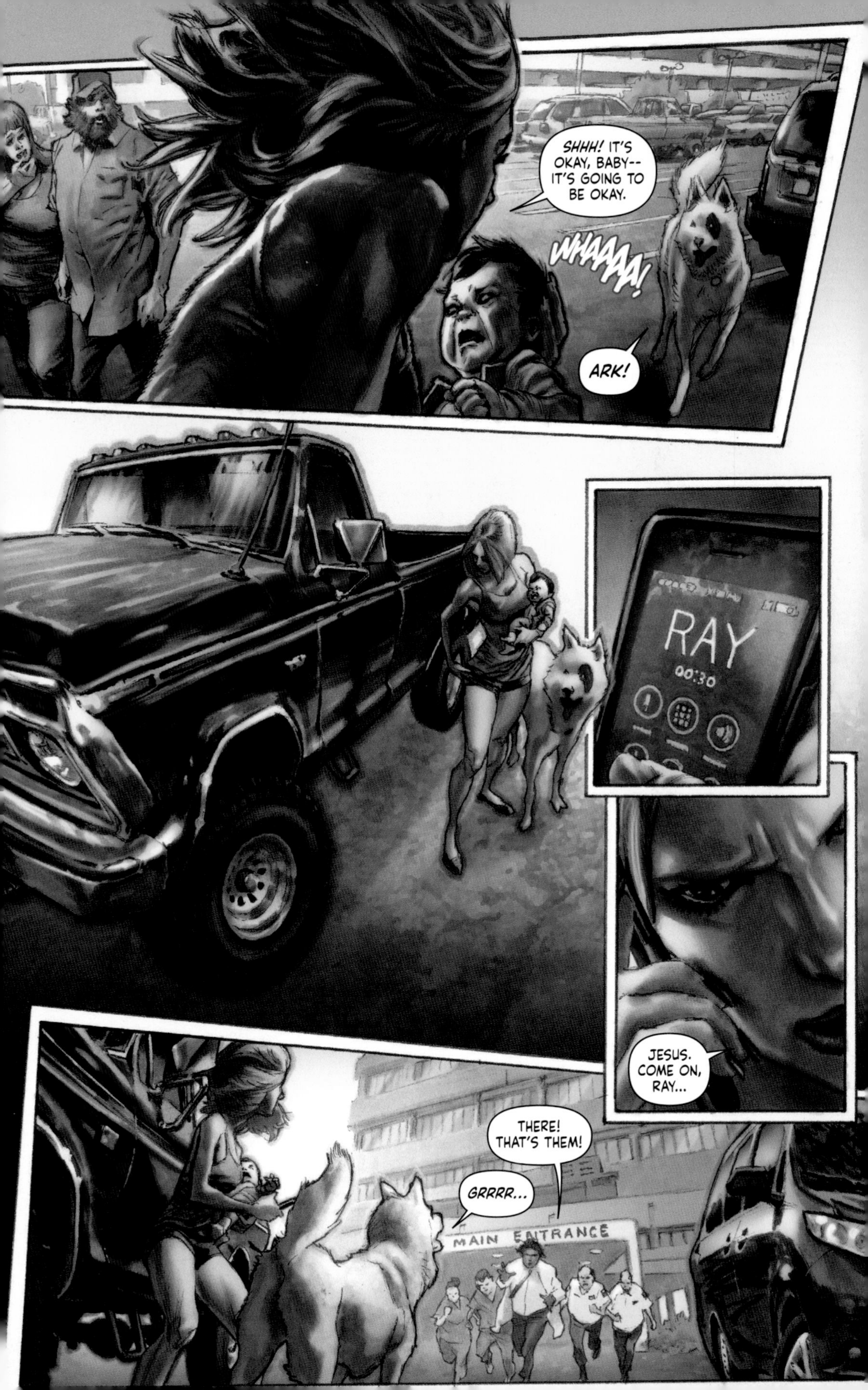
SHHH! IT'S OKAY, BABY-- IT'S GOING TO BE OKAY.
WHAAAAA!
ARK!
RAY
00:30
JESUS. COME ON, RAY...
THERE! THAT'S THEM!
GRRRR...
MAIN ENTRANCE

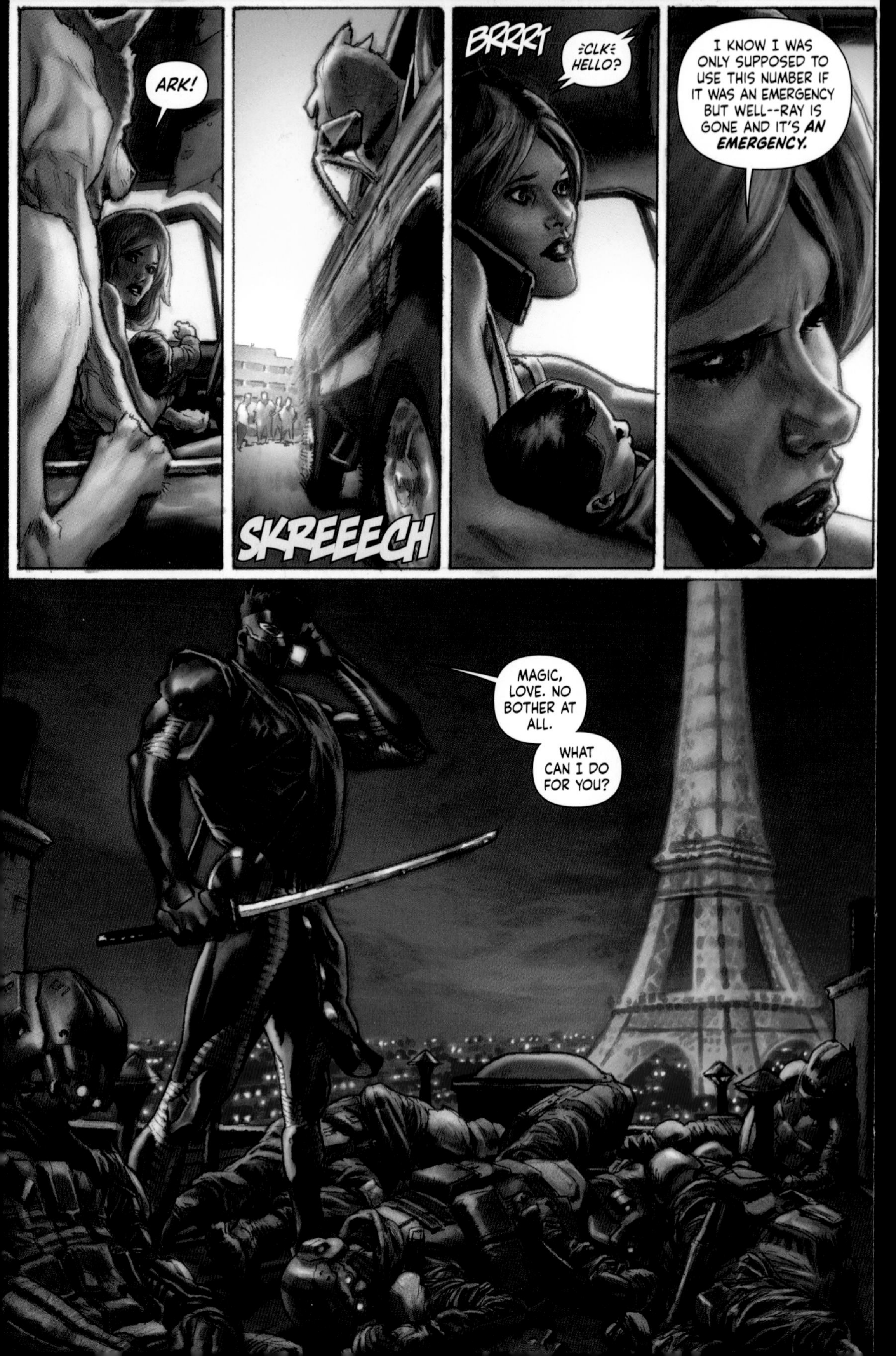
ARK!
SKREEECH
BRRRT
≡CLK≡ HELLO?
I KNOW I WAS ONLY SUPPOSED TO USE THIS NUMBER IF IT WAS AN EMERGENCY BUT WELL--RAY IS GONE AND IT'S **AN EMERGENCY.**
MAGIC, LOVE. NO BOTHER AT ALL.
WHAT CAN I DO FOR YOU?

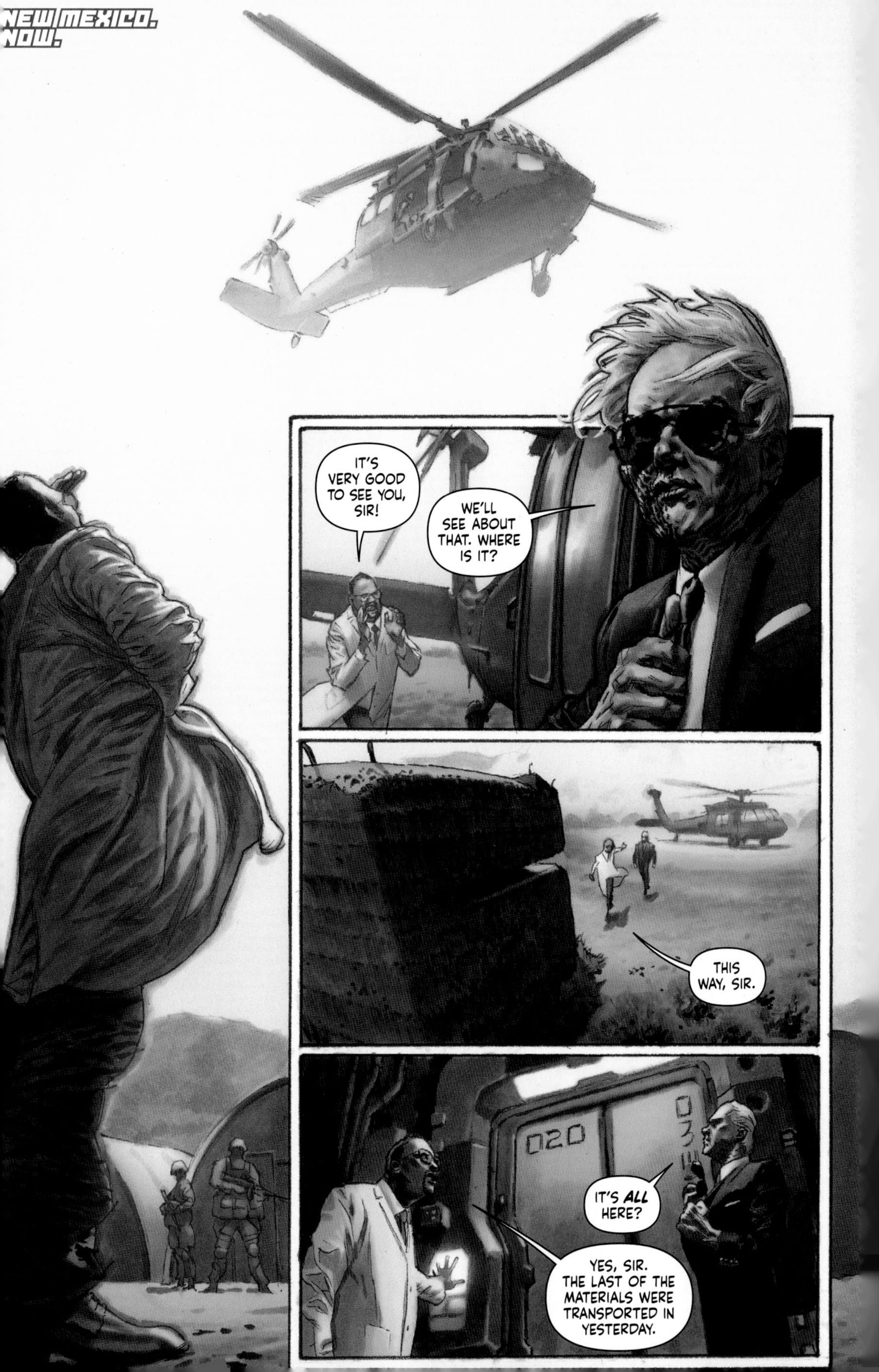
NEW MEXICO.
NOW.
IT'S VERY GOOD TO SEE YOU, SIR!
WE'LL SEE ABOUT THAT. WHERE IS IT?
THIS WAY, SIR.
IT'S ALL HERE?
YES, SIR. THE LAST OF THE MATERIALS WERE TRANSPORTED IN YESTERDAY.

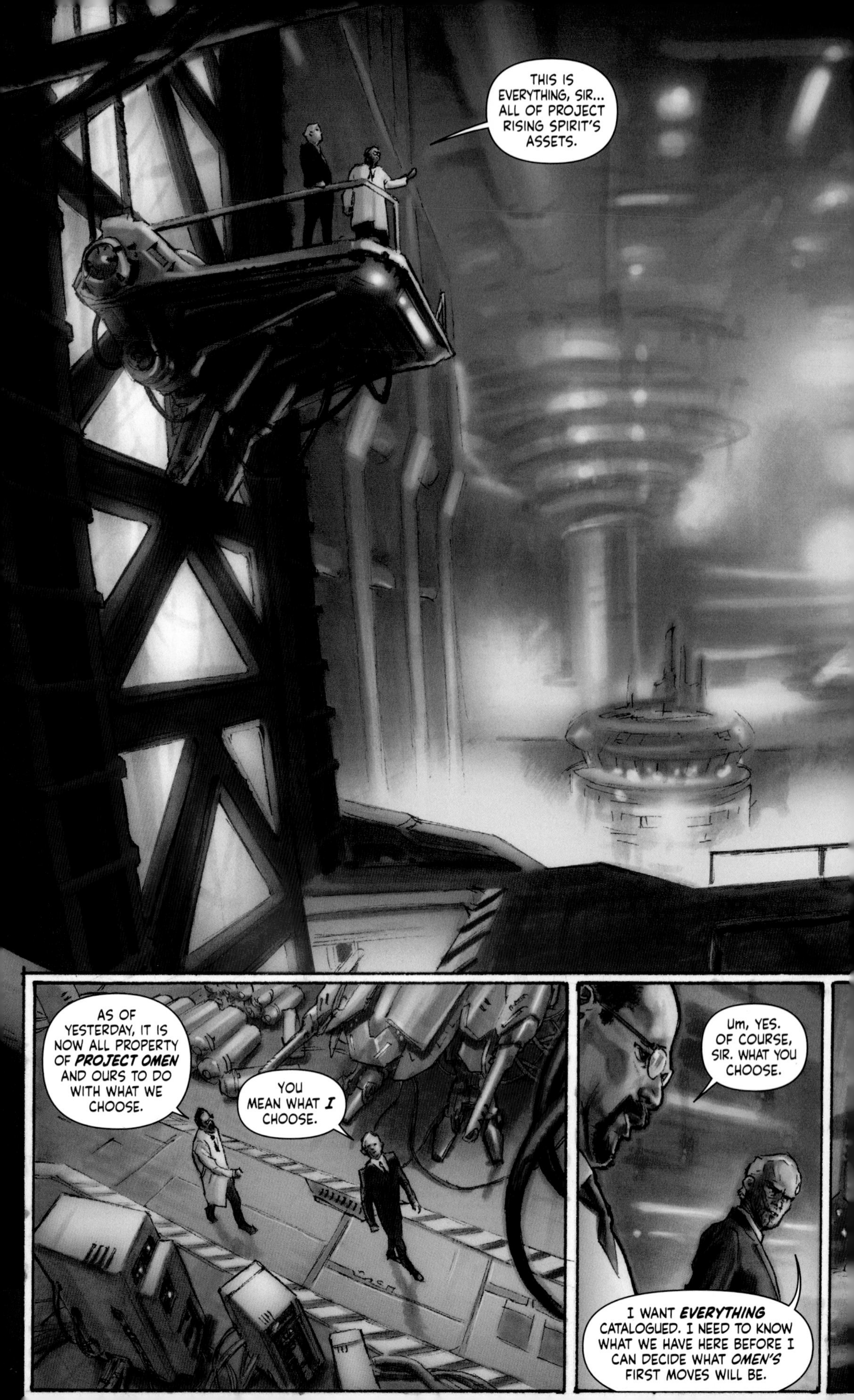
THIS IS EVERYTHING, SIR... ALL OF PROJECT RISING SPIRIT'S ASSETS.
AS OF YESTERDAY, IT IS NOW ALL PROPERTY OF ***PROJECT OMEN*** AND OURS TO DO WITH WHAT WE CHOOSE.
YOU MEAN WHAT ***I*** CHOOSE.
Um, YES. OF COURSE, SIR. WHAT YOU CHOOSE.
I WANT ***EVERYTHING*** CATALOGUED. I NEED TO KNOW WHAT WE HAVE HERE BEFORE I CAN DECIDE WHAT ***OMEN'S*** FIRST MOVES WILL BE.

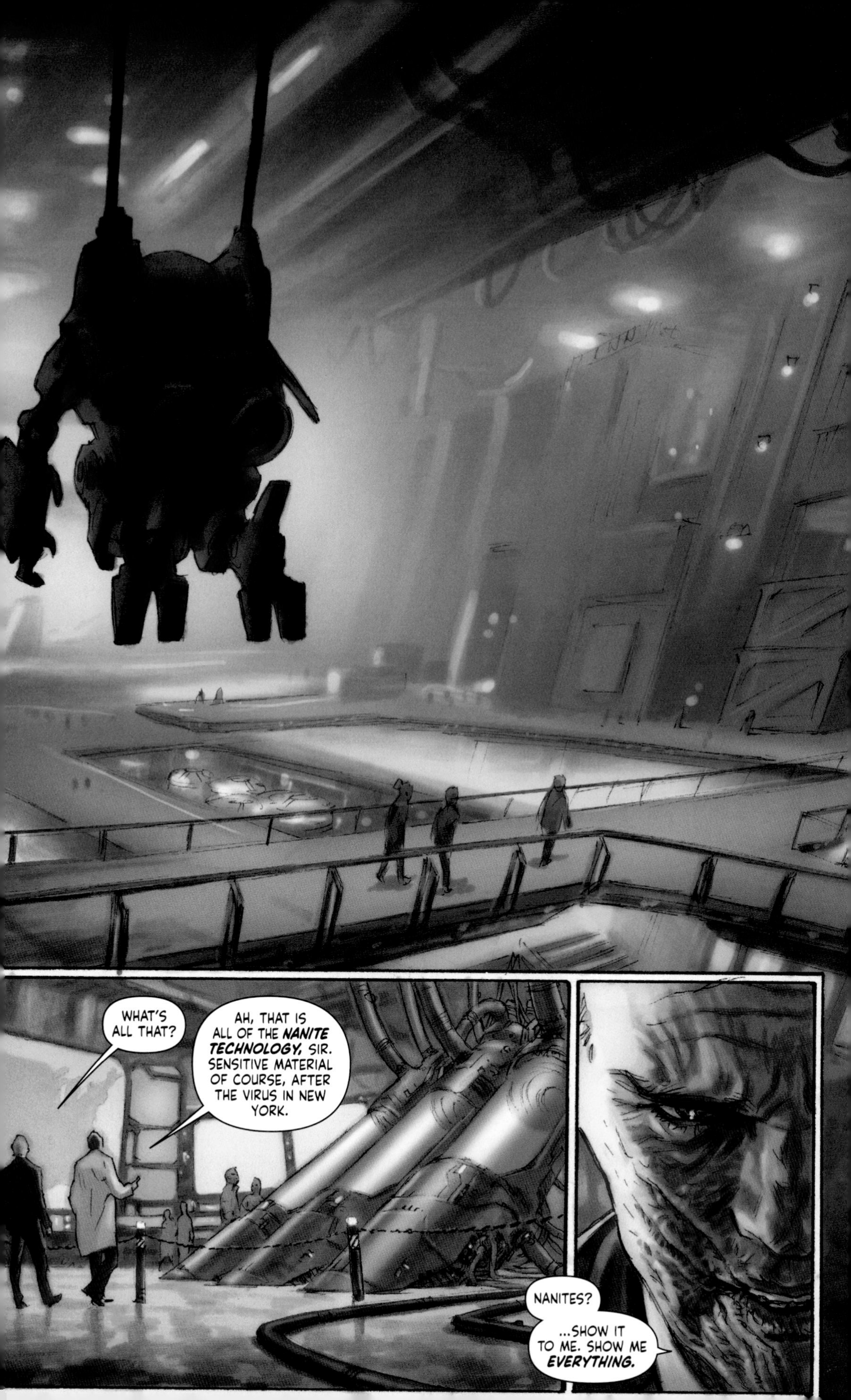
WHAT'S ALL THAT?
AH, THAT IS ALL OF THE NANITE TECHNOLOGY, SIR. SENSITIVE MATERIAL OF COURSE, AFTER THE VIRUS IN NEW YORK.
NANITES?
...SHOW IT TO ME. SHOW ME EVERYTHING.

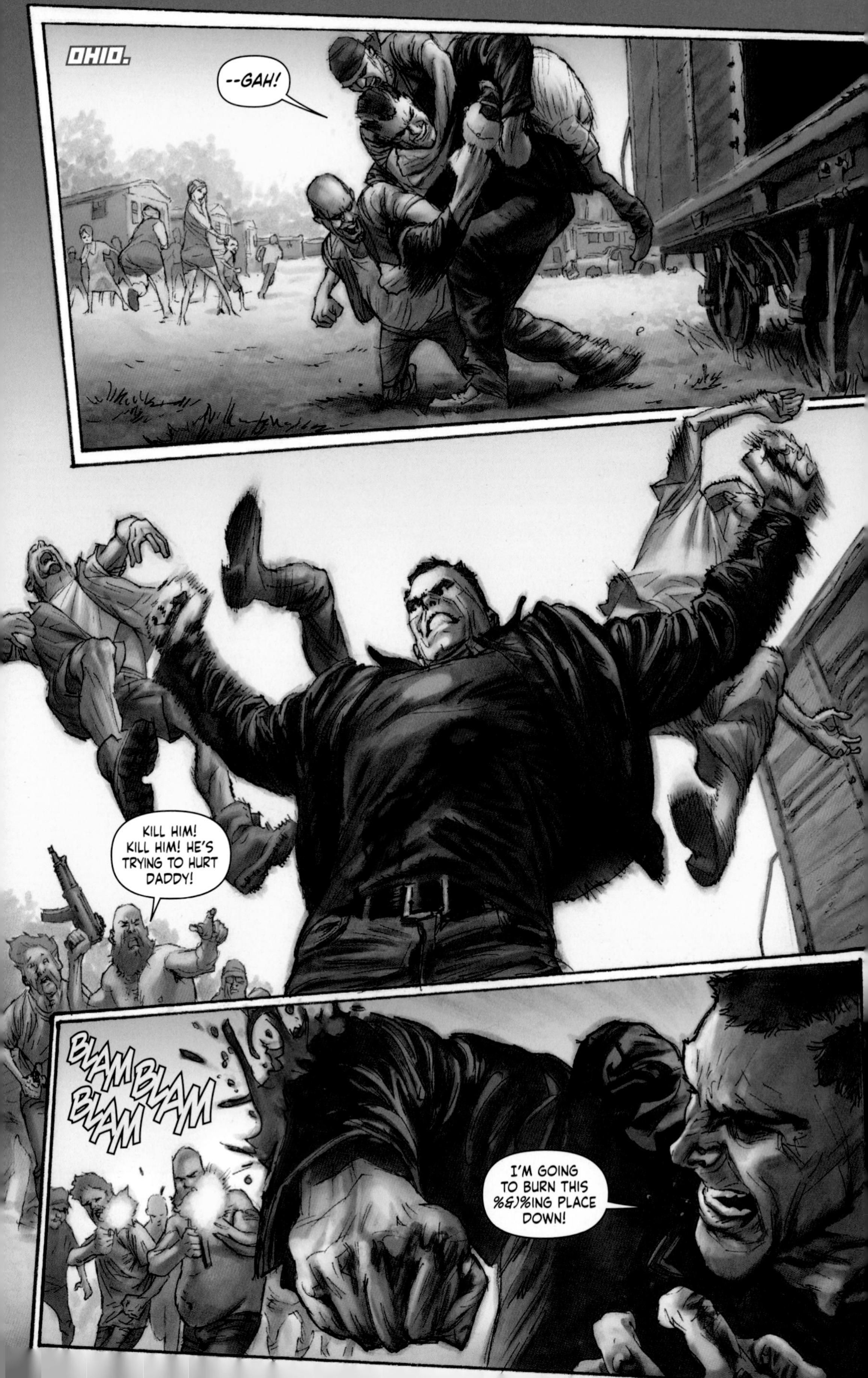
OHIO.
--GAH!
KILL HIM! KILL HIM! HE'S TRYING TO HURT DADDY!
BLAM BLAM BLAM
I'M GOING TO BURN THIS %&)%ING PLACE DOWN!

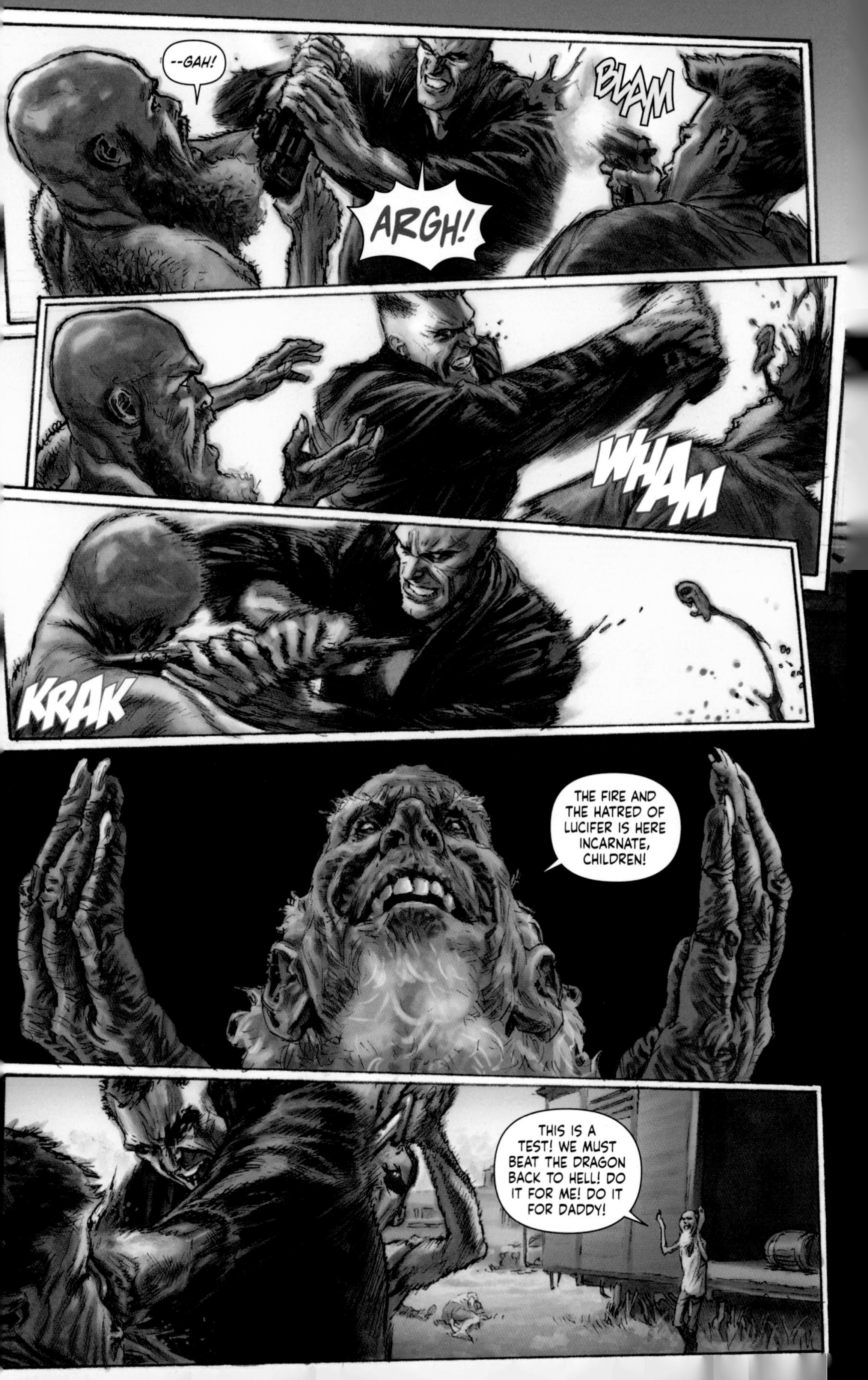
--GAH!
BLAM
ARGH!
WHAM
KRAK
THE FIRE AND THE HATRED OF LUCIFER IS HERE INCARNATE, CHILDREN!
THIS IS A TEST! WE MUST BEAT THE DRAGON BACK TO HELL! DO IT FOR ME! DO IT FOR DADDY!

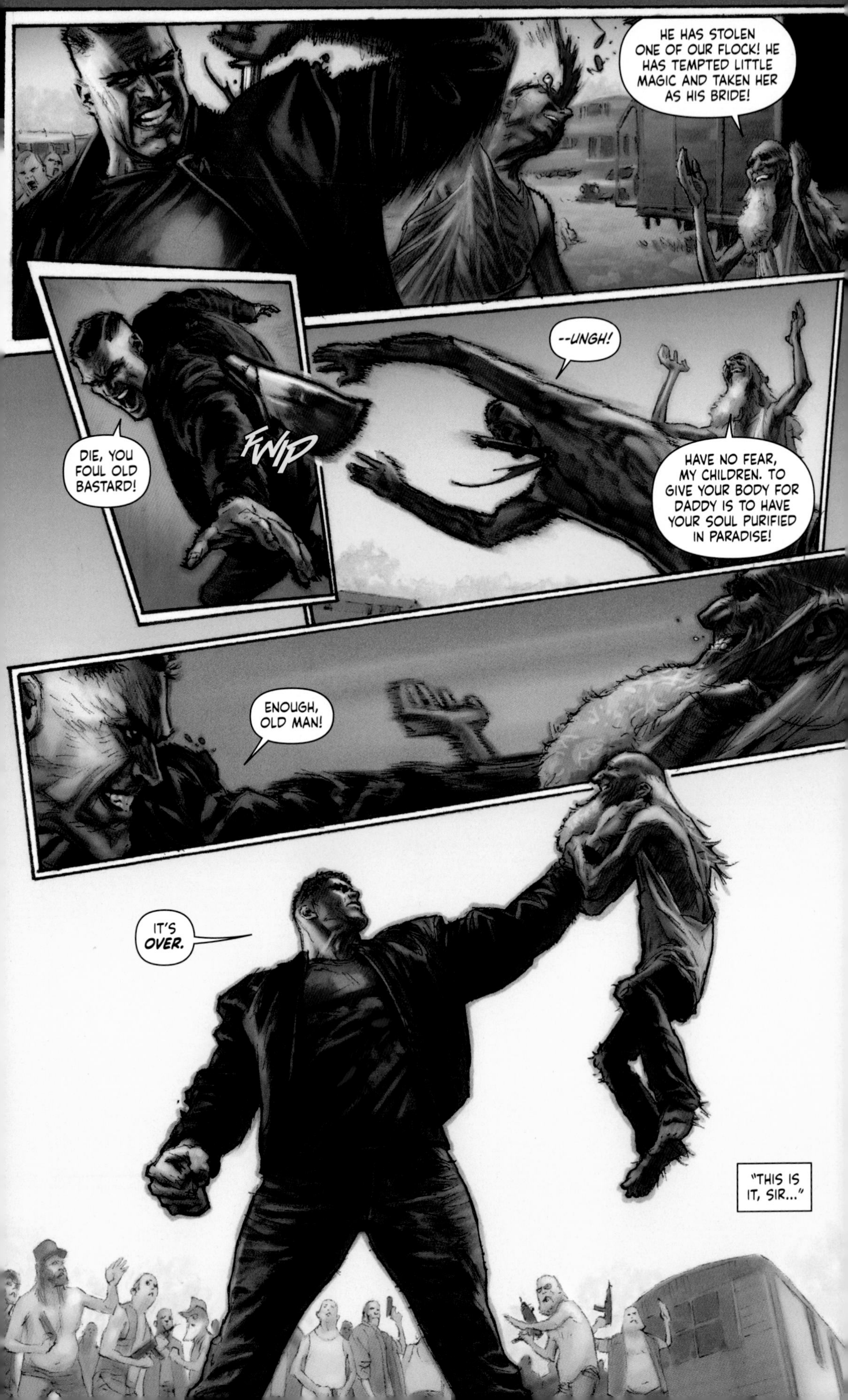
HE HAS STOLEN ONE OF OUR FLOCK! HE HAS TEMPTED LITTLE MAGIC AND TAKEN HER AS HIS BRIDE!
--UNGH!
DIE, YOU FOUL OLD BASTARD!
FWIP
HAVE NO FEAR, MY CHILDREN. TO GIVE YOUR BODY FOR DADDY IS TO HAVE YOUR SOUL PURIFIED IN PARADISE!
ENOUGH, OLD MAN!
IT'S OVER.
"THIS IS IT, SIR..."

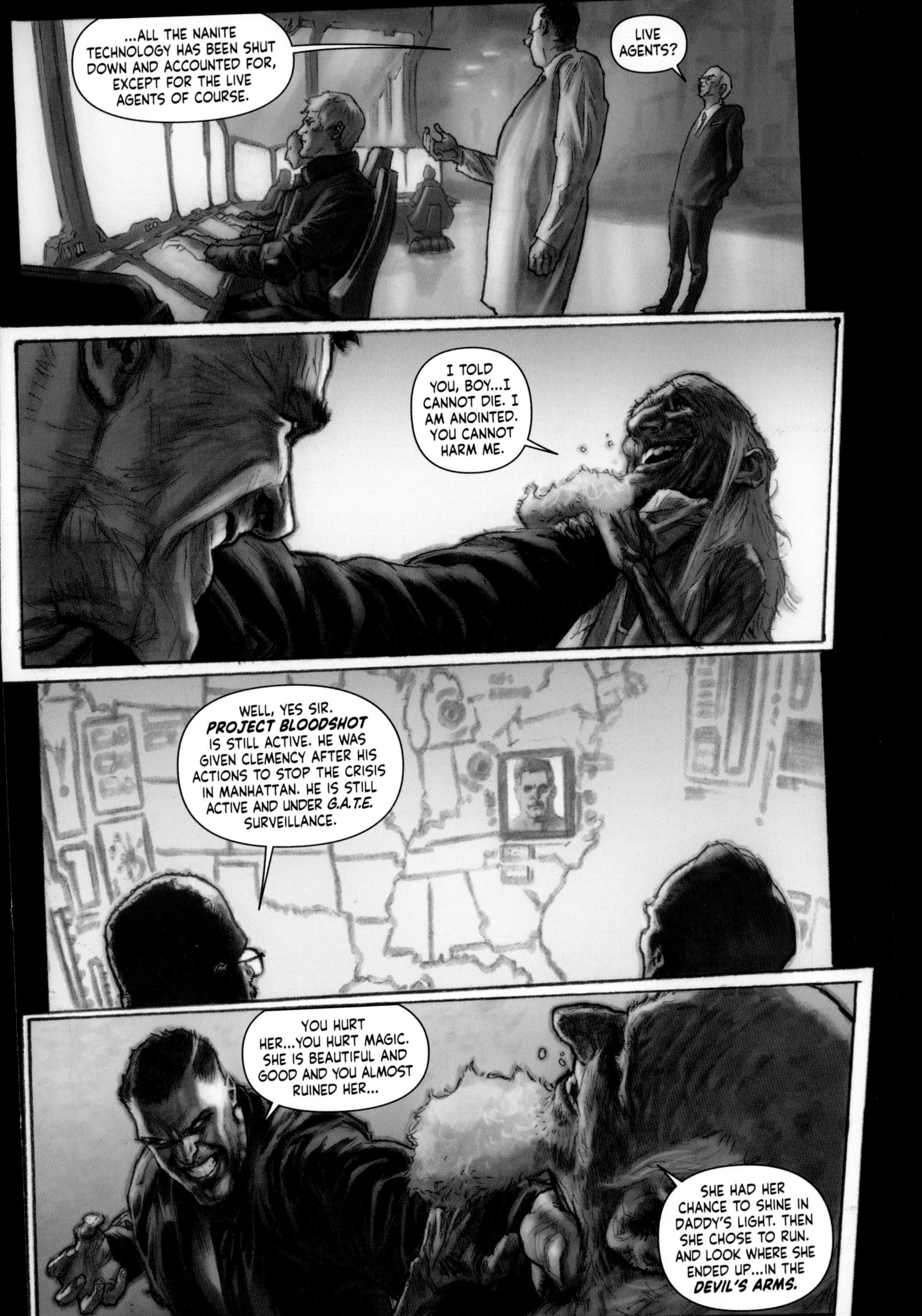
...ALL THE NANITE TECHNOLOGY HAS BEEN SHUT DOWN AND ACCOUNTED FOR, EXCEPT FOR THE LIVE AGENTS OF COURSE.
LIVE AGENTS?
I TOLD YOU, BOY...I CANNOT DIE. I AM ANOINTED. YOU CANNOT HARM ME.
WELL, YES SIR. PROJECT BLOODSHOT IS STILL ACTIVE. HE WAS GIVEN CLEMENCY AFTER HIS ACTIONS TO STOP THE CRISIS IN MANHATTAN. HE IS STILL ACTIVE AND UNDER G.A.T.E. SURVEILLANCE.
YOU HURT HER...YOU HURT MAGIC. SHE IS BEAUTIFUL AND GOOD AND YOU ALMOST RUINED HER...
SHE HAD HER CHANCE TO SHINE IN DADDY'S LIGHT. THEN SHE CHOSE TO RUN. AND LOOK WHERE SHE ENDED UP...IN THE DEVIL'S ARMS.

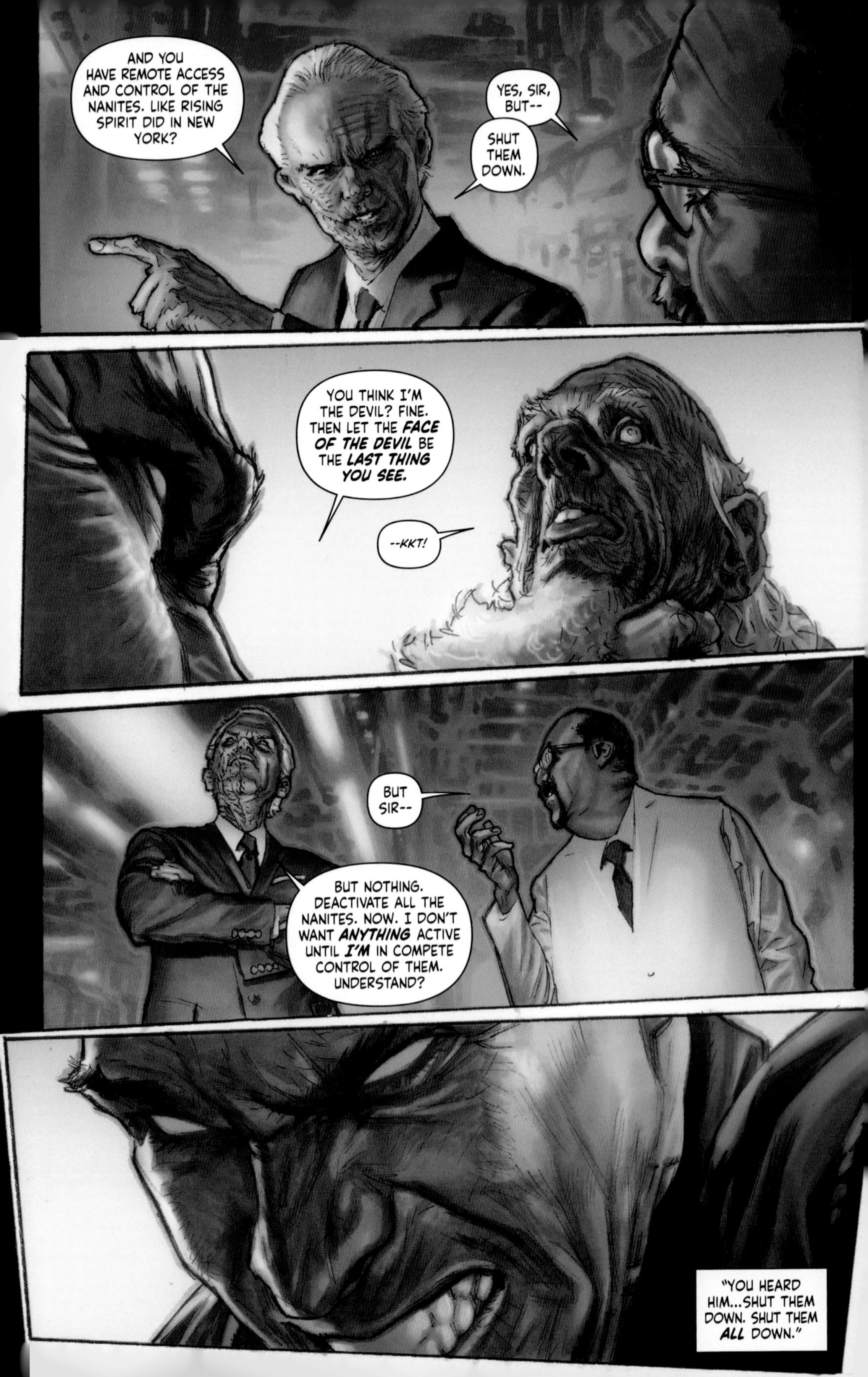
AND YOU HAVE REMOTE ACCESS AND CONTROL OF THE NANITES. LIKE RISING SPIRIT DID IN NEW YORK?
YES, SIR, BUT--
SHUT THEM DOWN.
YOU THINK I'M THE DEVIL? FINE. THEN LET THE ***FACE OF THE DEVIL*** BE THE ***LAST THING YOU SEE.***
--KKT!
BUT SIR--
BUT NOTHING. DEACTIVATE ALL THE NANITES. NOW. I DON'T WANT ***ANYTHING*** ACTIVE UNTIL ***I'M*** IN COMPETE CONTROL OF THEM. UNDERSTAND?
"YOU HEARD HIM...SHUT THEM DOWN. SHUT THEM ***ALL*** DOWN."

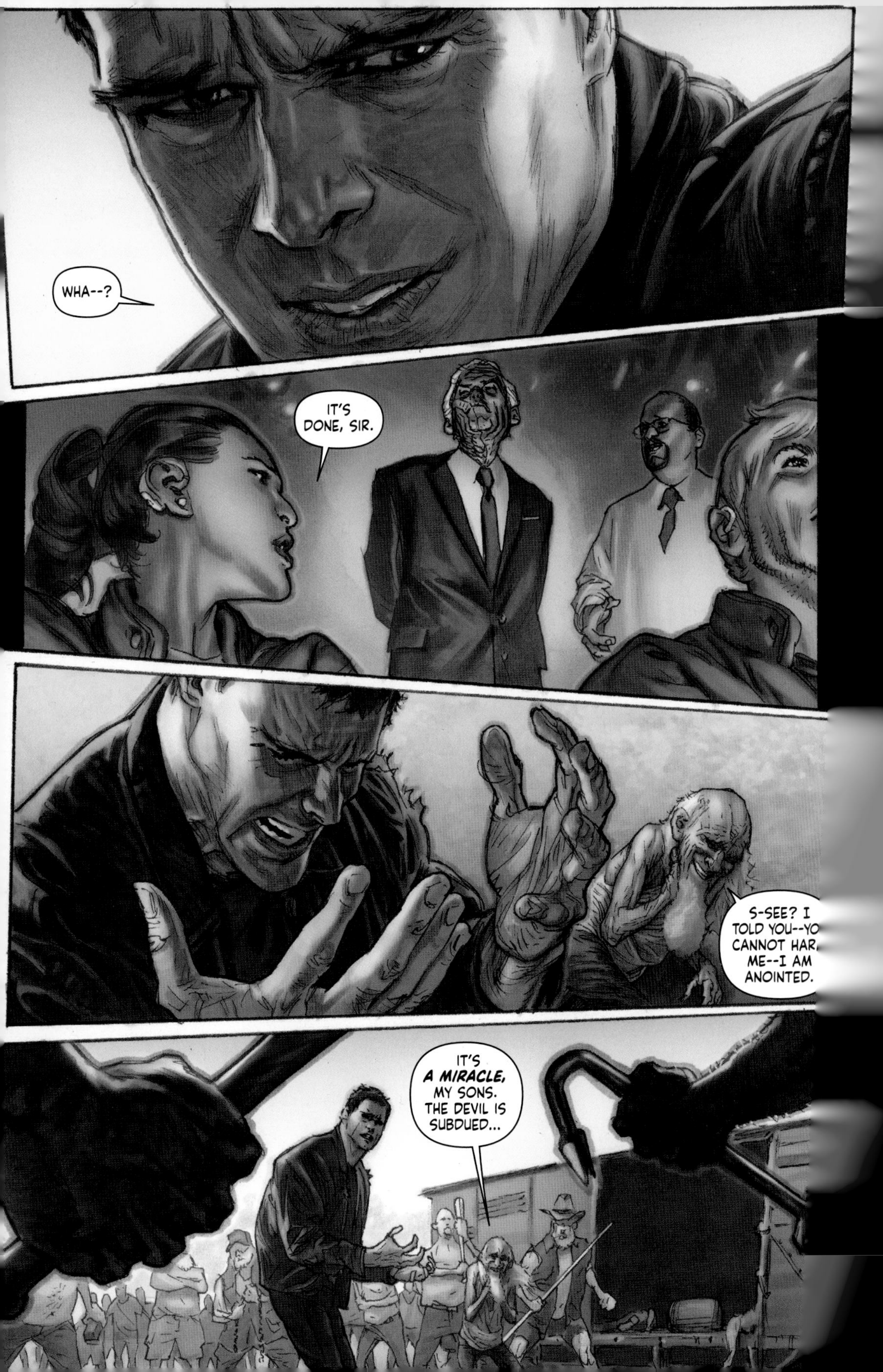
WHA--?
IT'S DONE, SIR.
S-SEE? I TOLD YOU--YO CANNOT HAR ME--I AM ANOINTED.
IT'S A MIRACLE, MY SONS. THE DEVIL IS SUBDUED...

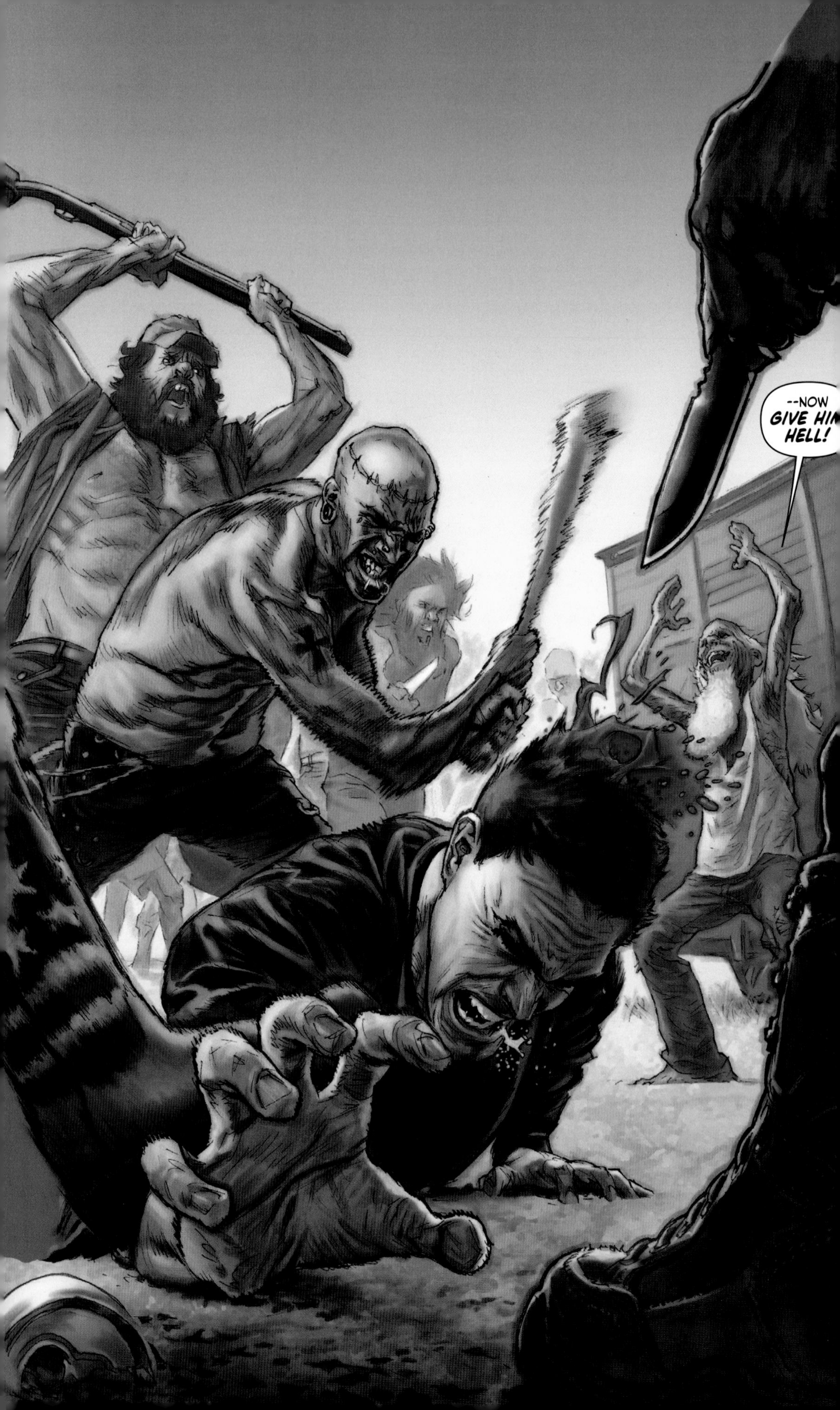
--NOW
GIVE HIM
HELL!

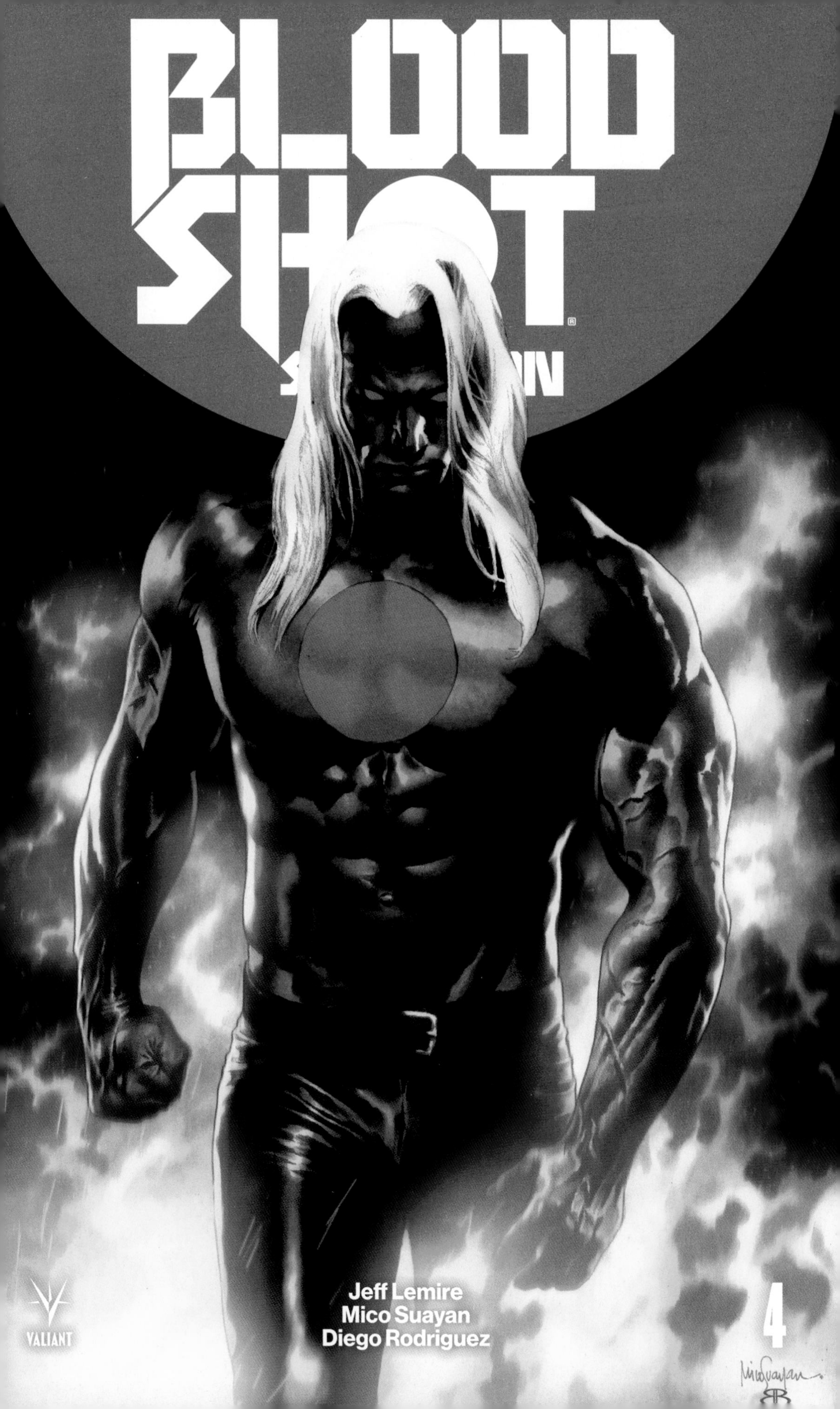

BLOODSHOT
Jeff Lemire
Mico Suayan
Diego Rodriguez
4
VALIANT

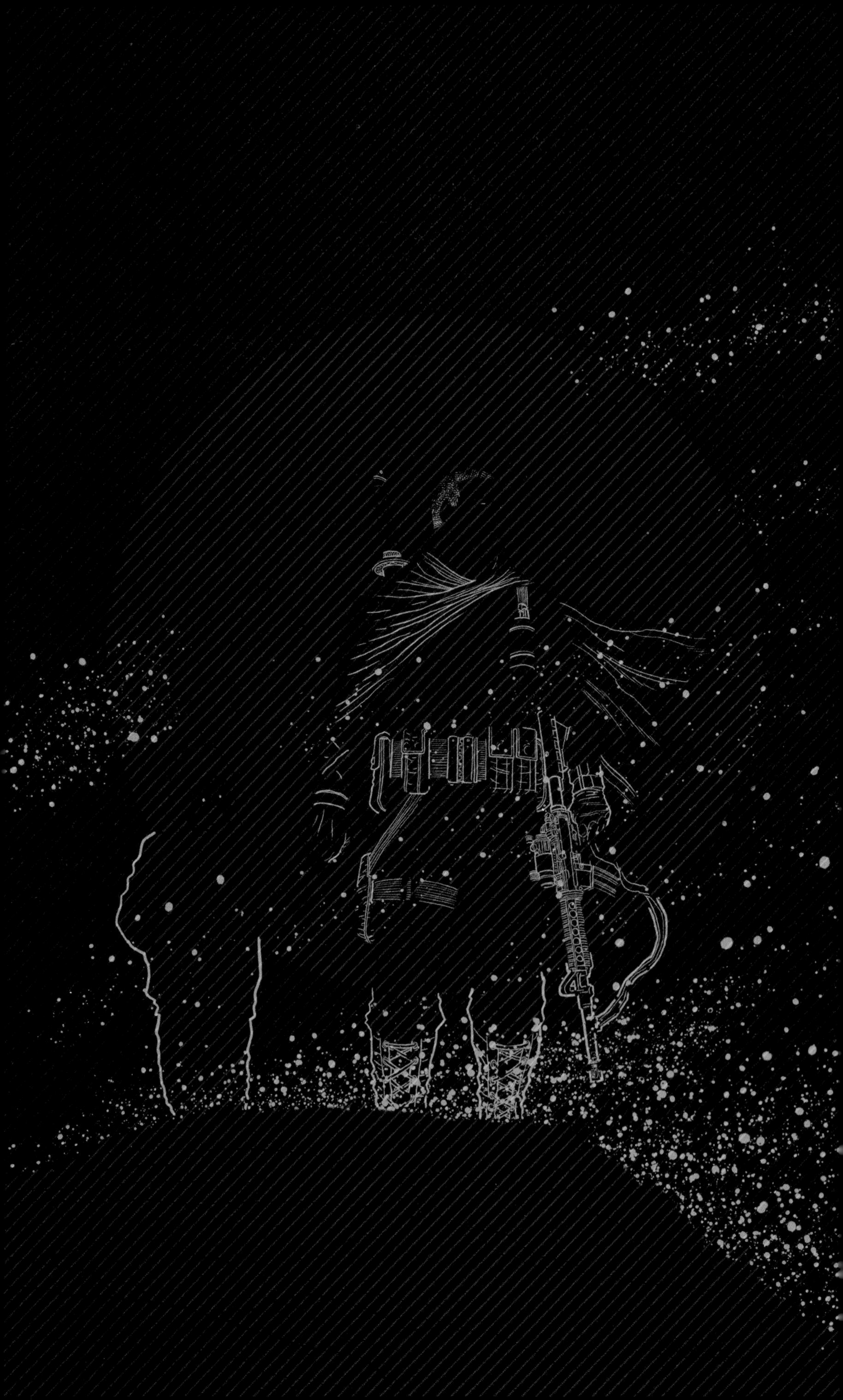

THIS IS THE BEST ONE WE'VE EVER BUILT!

I THINK YOU'RE RIGHT, DANNY. I COULDN'T HAVE DONE IT WITHOUT YOU. NEVER WOULD HAVE BEEN ABLE TO LIFT ALL THE BAILS CLEAR.

TOMORROW WE SHOULD BUILD MORE TUNNELS. JUST KEEP GOING DEEPER AND DEEPER.

CAN'T GO ANY DEEPER, DANNY. THE FLOOR IS RIGHT BENEATH, REMEMBER?

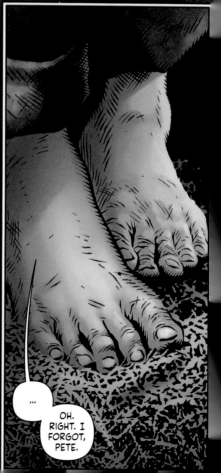

...

OH. RIGHT. I FORGOT, PETE.

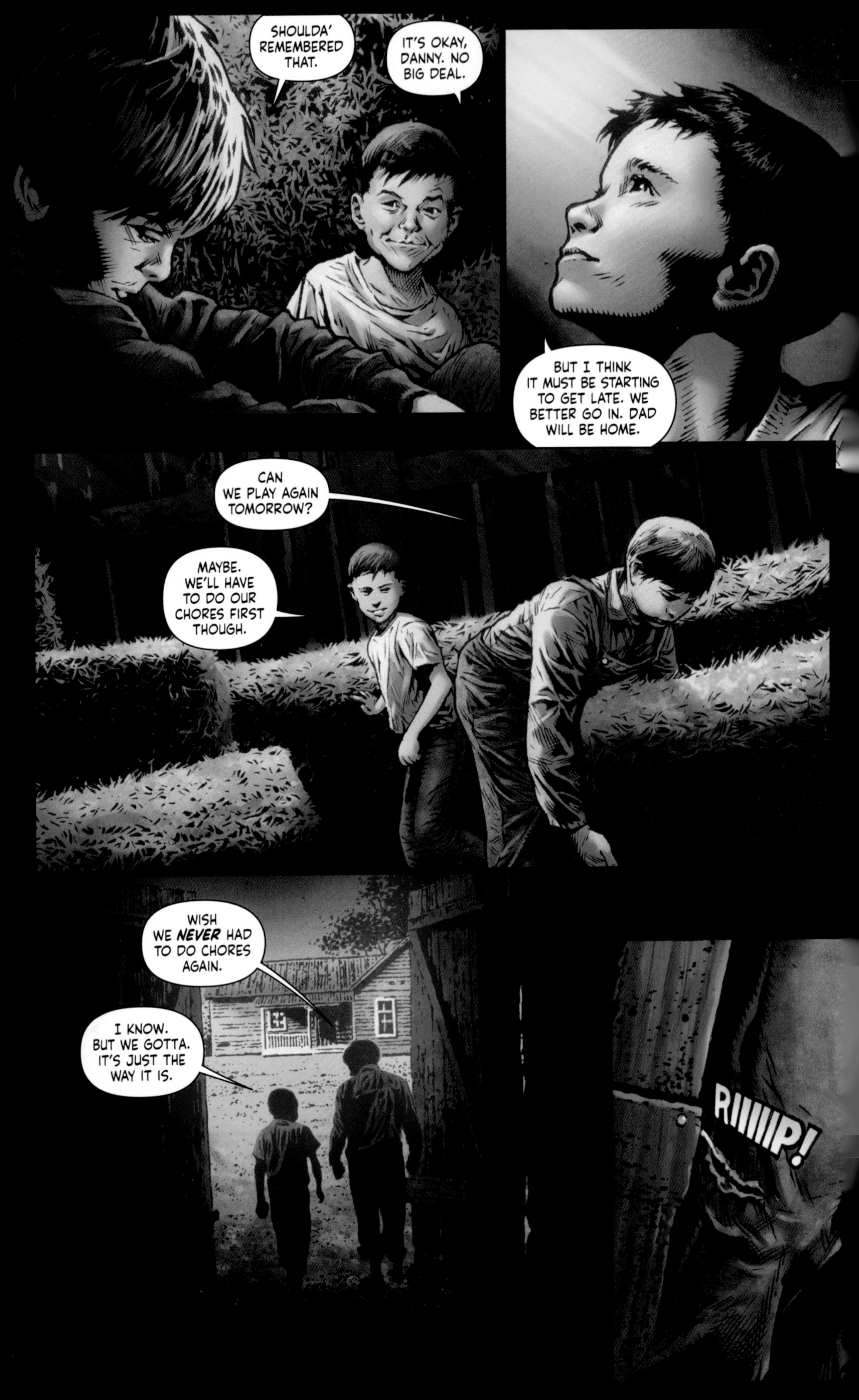
SHOULDA' REMEMBERED THAT.
IT'S OKAY, DANNY. NO BIG DEAL.
BUT I THINK IT MUST BE STARTING TO GET LATE. WE BETTER GO IN. DAD WILL BE HOME.
CAN WE PLAY AGAIN TOMORROW?
MAYBE. WE'LL HAVE TO DO OUR CHORES FIRST THOUGH.
WISH WE NEVER HAD TO DO CHORES AGAIN.
I KNOW. BUT WE GOTTA. IT'S JUST THE WAY IT IS.
RIIIIIP!

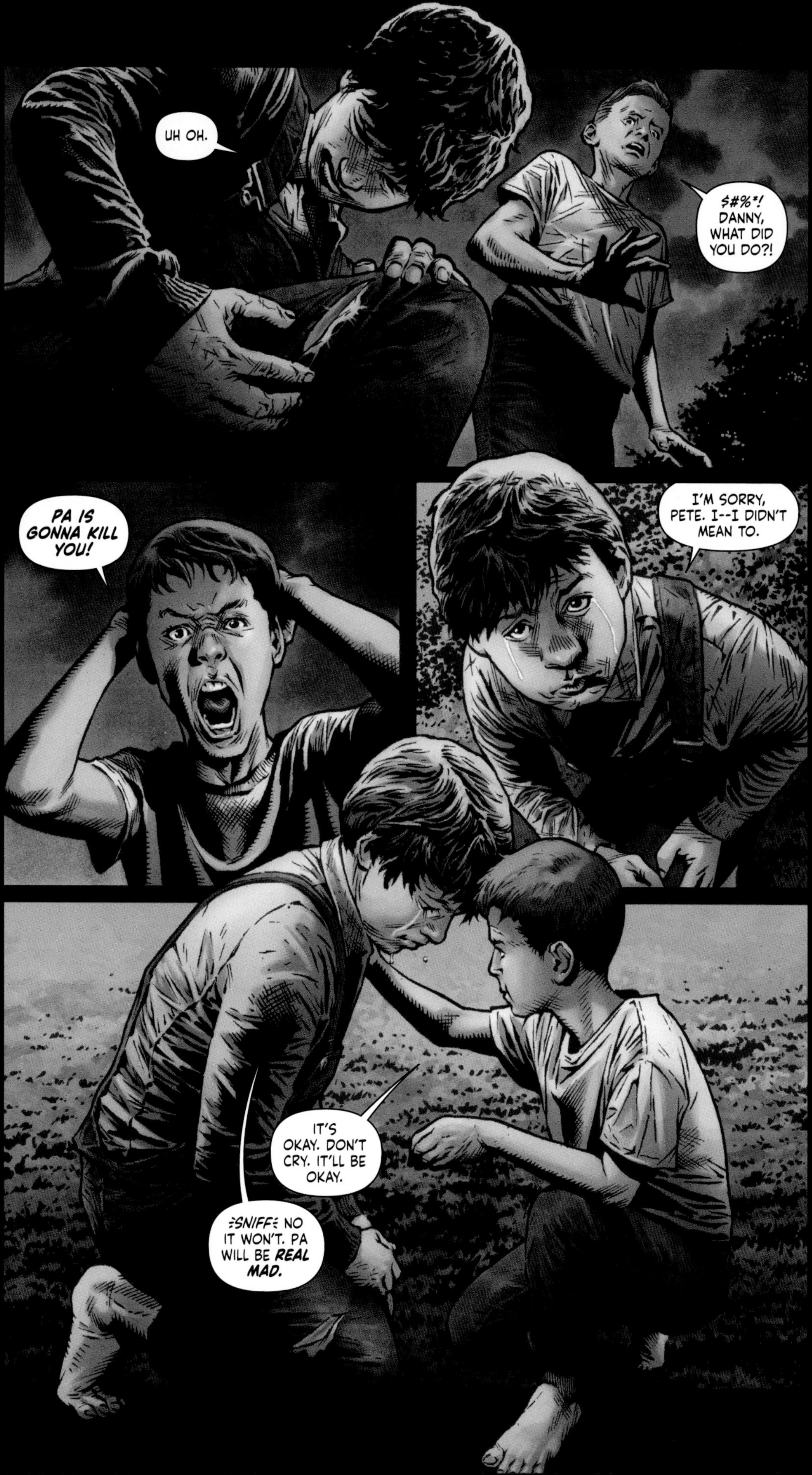

UH OH.
$#%*! DANNY, WHAT DID YOU DO?!
PA IS GONNA KILL YOU!
I'M SORRY, PETE. I--I DIDN'T MEAN TO.
IT'S OKAY. DON'T CRY. IT'LL BE OKAY.
SNIFF NO IT WON'T. PA WILL BE REAL MAD.

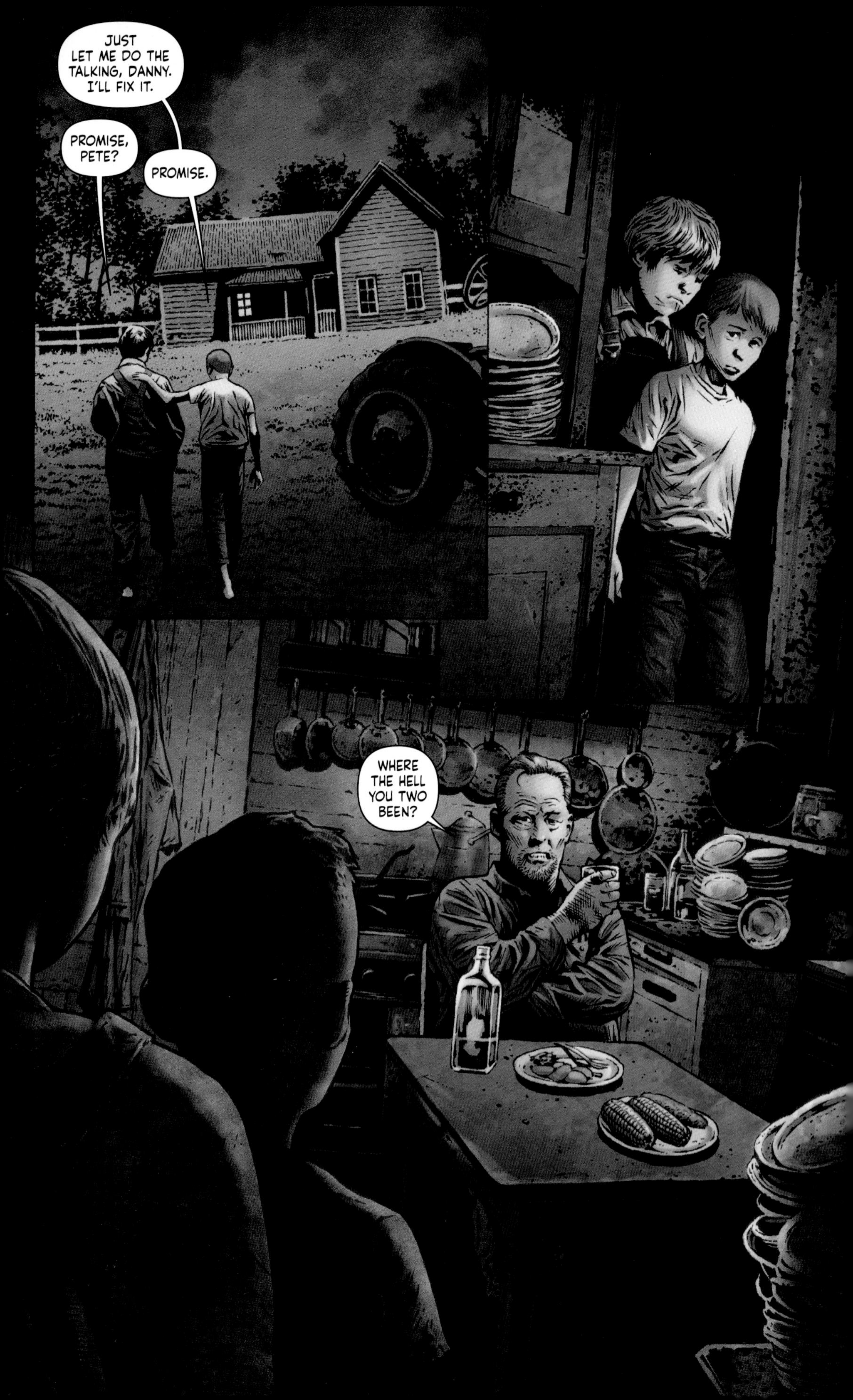
JUST LET ME DO THE TALKING, DANNY. I'LL FIX IT.
PROMISE, PETE?
PROMISE.
WHERE THE HELL YOU TWO BEEN?

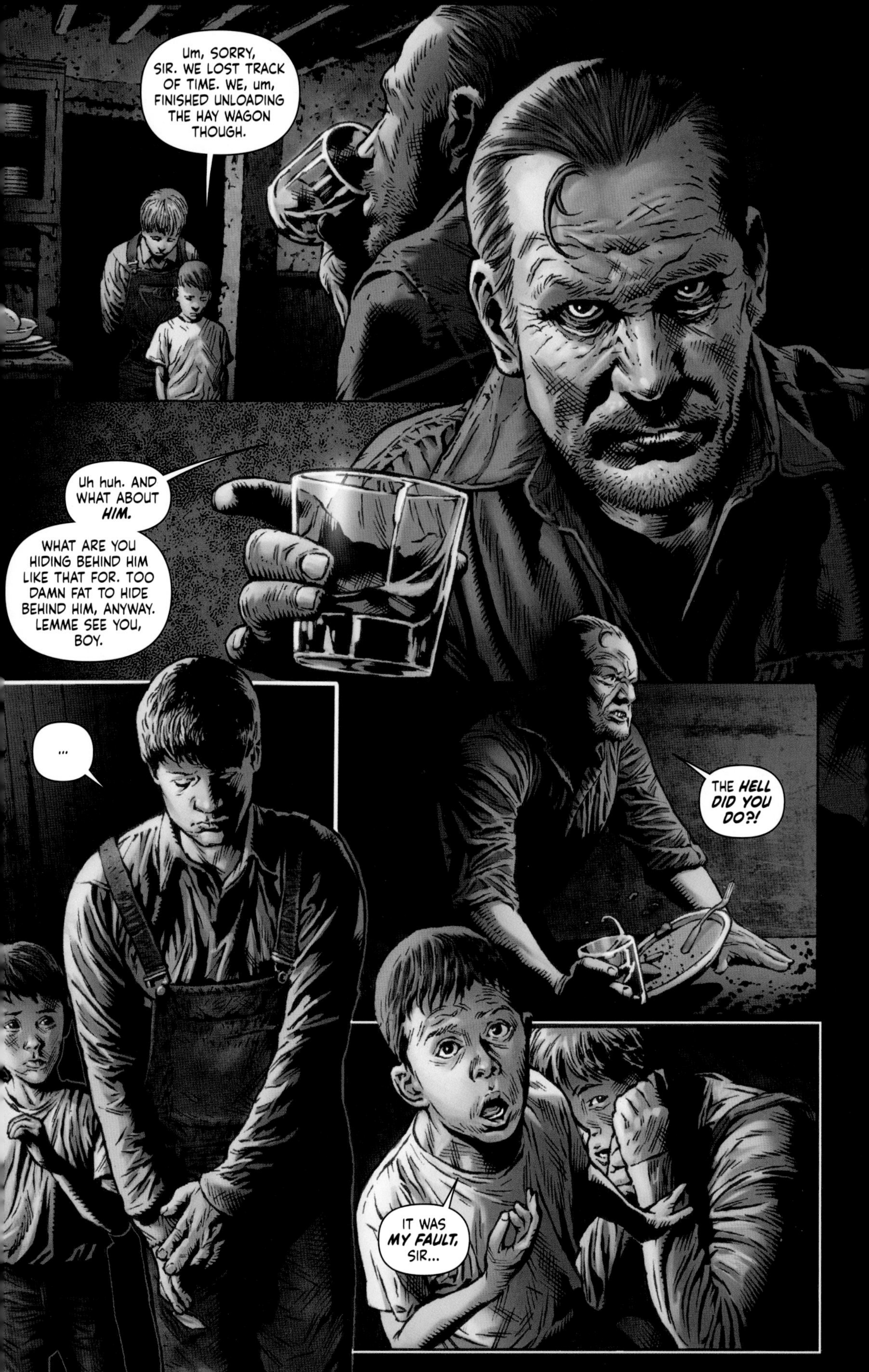
Um, SORRY, SIR. WE LOST TRACK OF TIME. WE, um, FINISHED UNLOADING THE HAY WAGON THOUGH.
Uh huh. AND WHAT ABOUT *HIM.*
WHAT ARE YOU HIDING BEHIND HIM LIKE THAT FOR. TOO DAMN FAT TO HIDE BEHIND HIM, ANYWAY. LEMME SEE YOU, BOY.
...
THE *HELL DID YOU DO?!*
IT WAS *MY FAULT,* SIR...

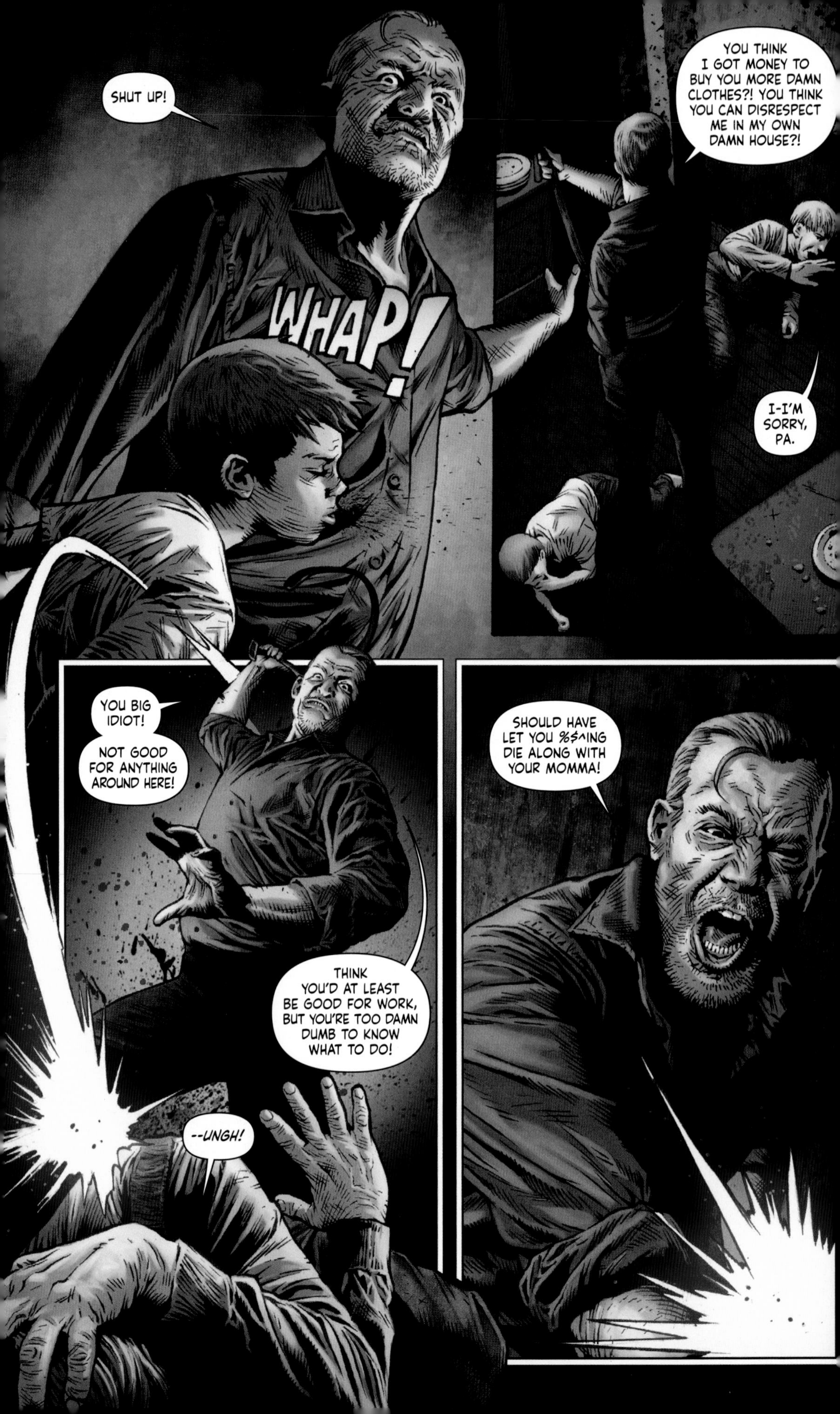
SHUT UP!
YOU THINK I GOT MONEY TO BUY YOU MORE DAMN CLOTHES?! YOU THINK YOU CAN DISRESPECT ME IN MY OWN DAMN HOUSE?!
WHAP!
I-I'M SORRY, PA.
YOU BIG IDIOT!
NOT GOOD FOR ANYTHING AROUND HERE!
THINK YOU'D AT LEAST BE GOOD FOR WORK, BUT YOU'RE TOO DAMN DUMB TO KNOW WHAT TO DO!
--UNGH!
SHOULD HAVE LET YOU %$^ING DIE ALONG WITH YOUR MOMMA!

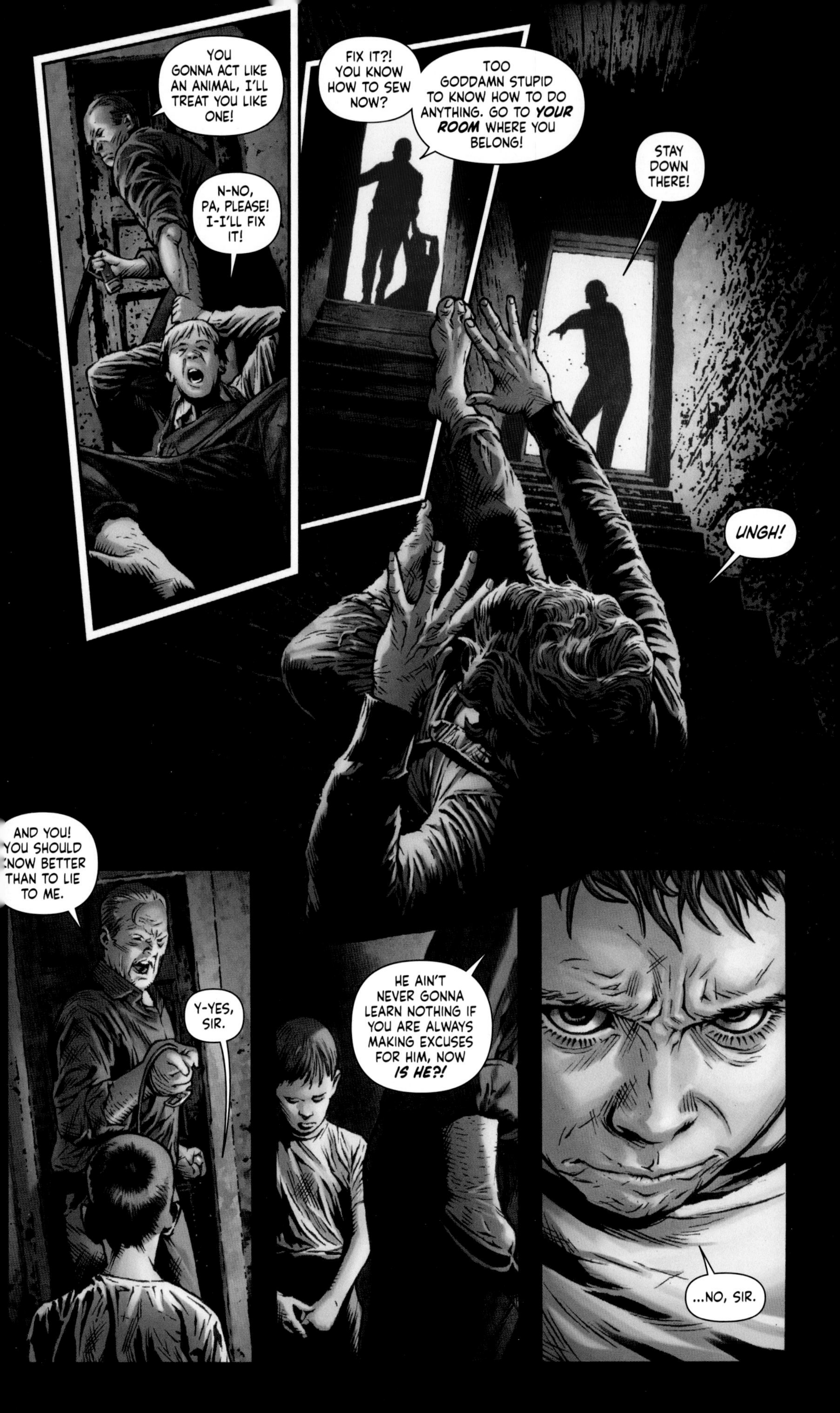
YOU GONNA ACT LIKE AN ANIMAL, I'LL TREAT YOU LIKE ONE!
N-NO, PA, PLEASE! I-I'LL FIX IT!
FIX IT?! YOU KNOW HOW TO SEW NOW?
TOO GODDAMN STUPID TO KNOW HOW TO DO ANYTHING. GO TO *YOUR ROOM* WHERE YOU BELONG!
STAY DOWN THERE!
*UNGH!*
AND YOU! YOU SHOULD KNOW BETTER THAN TO LIE TO ME.
Y-YES, SIR.
HE AIN'T NEVER GONNA LEARN NOTHING IF YOU ARE ALWAYS MAKING EXCUSES FOR HIM, NOW *IS HE?!*
...NO, SIR.

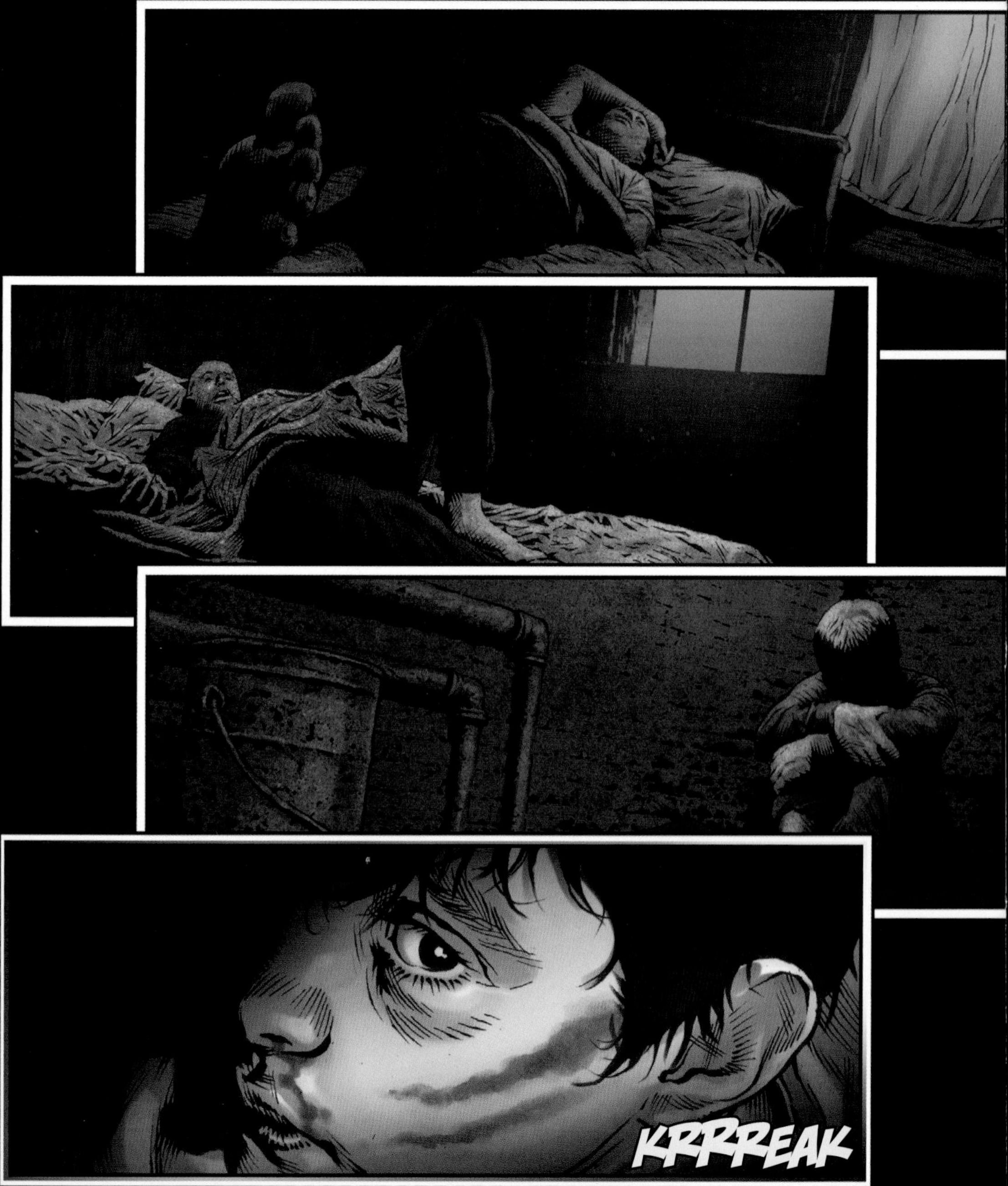
KRRREAK

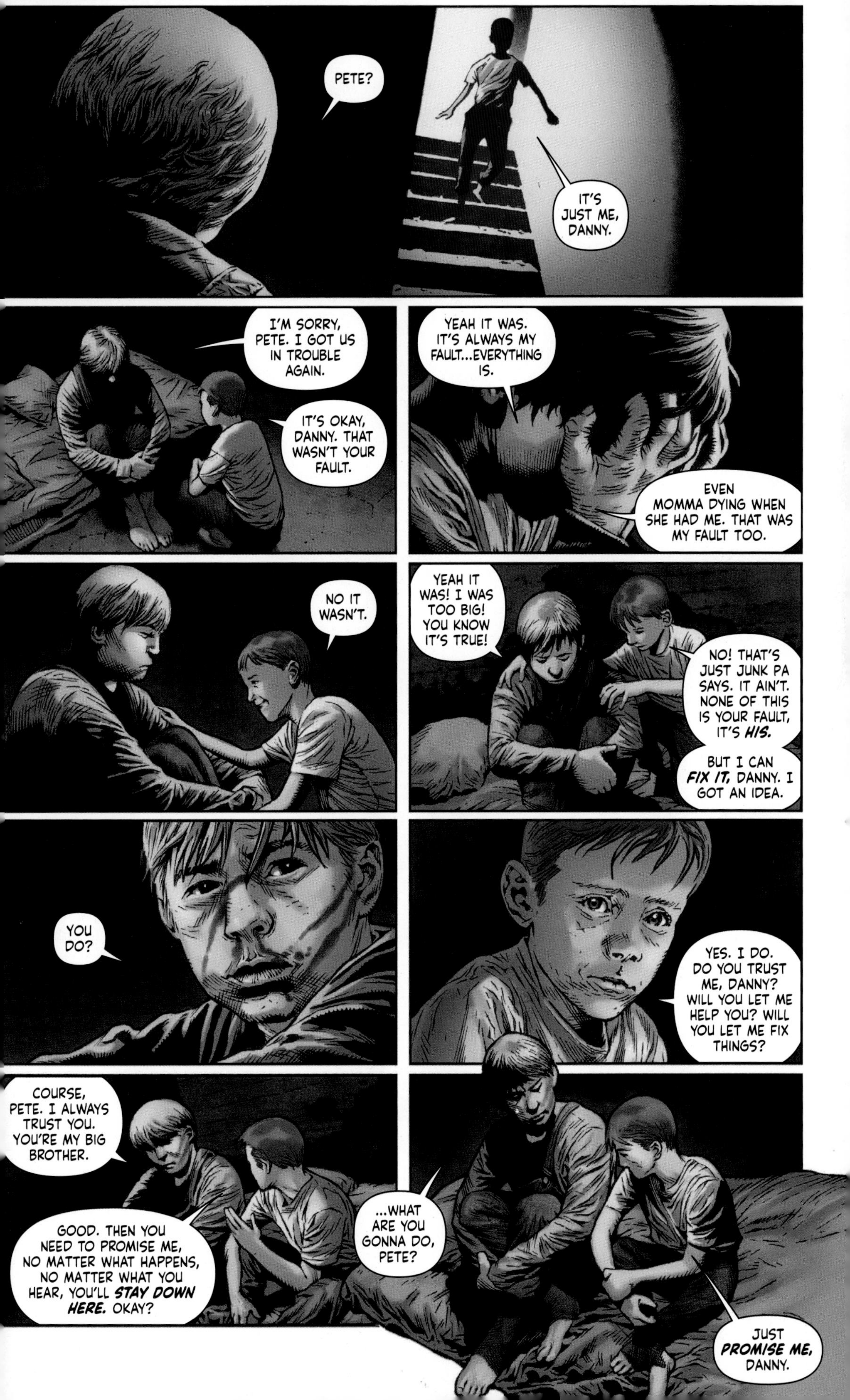
PETE?
IT'S JUST ME, DANNY.
I'M SORRY, PETE. I GOT US IN TROUBLE AGAIN.
IT'S OKAY, DANNY. THAT WASN'T YOUR FAULT.
YEAH IT WAS. IT'S ALWAYS MY FAULT...EVERYTHING IS.
EVEN MOMMA DYING WHEN SHE HAD ME. THAT WAS MY FAULT TOO.
NO IT WASN'T.
YEAH IT WAS! I WAS TOO BIG! YOU KNOW IT'S TRUE!
NO! THAT'S JUST JUNK PA SAYS. IT AIN'T. NONE OF THIS IS YOUR FAULT, IT'S ***HIS.***
BUT I CAN ***FIX IT,*** DANNY. I GOT AN IDEA.
YOU DO?
YES. I DO. DO YOU TRUST ME, DANNY? WILL YOU LET ME HELP YOU? WILL YOU LET ME FIX THINGS?
COURSE, PETE. I ALWAYS TRUST YOU. YOU'RE MY BIG BROTHER.
GOOD. THEN YOU NEED TO PROMISE ME, NO MATTER WHAT HAPPENS, NO MATTER WHAT YOU HEAR, YOU'LL ***STAY DOWN HERE.*** OKAY?
...WHAT ARE YOU GONNA DO, PETE?
JUST ***PROMISE ME,*** DANNY.

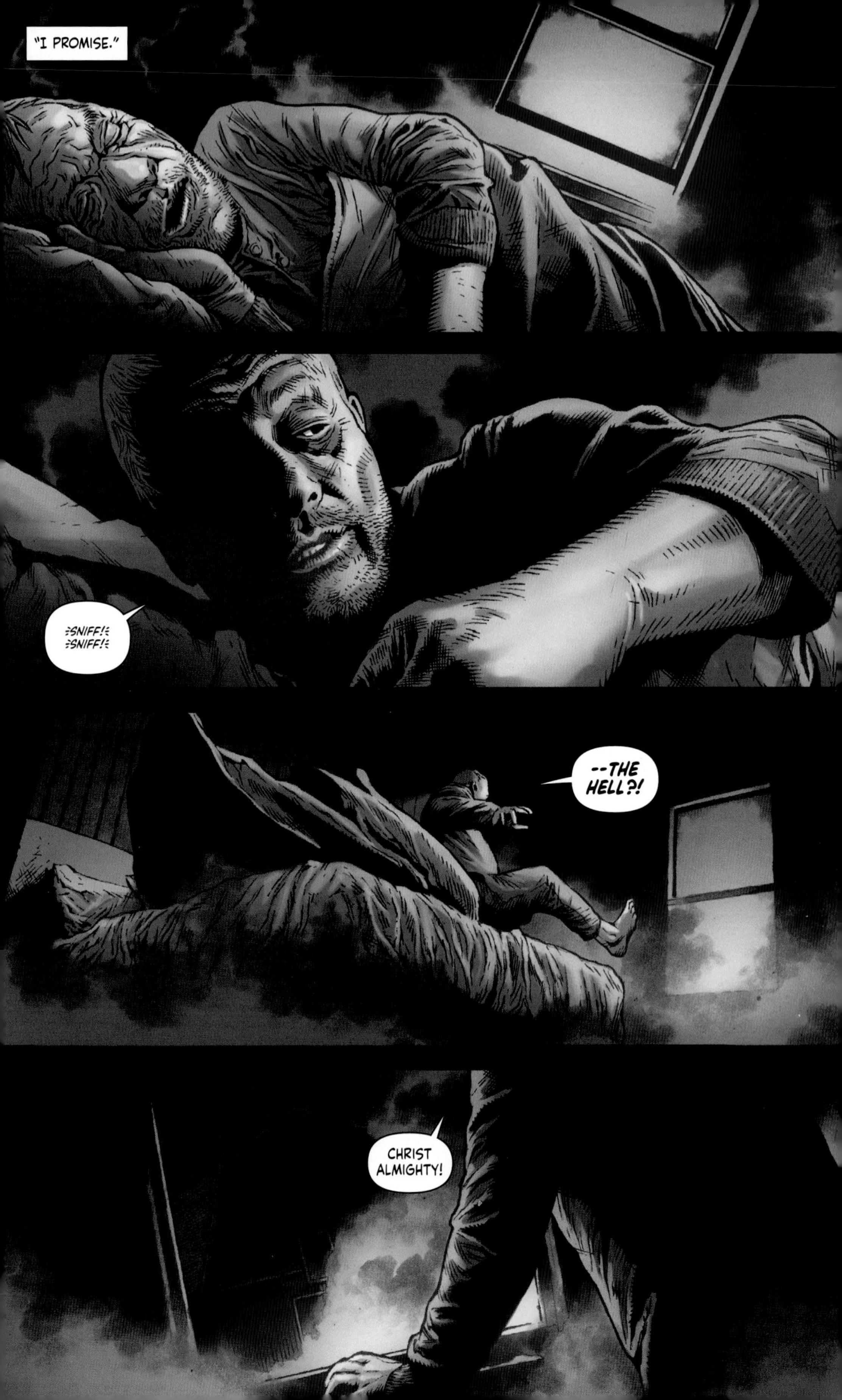
"I PROMISE."
SNIFF! SNIFF!
--THE HELL?!
CHRIST ALMIGHTY!

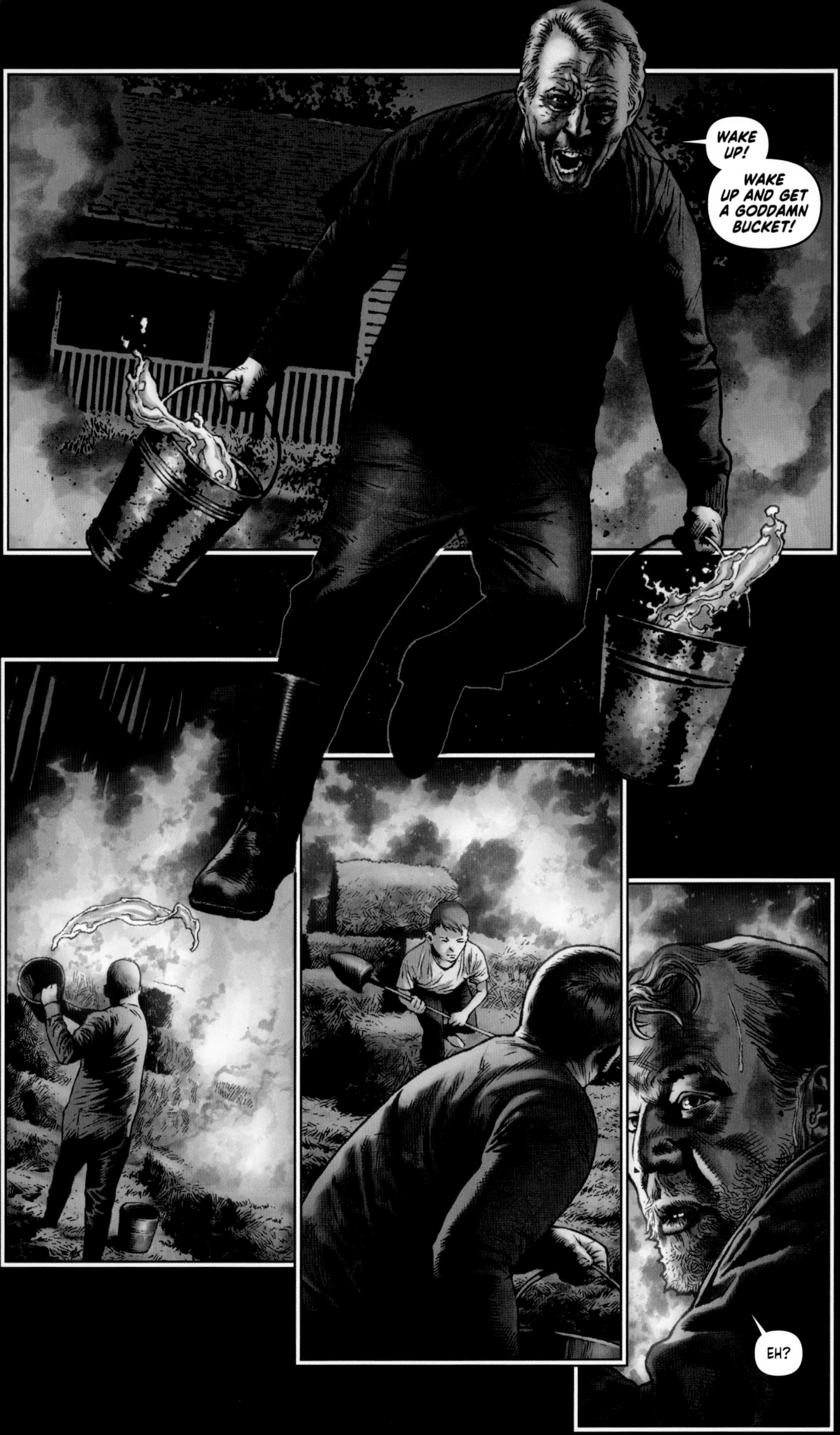
WAKE UP!
WAKE UP AND GET A GODDAMN BUCKET!
EH?

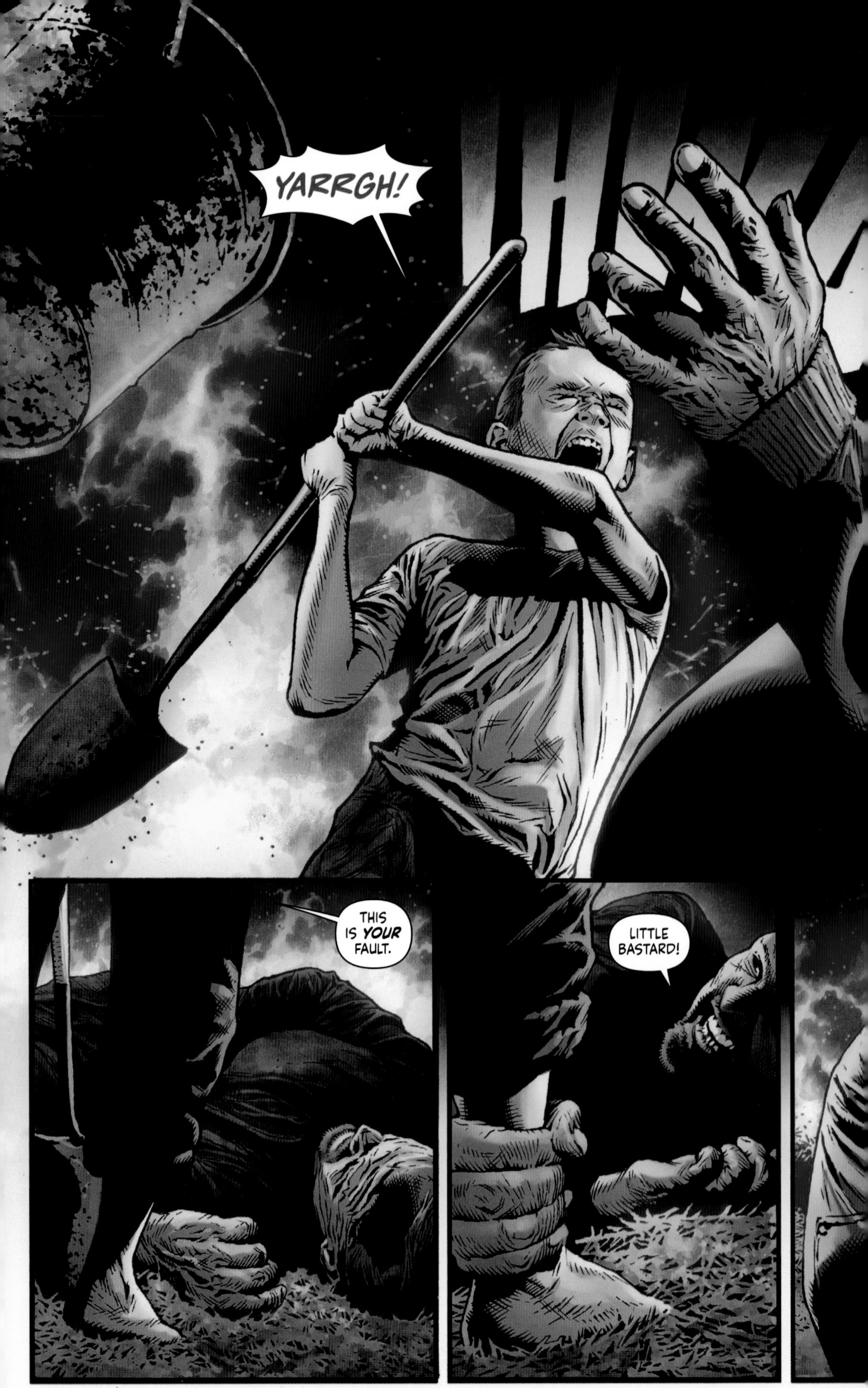
YARRGH!
THIS IS YOUR FAULT.
LITTLE BASTARD!

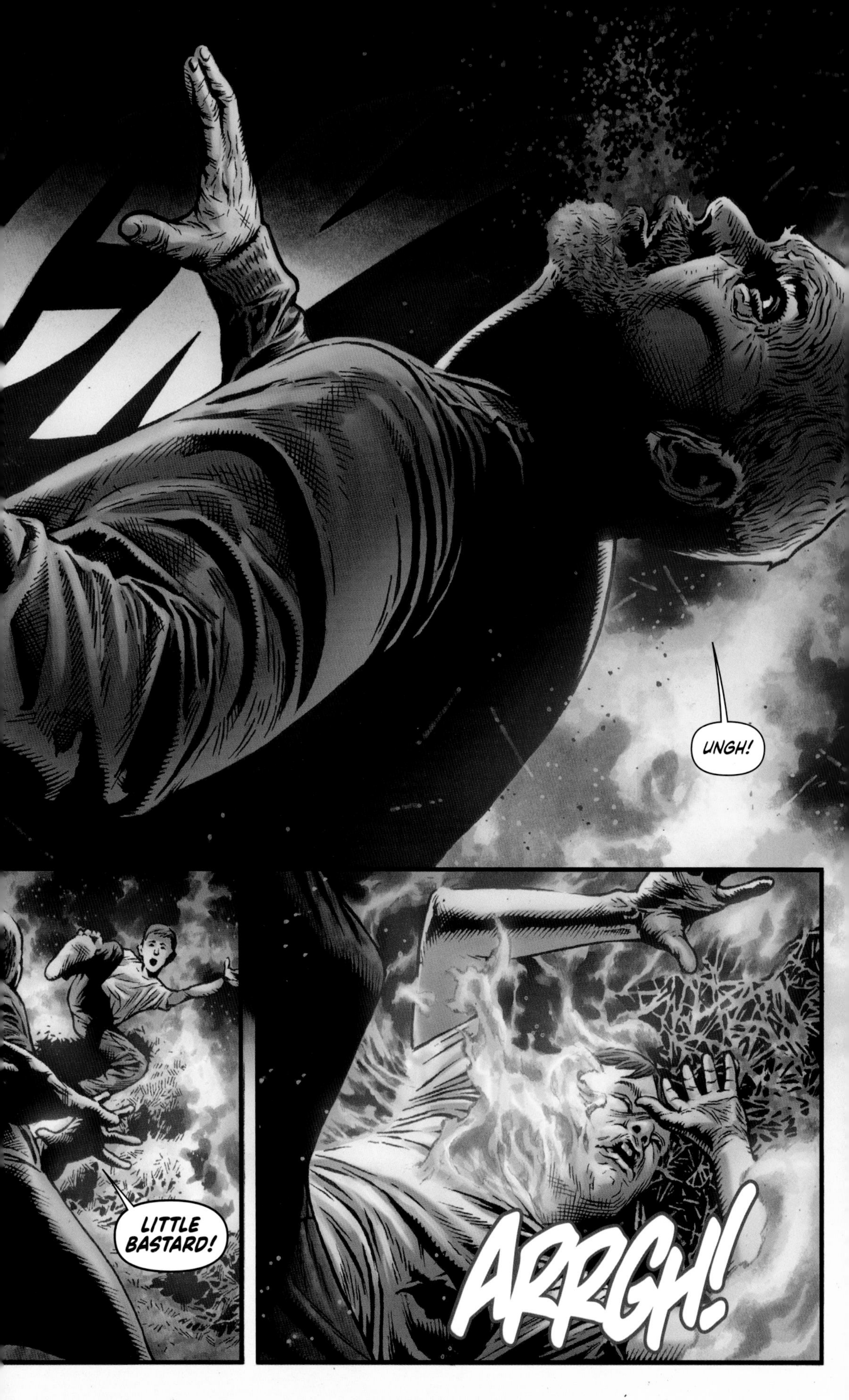
UNGH!
LITTLE BASTARD!
ARRGH!

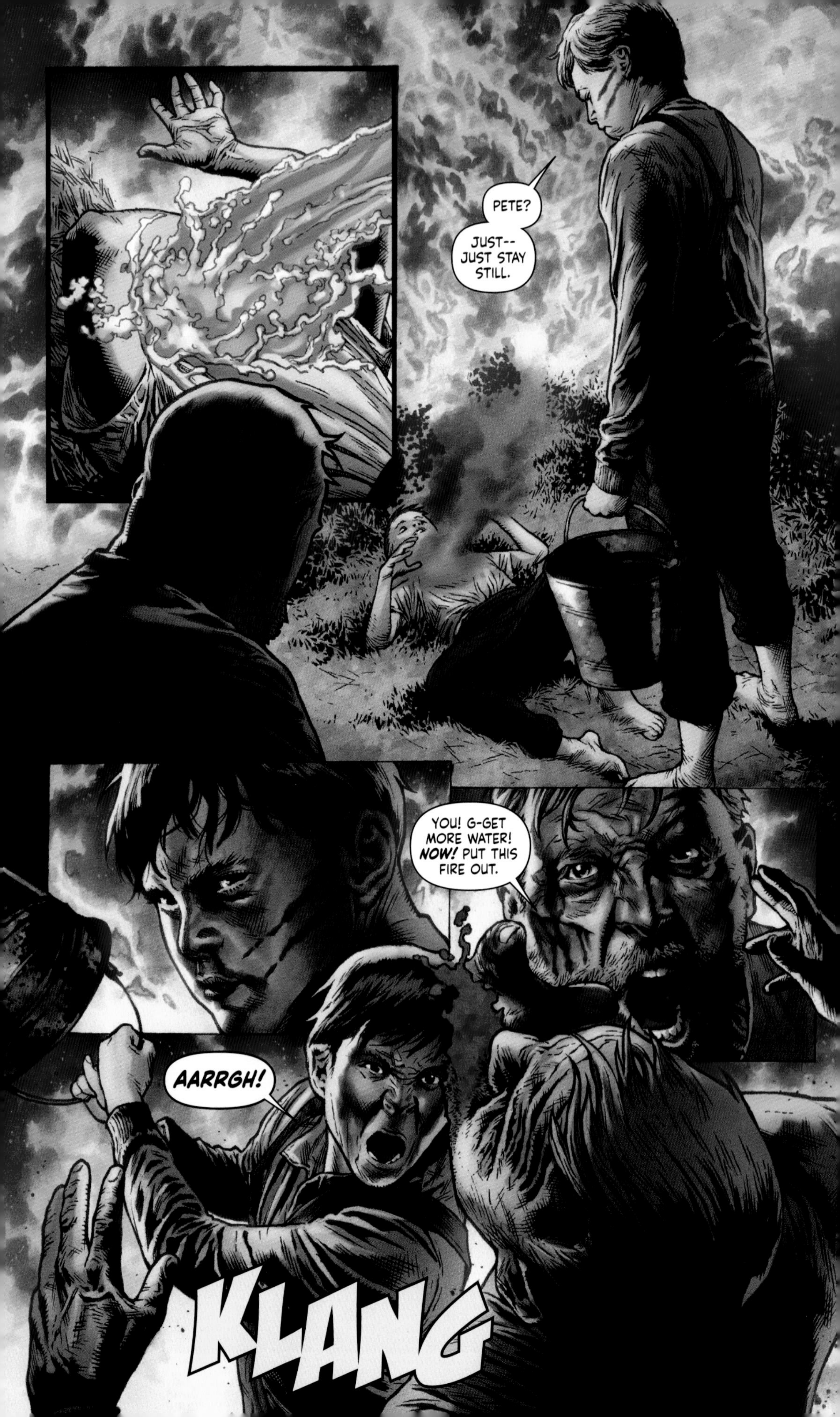
PETE?
JUST--
JUST STAY
STILL.
YOU! G-GET
MORE WATER!
*NOW!* PUT THIS
FIRE OUT.
AARRGH!
KLANG

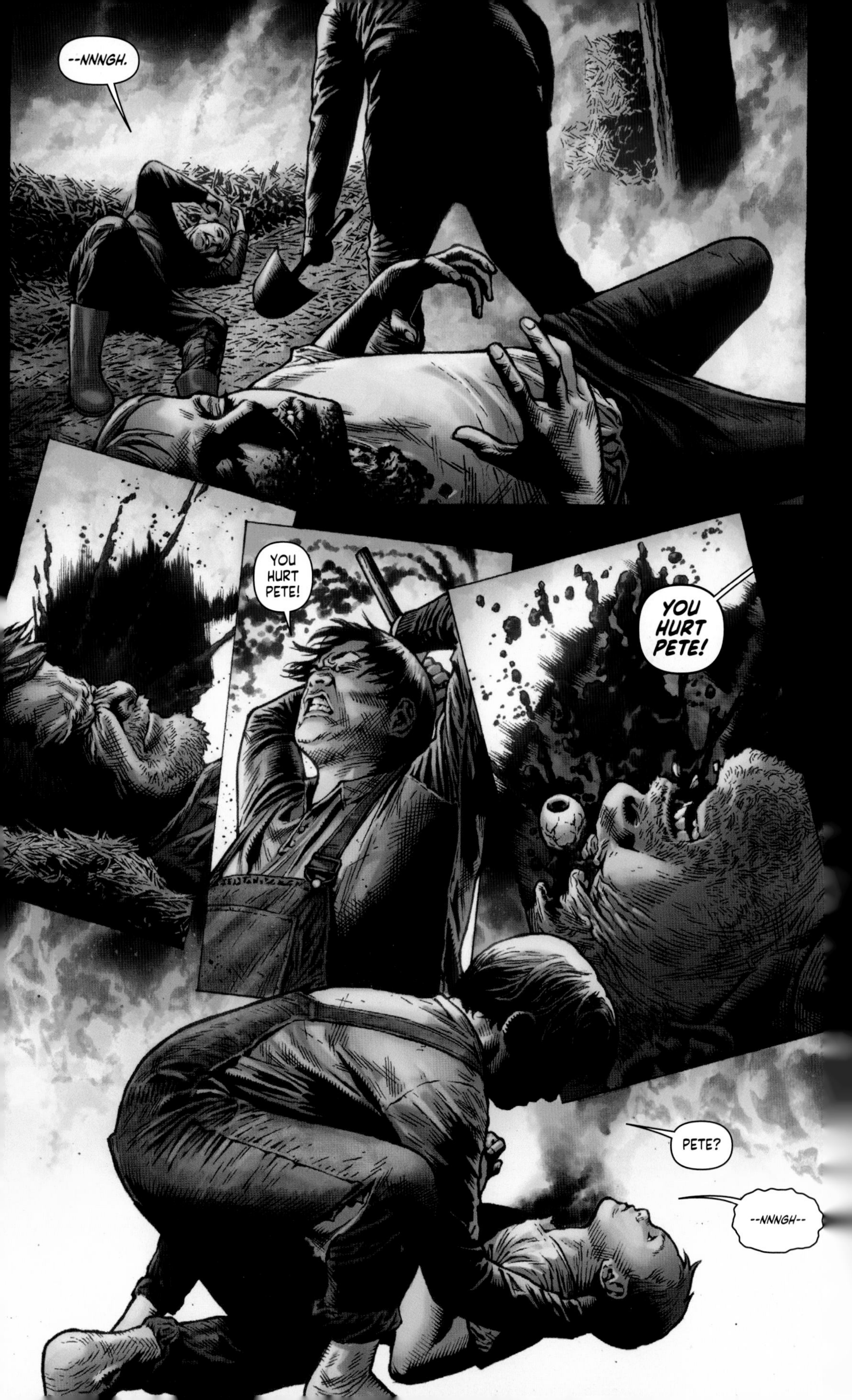
--NNNGH.
YOU HURT PETE!
YOU HURT PETE!
PETE?
--NNNGH--

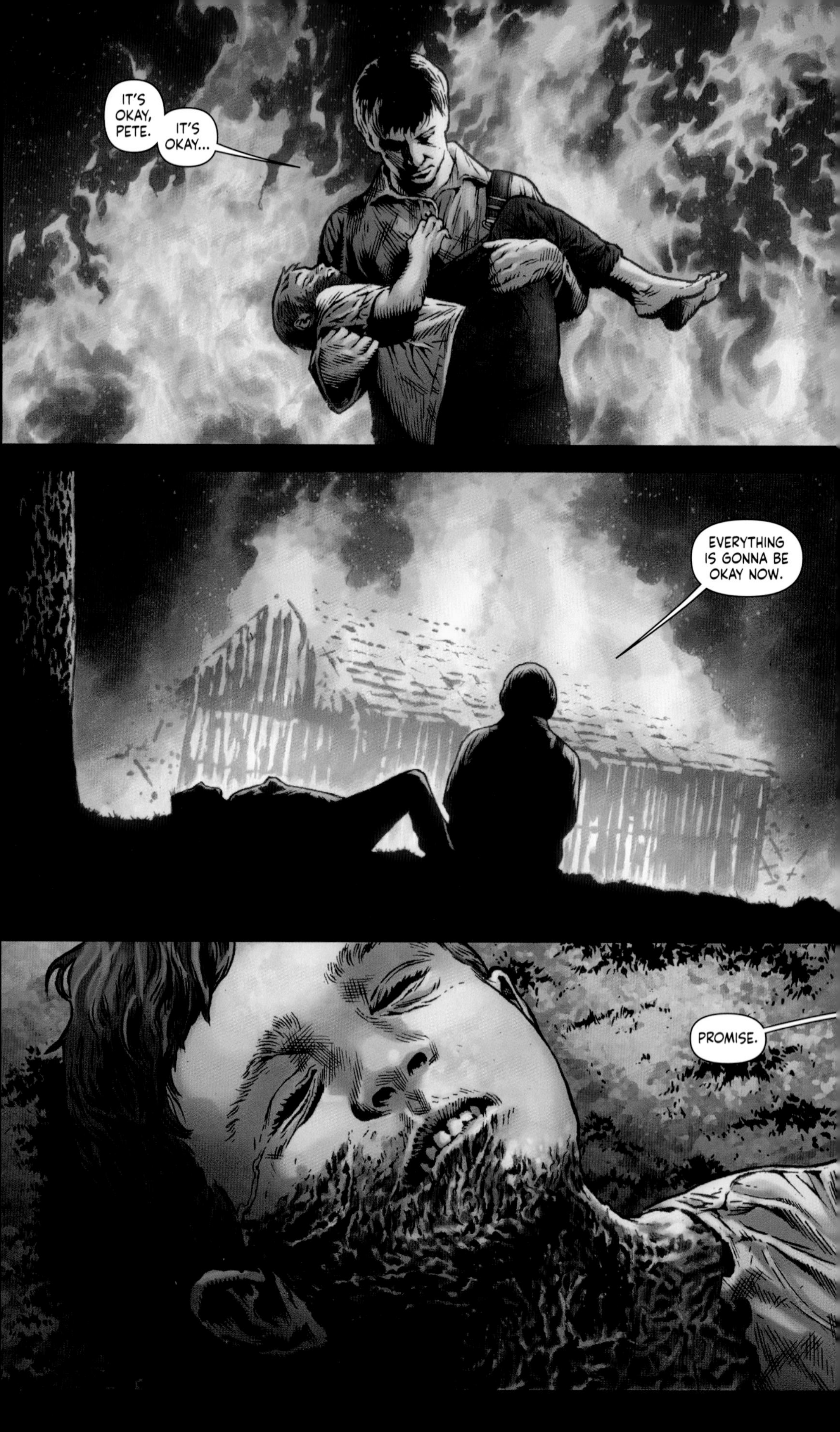
IT'S OKAY, PETE.
IT'S OKAY...
EVERYTHING IS GONNA BE OKAY NOW.
PROMISE.

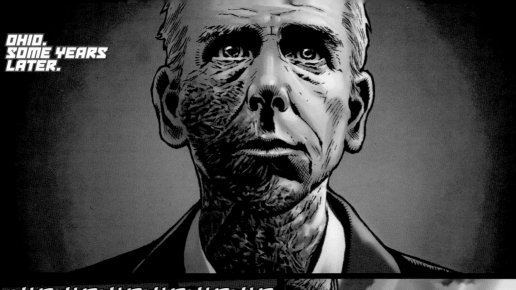

WHUP WHUP WHUP WHUP WHUP WHUP

WHUP WHUP WHUP
WHUP WHUP WHUP

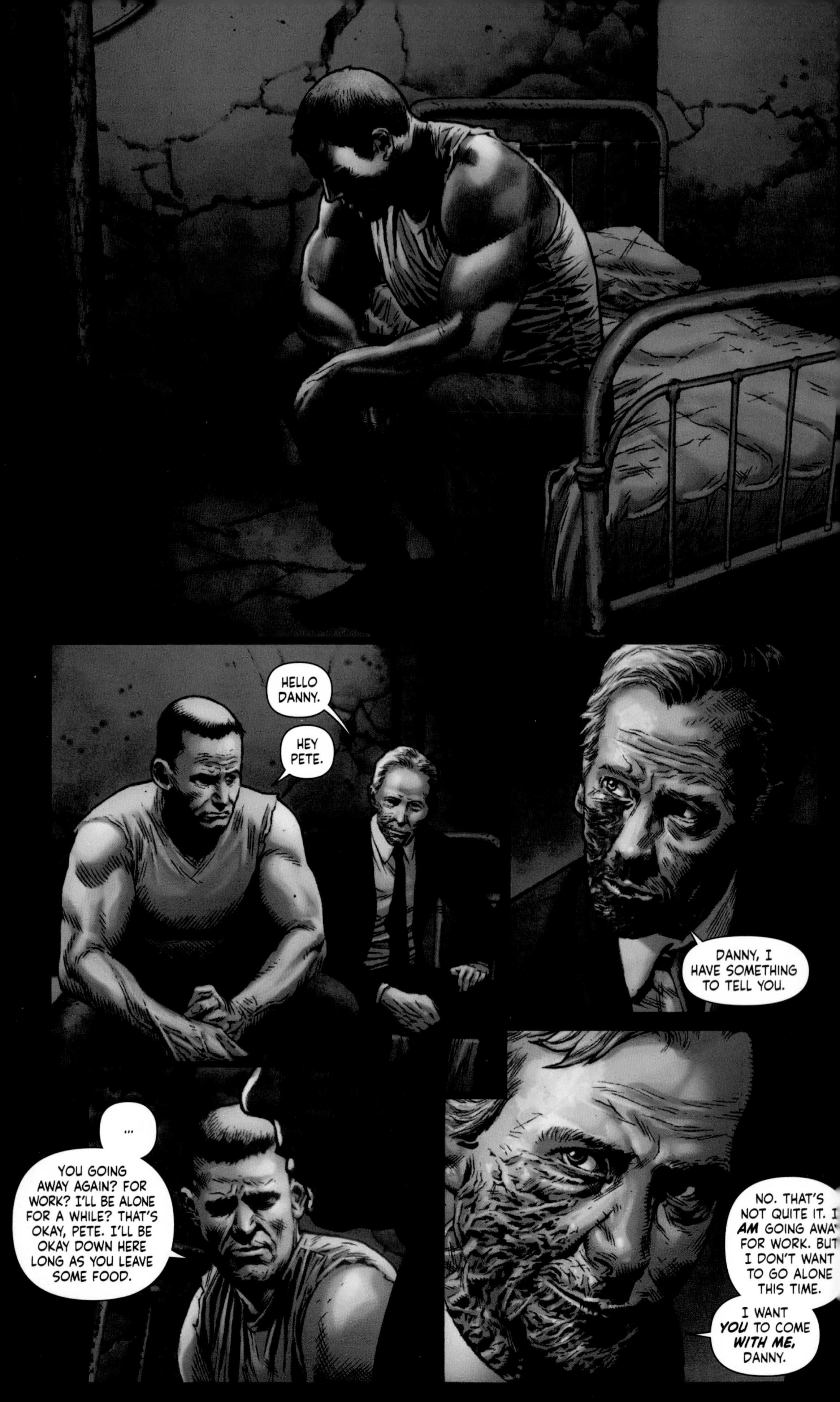
HELLO DANNY.
HEY PETE.
DANNY, I HAVE SOMETHING TO TELL YOU.
...
YOU GOING AWAY AGAIN? FOR WORK? I'LL BE ALONE FOR A WHILE? THAT'S OKAY, PETE. I'LL BE OKAY DOWN HERE LONG AS YOU LEAVE SOME FOOD.
NO. THAT'S NOT QUITE IT. I **AM** GOING AWA FOR WORK. BUT I DON'T WANT TO GO ALONE THIS TIME.
I WANT ***YOU*** TO COME ***WITH ME,*** DANNY.

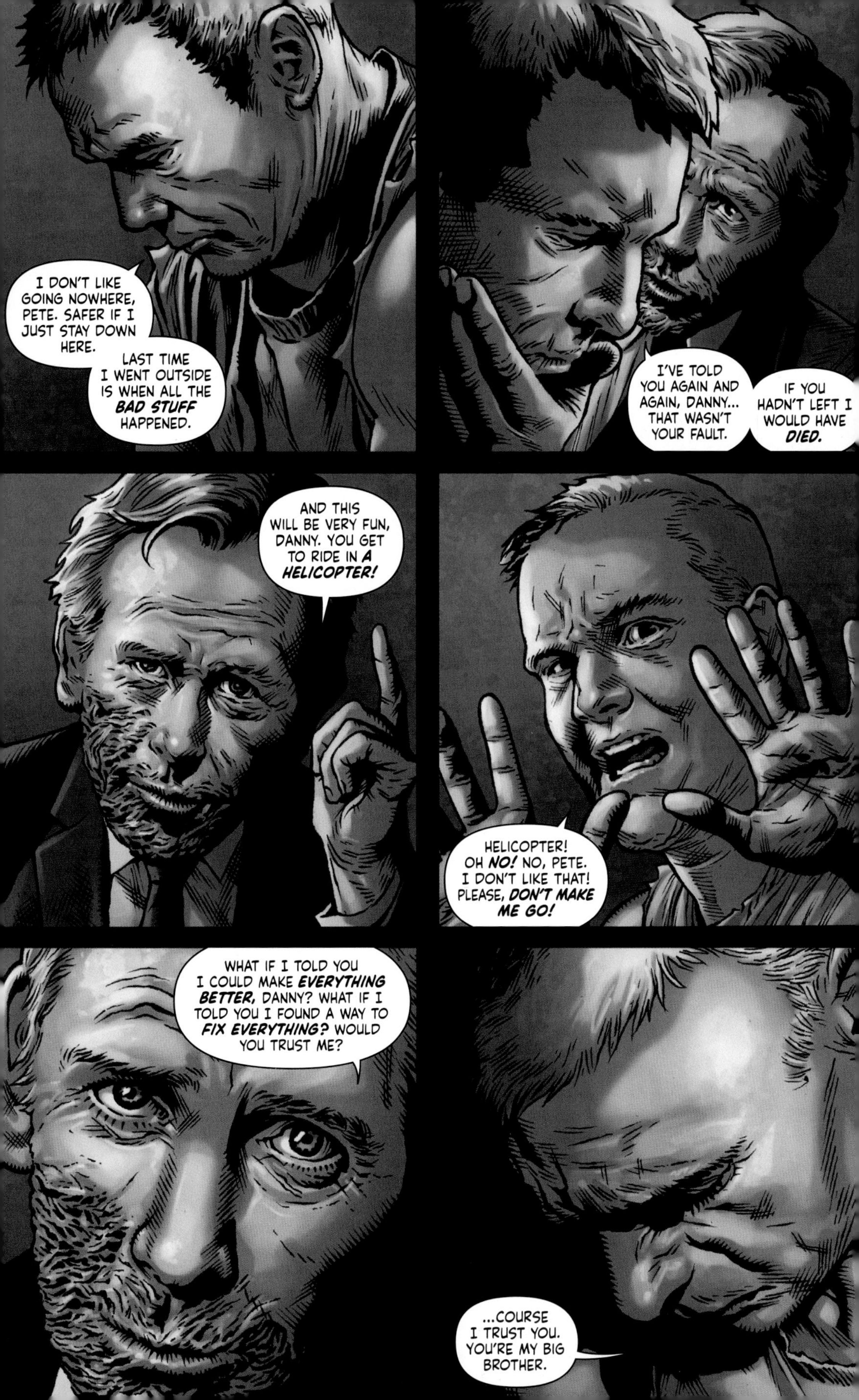
I DON'T LIKE GOING NOWHERE, PETE. SAFER IF I JUST STAY DOWN HERE.
LAST TIME I WENT OUTSIDE IS WHEN ALL THE BAD STUFF HAPPENED.
I'VE TOLD YOU AGAIN AND AGAIN, DANNY... THAT WASN'T YOUR FAULT.
IF YOU HADN'T LEFT I WOULD HAVE DIED.
AND THIS WILL BE VERY FUN, DANNY. YOU GET TO RIDE IN A HELICOPTER!
HELICOPTER! OH NO! NO, PETE. I DON'T LIKE THAT! PLEASE, DON'T MAKE ME GO!
WHAT IF I TOLD YOU I COULD MAKE EVERYTHING BETTER, DANNY? WHAT IF I TOLD YOU I FOUND A WAY TO FIX EVERYTHING? WOULD YOU TRUST ME?
...COURSE I TRUST YOU. YOU'RE MY BIG BROTHER.

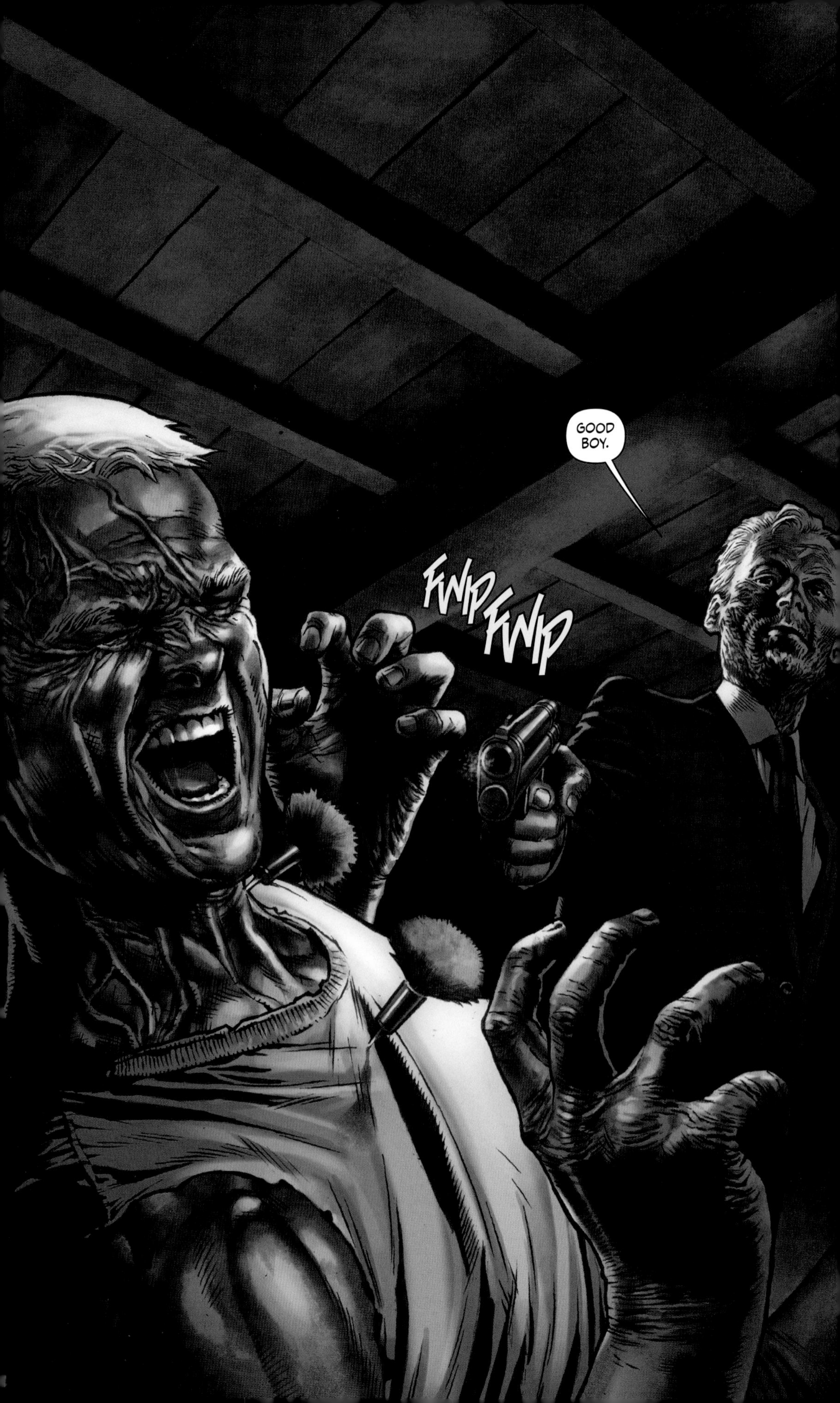
GOOD BOY.
FWIP FWIP

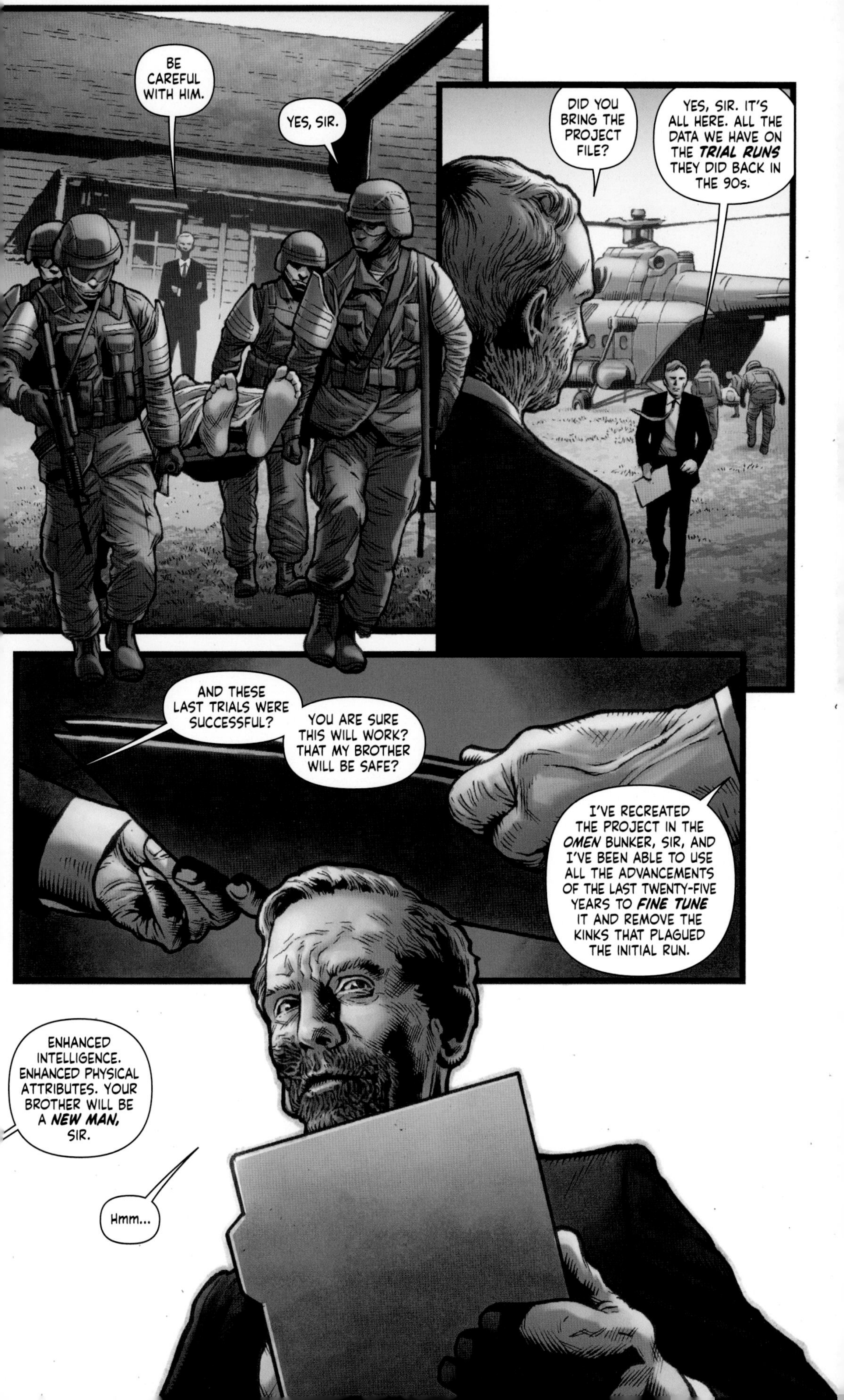
BE CAREFUL WITH HIM.
YES, SIR.
DID YOU BRING THE PROJECT FILE?
YES, SIR. IT'S ALL HERE. ALL THE DATA WE HAVE ON THE ***TRIAL RUNS*** THEY DID BACK IN THE 90s.
AND THESE LAST TRIALS WERE SUCCESSFUL?
YOU ARE SURE THIS WILL WORK? THAT MY BROTHER WILL BE SAFE?
I'VE RECREATED THE PROJECT IN THE *OMEN* BUNKER, SIR, AND I'VE BEEN ABLE TO USE ALL THE ADVANCEMENTS OF THE LAST TWENTY-FIVE YEARS TO ***FINE TUNE*** IT AND REMOVE THE KINKS THAT PLAGUED THE INITIAL RUN.
ENHANCED INTELLIGENCE. ENHANCED PHYSICAL ATTRIBUTES. YOUR BROTHER WILL BE A ***NEW MAN,*** SIR.
Hmm...

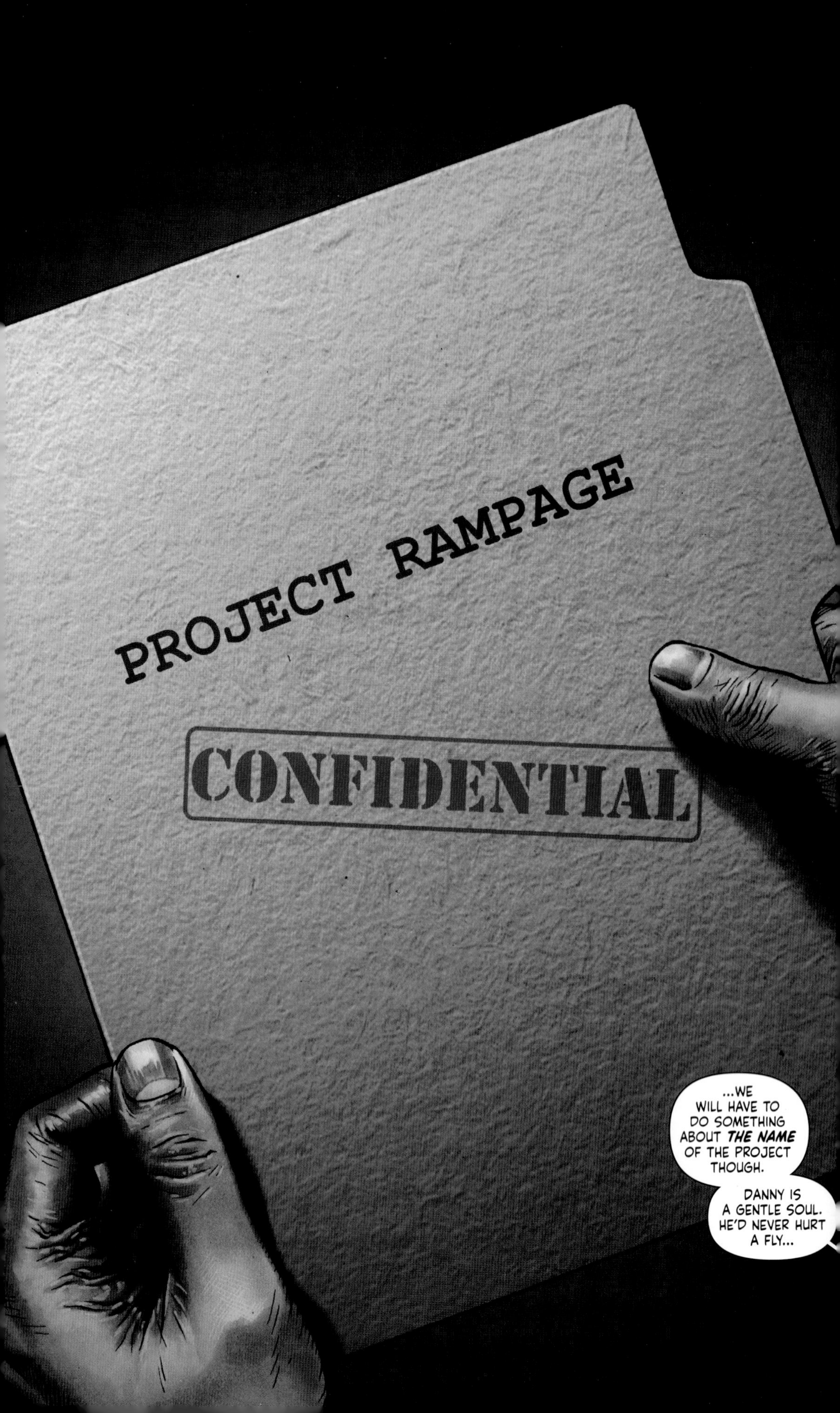
PROJECT RAMPAGE
CONFIDENTIAL
...WE WILL HAVE TO DO SOMETHING ABOUT ***THE NAME*** OF THE PROJECT THOUGH.
DANNY IS A GENTLE SOUL. HE'D NEVER HURT A FLY...

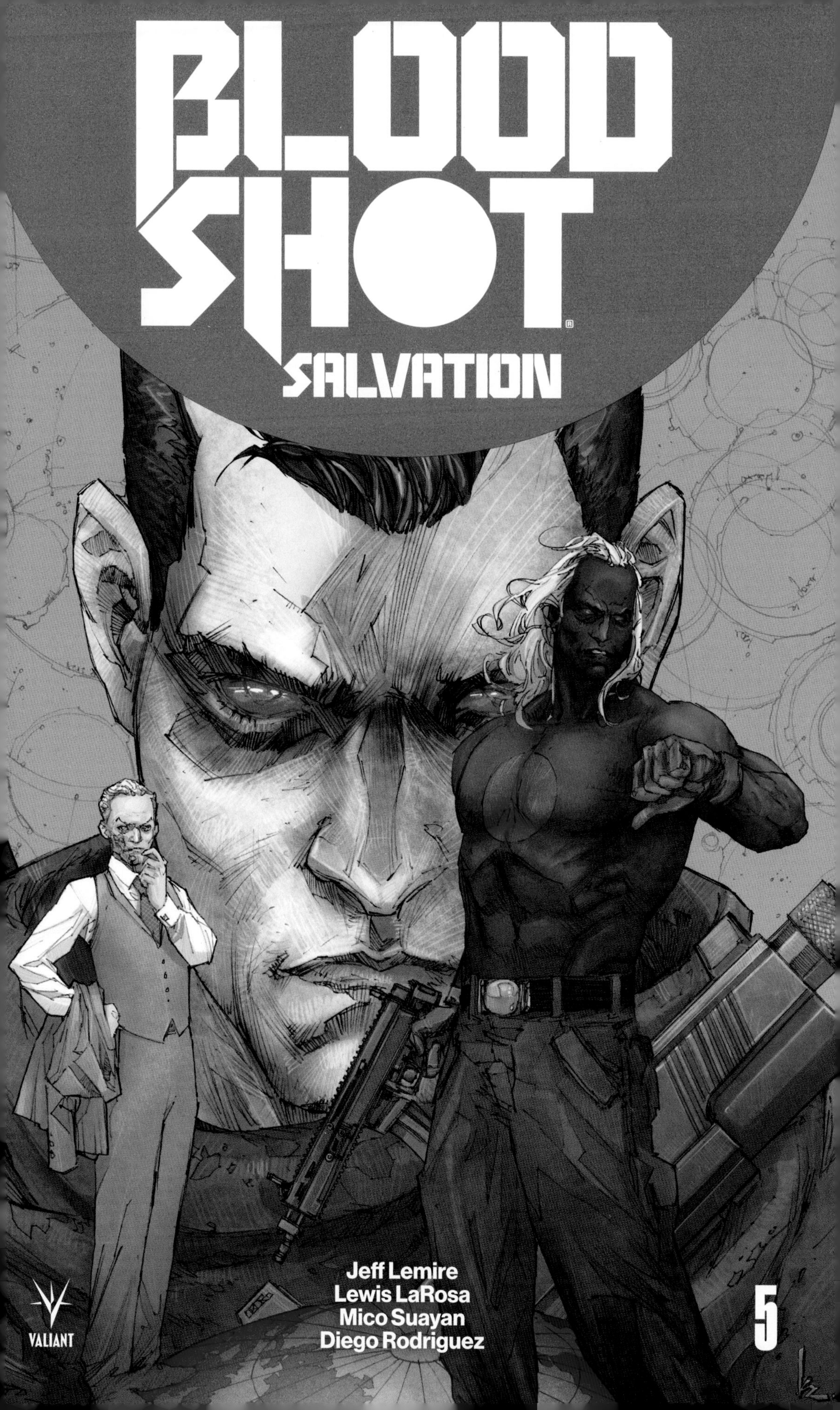
BLOODSHOT®
SALVATION
Jeff Lemire
Lewis LaRosa
Mico Suayan
Diego Rodriguez
VALIANT
5

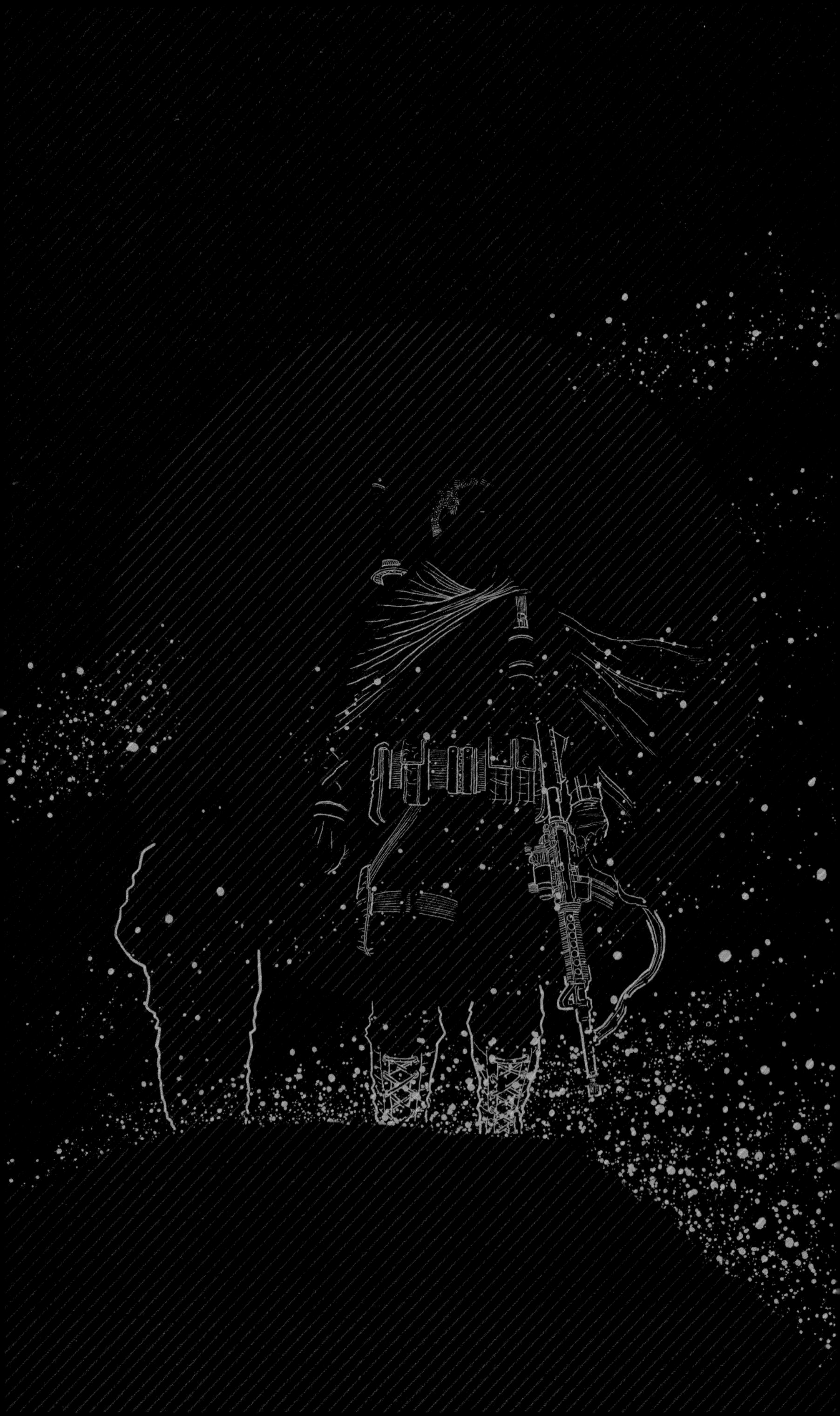

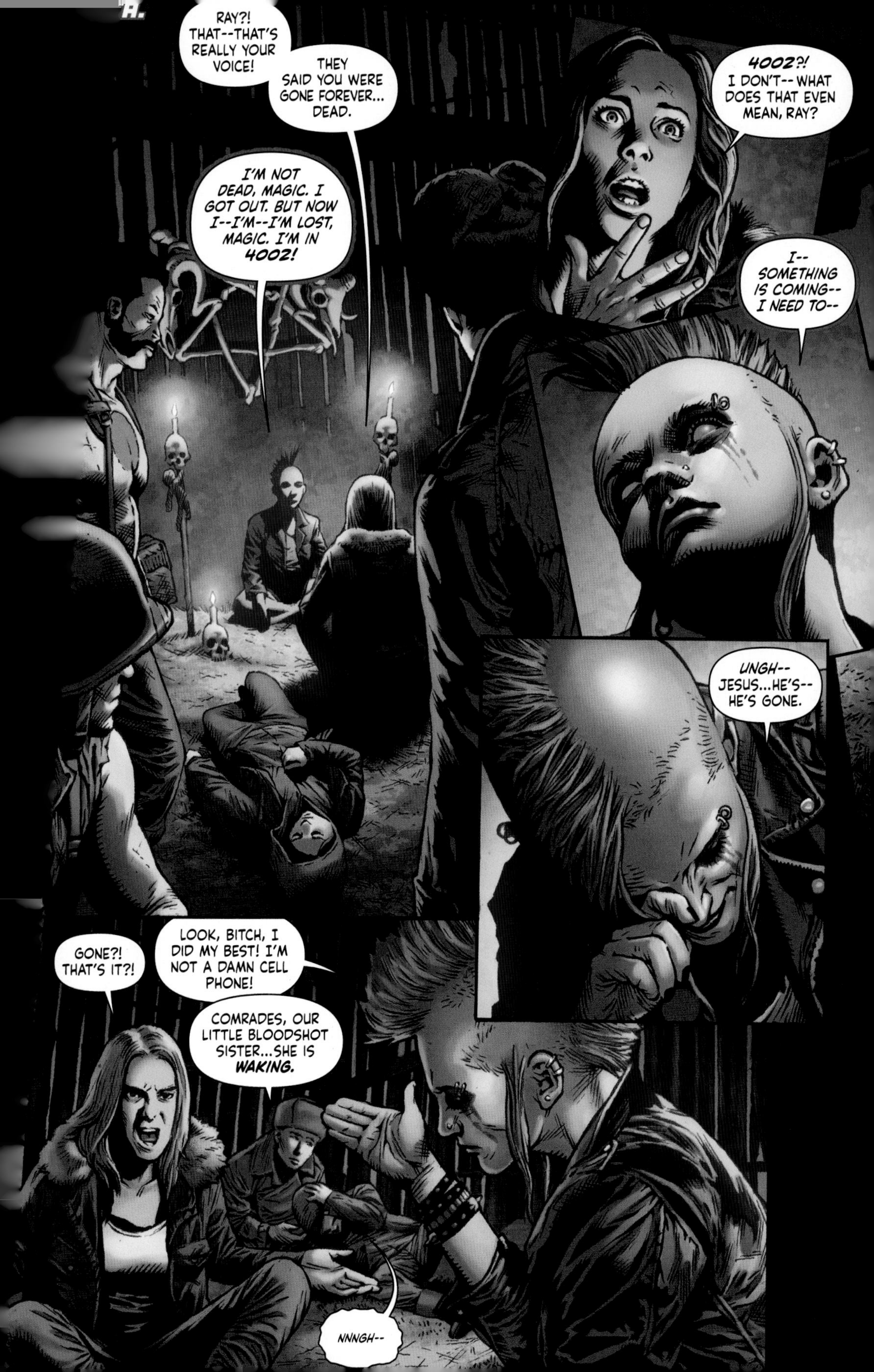
RAY?! THAT--THAT'S REALLY YOUR VOICE!
THEY SAID YOU WERE GONE FOREVER... DEAD.
I'M NOT DEAD, MAGIC. I GOT OUT. BUT NOW I--I'M--I'M LOST, MAGIC. I'M IN 4002!
4002?! I DON'T--WHAT DOES THAT EVEN MEAN, RAY?
I-- SOMETHING IS COMING-- I NEED TO--
UNGH-- JESUS...HE'S-- HE'S GONE.
GONE?! THAT'S IT?!
LOOK, BITCH, I DID MY BEST! I'M NOT A DAMN CELL PHONE!
COMRADES, OUR LITTLE BLOODSHOT SISTER...SHE IS WAKING.
NNNGH--

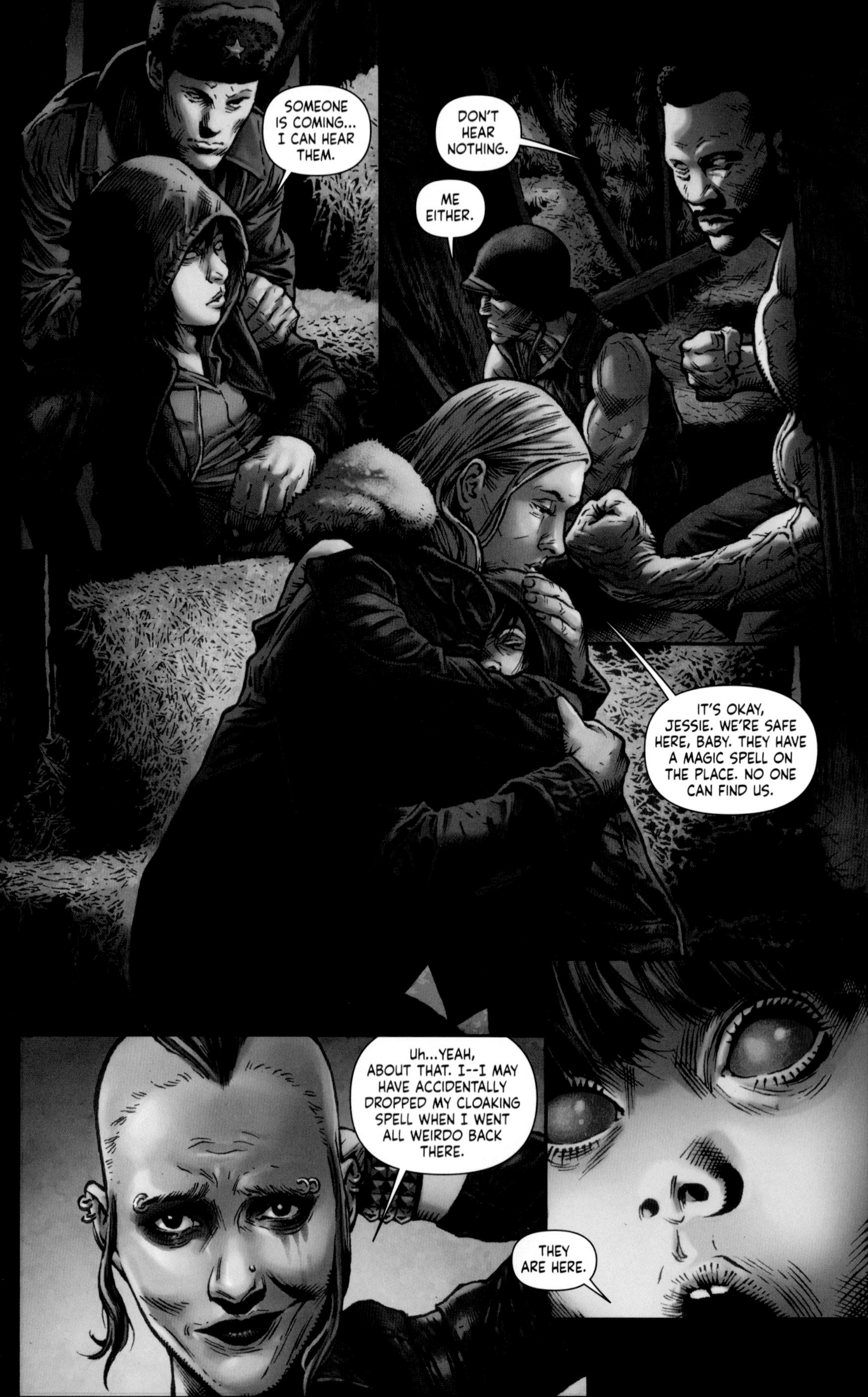
SOMEONE IS COMING... I CAN HEAR THEM.
DON'T HEAR NOTHING.
ME EITHER.
IT'S OKAY, JESSIE. WE'RE SAFE HERE, BABY. THEY HAVE A MAGIC SPELL ON THE PLACE. NO ONE CAN FIND US.
Uh...YEAH, ABOUT THAT. I--I MAY HAVE ACCIDENTALLY DROPPED MY CLOAKING SPELL WHEN I WENT ALL WEIRDO BACK THERE.
THEY ARE HERE.

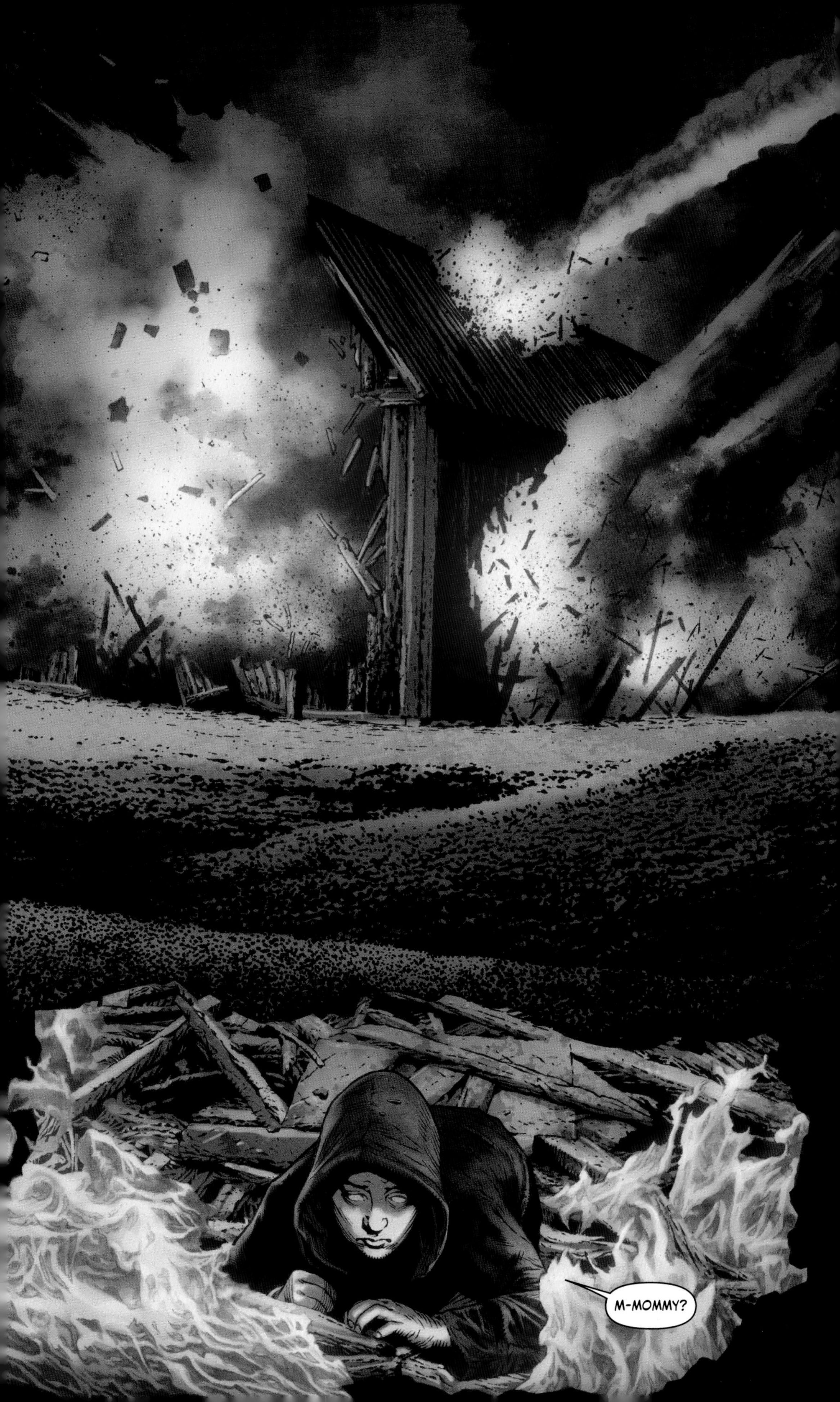
M-MOMMY?

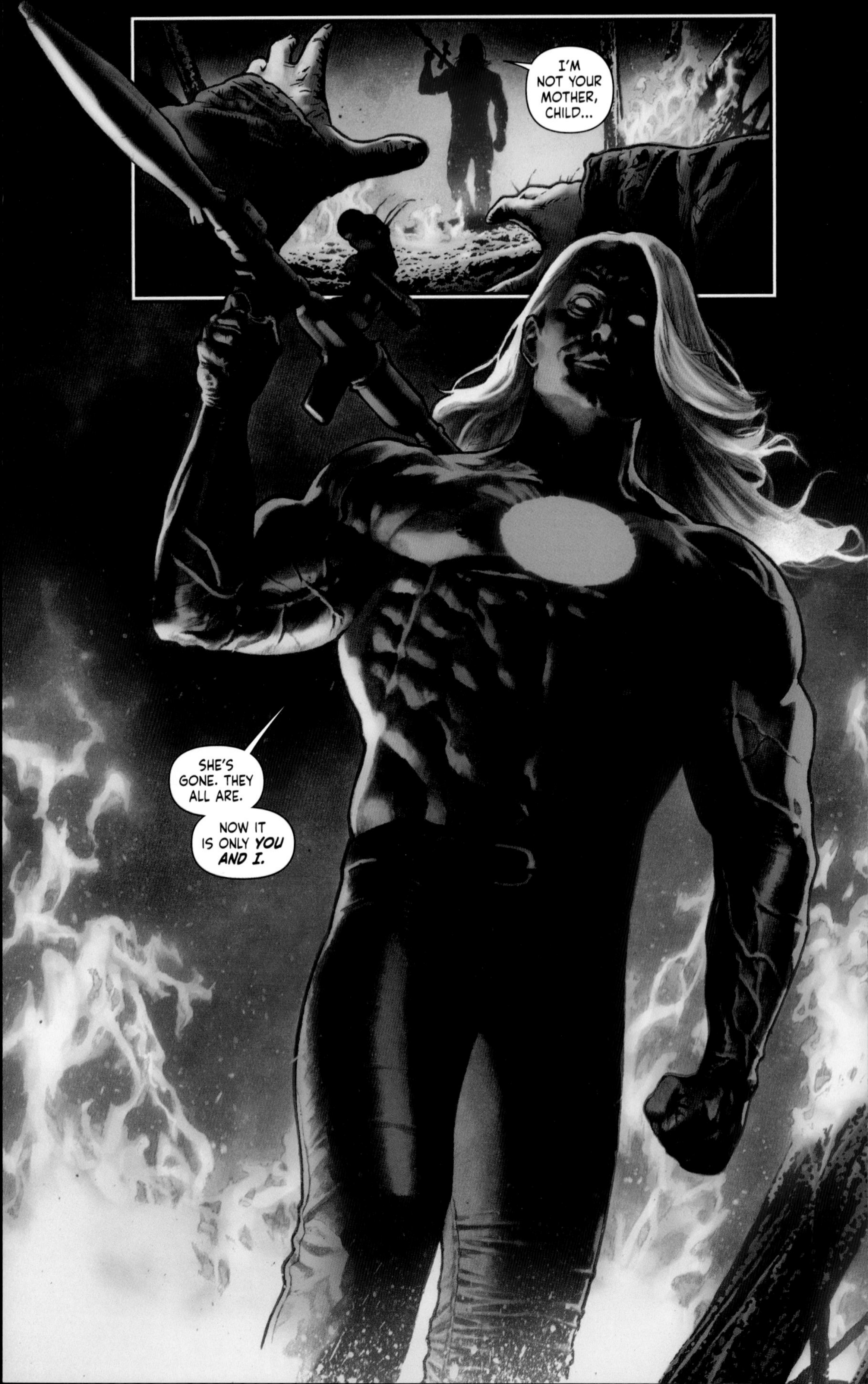
I'M NOT YOUR MOTHER, CHILD...
SHE'S GONE. THEY ALL ARE.
NOW IT IS ONLY *YOU AND I.*

OHIO.
NOW.

WAKE UP.

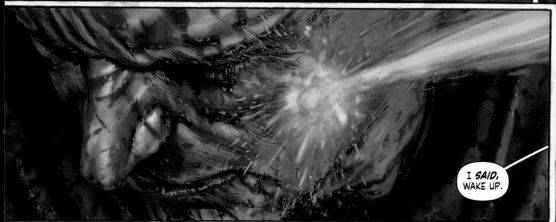

I *SAID*,
WAKE UP.

THAT GOT HIS
ATTENTION.

RISE
AND SHINE,
BIG BOY.

ZZIP

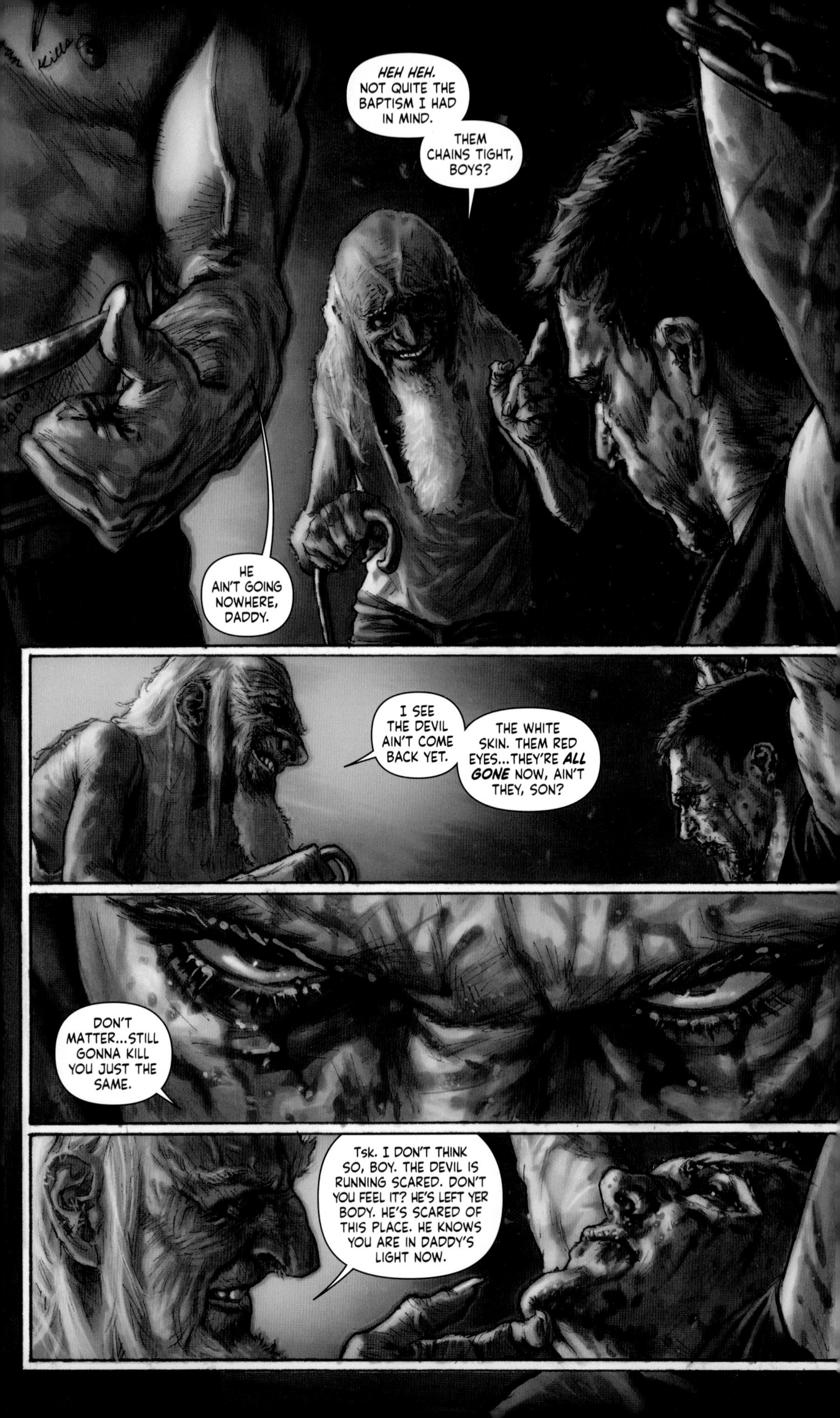
HEH HEH. NOT QUITE THE BAPTISM I HAD IN MIND.
THEM CHAINS TIGHT, BOYS?
HE AIN'T GOING NOWHERE, DADDY.
I SEE THE DEVIL AIN'T COME BACK YET.
THE WHITE SKIN. THEM RED EYES...THEY'RE ALL GONE NOW, AIN'T THEY, SON?
DON'T MATTER...STILL GONNA KILL YOU JUST THE SAME.
Tsk. I DON'T THINK SO, BOY. THE DEVIL IS RUNNING SCARED. DON'T YOU FEEL IT? HE'S LEFT YER BODY. HE'S SCARED OF THIS PLACE. HE KNOWS YOU ARE IN DADDY'S LIGHT NOW.

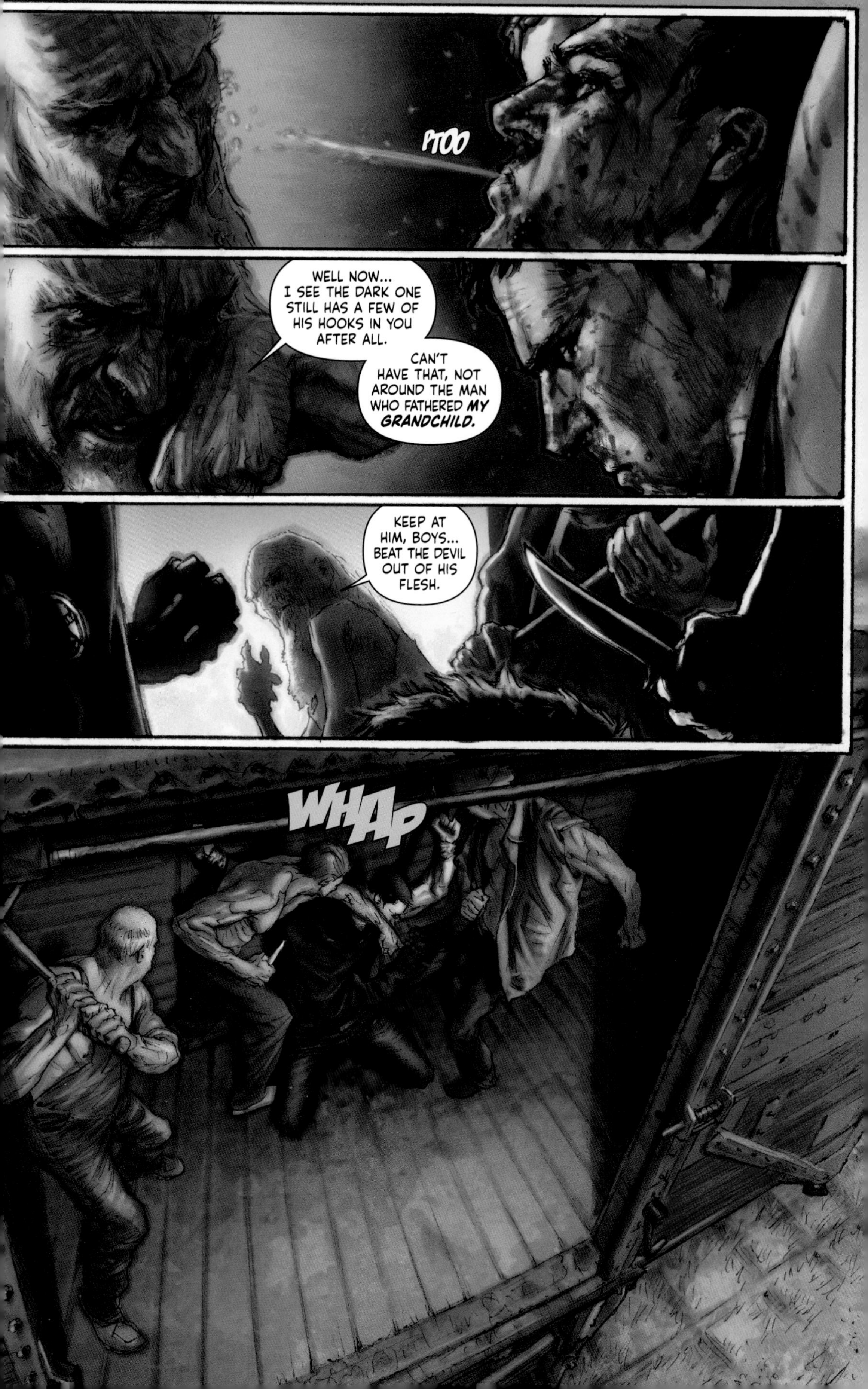
PTOO
WELL NOW... I SEE THE DARK ONE STILL HAS A FEW OF HIS HOOKS IN YOU AFTER ALL.
CAN'T HAVE THAT, NOT AROUND THE MAN WHO FATHERED **MY GRANDCHILD.**
KEEP AT HIM, BOYS... BEAT THE DEVIL OUT OF HIS FLESH.
WHAP

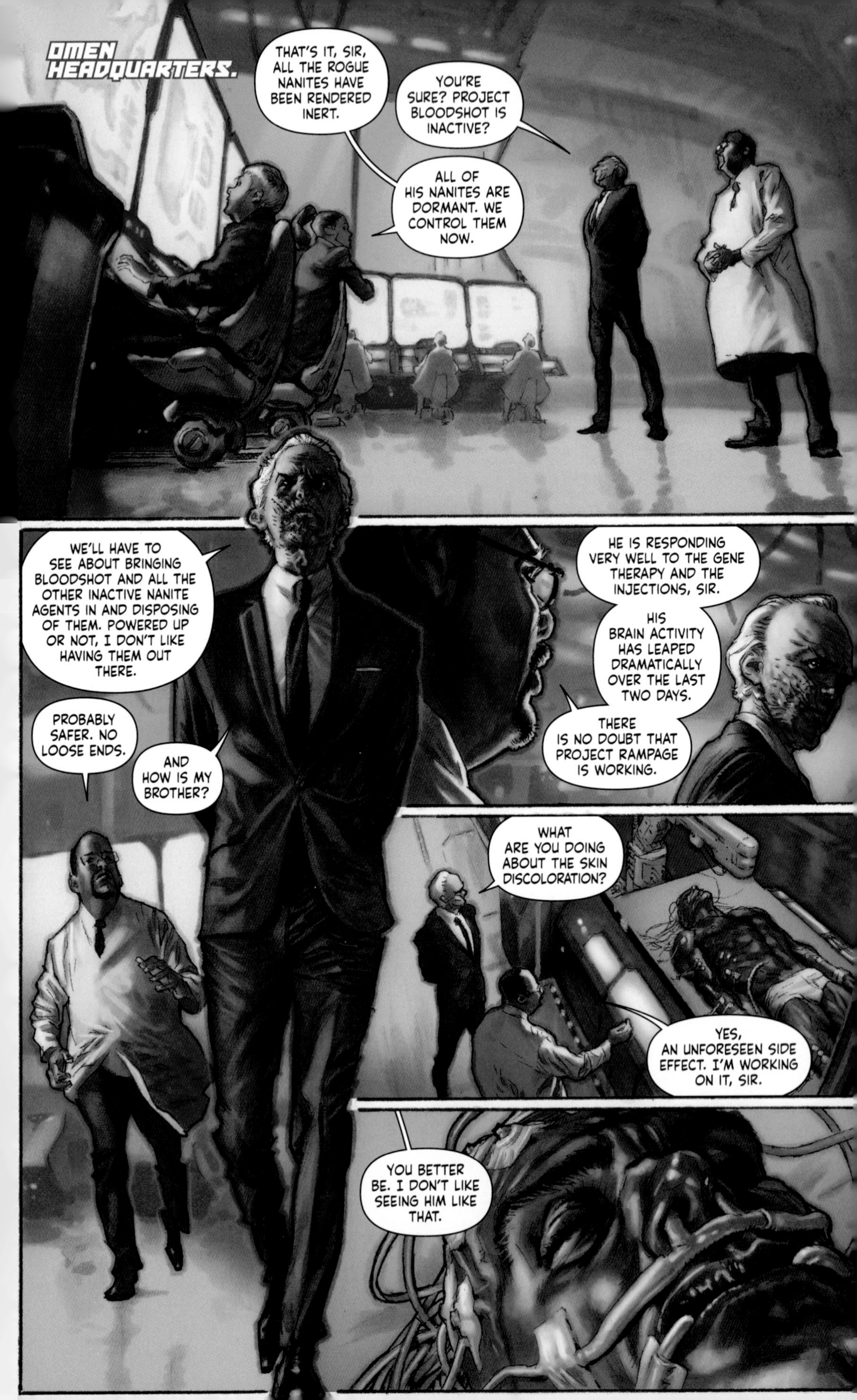
OMEN HEADQUARTERS.
THAT'S IT, SIR, ALL THE ROGUE NANITES HAVE BEEN RENDERED INERT.
YOU'RE SURE? PROJECT BLOODSHOT IS INACTIVE?
ALL OF HIS NANITES ARE DORMANT. WE CONTROL THEM NOW.
WE'LL HAVE TO SEE ABOUT BRINGING BLOODSHOT AND ALL THE OTHER INACTIVE NANITE AGENTS IN AND DISPOSING OF THEM. POWERED UP OR NOT, I DON'T LIKE HAVING THEM OUT THERE.
PROBABLY SAFER. NO LOOSE ENDS.
AND HOW IS MY BROTHER?
HE IS RESPONDING VERY WELL TO THE GENE THERAPY AND THE INJECTIONS, SIR.
HIS BRAIN ACTIVITY HAS LEAPED DRAMATICALLY OVER THE LAST TWO DAYS.
THERE IS NO DOUBT THAT PROJECT RAMPAGE IS WORKING.
WHAT ARE YOU DOING ABOUT THE SKIN DISCOLORATION?
YES, AN UNFORESEEN SIDE EFFECT. I'M WORKING ON IT, SIR.
YOU BETTER BE. I DON'T LIKE SEEING HIM LIKE THAT.

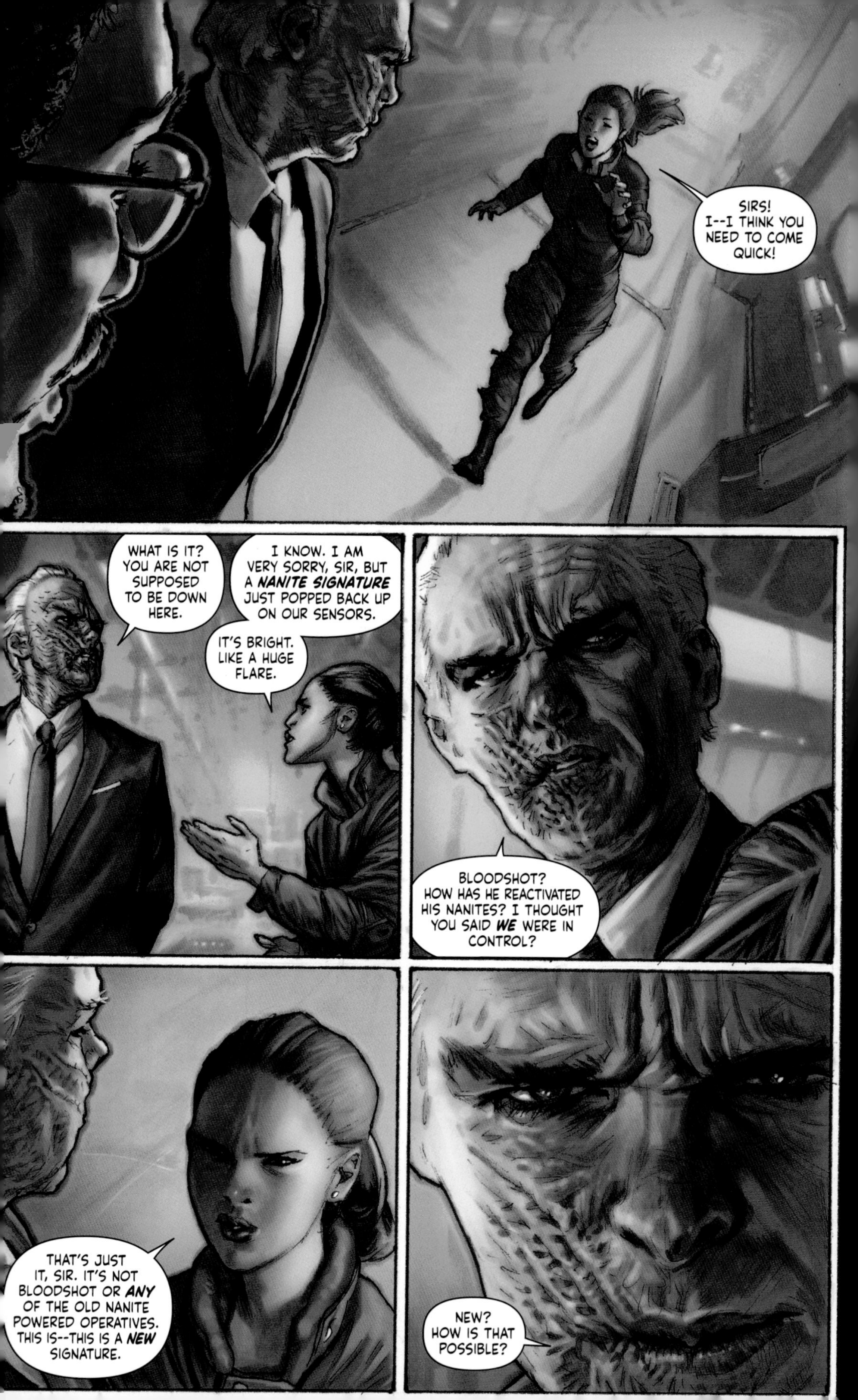
SIRS! I--I THINK YOU NEED TO COME QUICK!
WHAT IS IT? YOU ARE NOT SUPPOSED TO BE DOWN HERE.
I KNOW. I AM VERY SORRY, SIR, BUT A ***NANITE SIGNATURE*** JUST POPPED BACK UP ON OUR SENSORS.
IT'S BRIGHT. LIKE A HUGE FLARE.
BLOODSHOT? HOW HAS HE REACTIVATED HIS NANITES? I THOUGHT YOU SAID ***WE*** WERE IN CONTROL?
THAT'S JUST IT, SIR. IT'S NOT BLOODSHOT OR ***ANY*** OF THE OLD NANITE POWERED OPERATIVES. THIS IS--THIS IS A ***NEW*** SIGNATURE.
NEW? HOW IS THAT POSSIBLE?

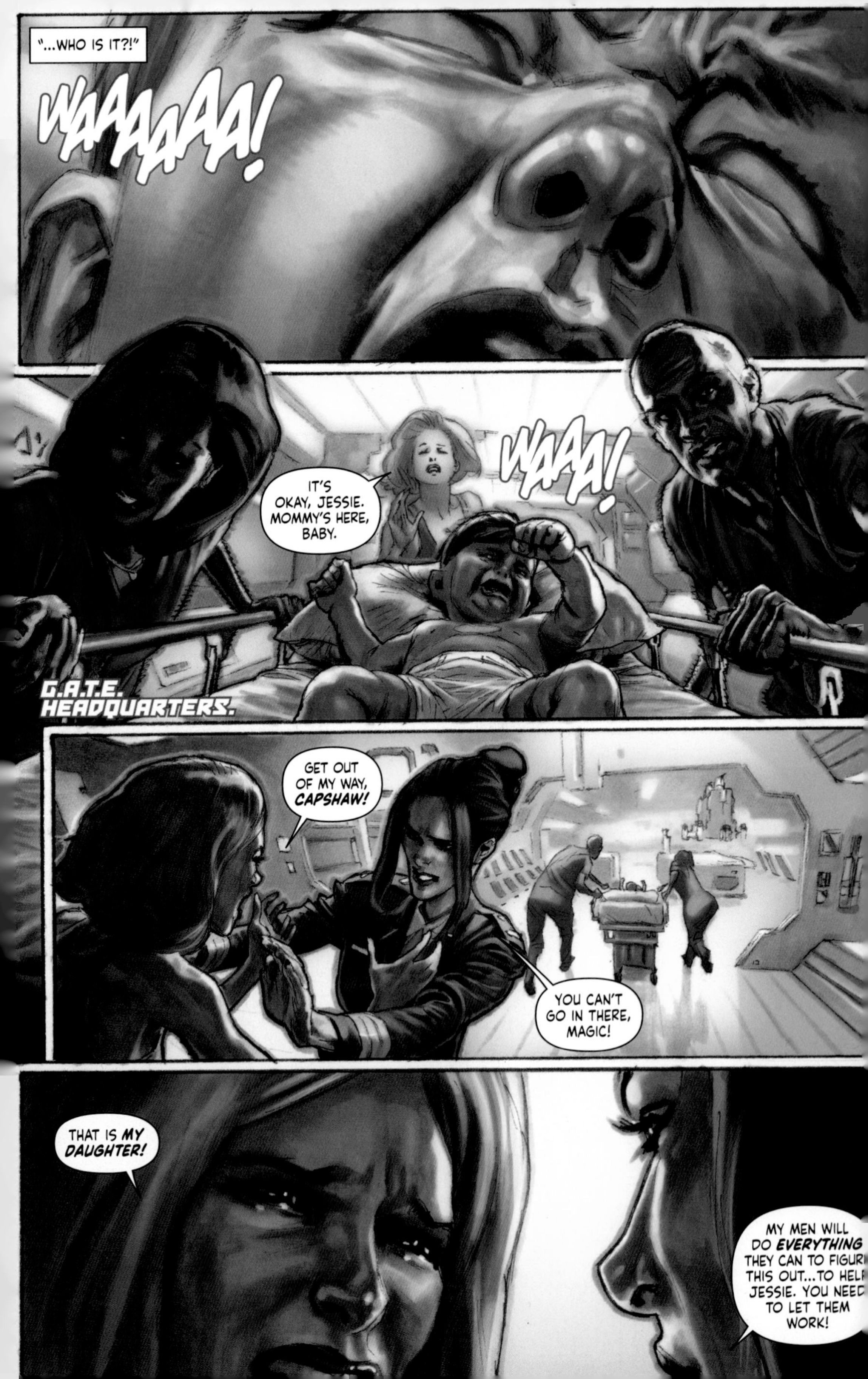
"...WHO IS IT?!"
WAAAAAAA!
G.A.T.E. HEADQUARTERS.
IT'S OKAY, JESSIE. MOMMY'S HERE, BABY.
WAAAA!
GET OUT OF MY WAY, CAPSHAW!
YOU CAN'T GO IN THERE, MAGIC!
THAT IS MY DAUGHTER!
MY MEN WILL DO EVERYTHING THEY CAN TO FIGUR THIS OUT...TO HELP JESSIE. YOU NEED TO LET THEM WORK!

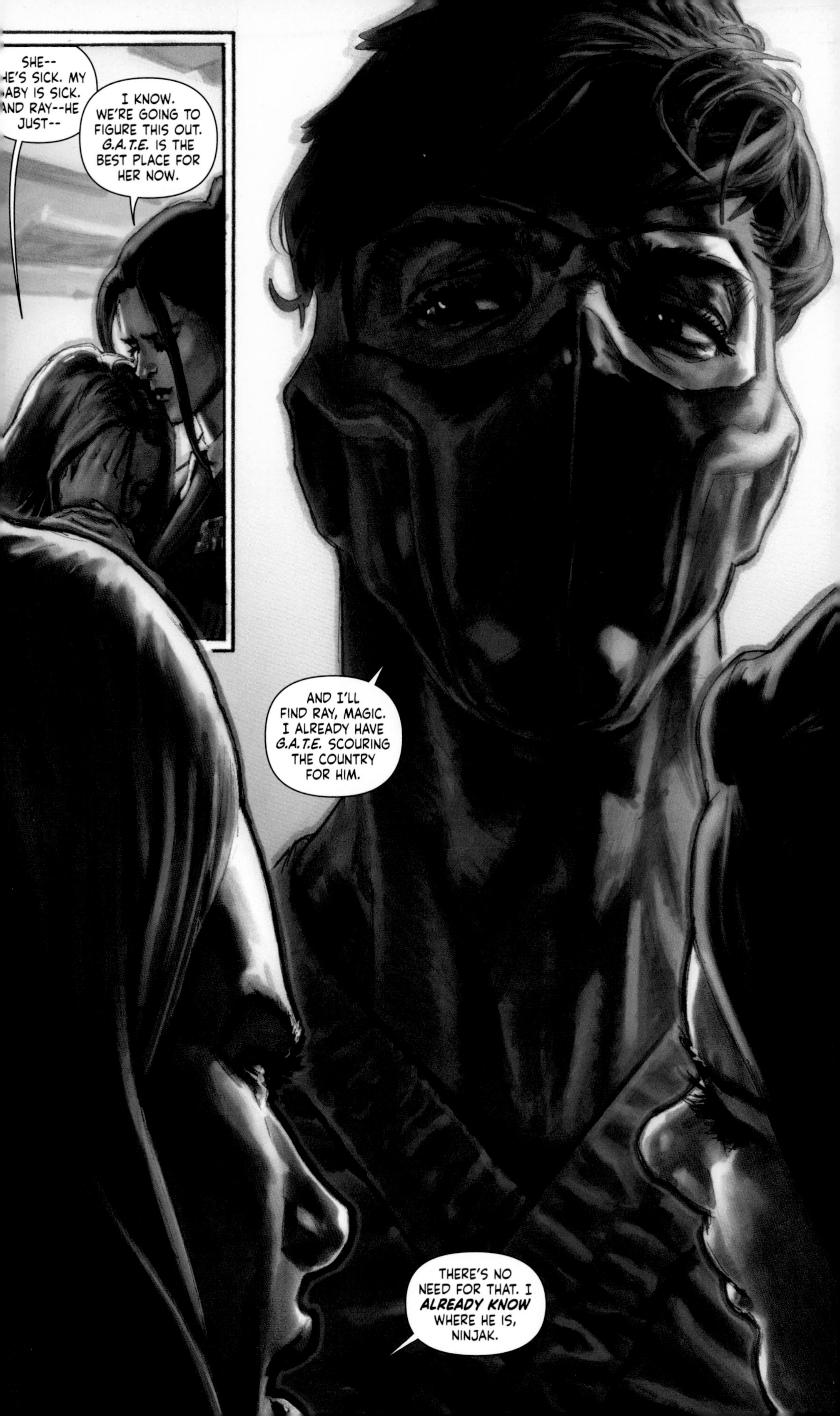
SHE--
HE'S SICK. MY
ABY IS SICK.
AND RAY--HE
JUST--
I KNOW. WE'RE GOING TO FIGURE THIS OUT. *G.A.T.E.* IS THE BEST PLACE FOR HER NOW.
AND I'LL FIND RAY, MAGIC. I ALREADY HAVE *G.A.T.E.* SCOURING THE COUNTRY FOR HIM.
THERE'S NO NEED FOR THAT. I ***ALREADY KNOW*** WHERE HE IS, NINJAK.

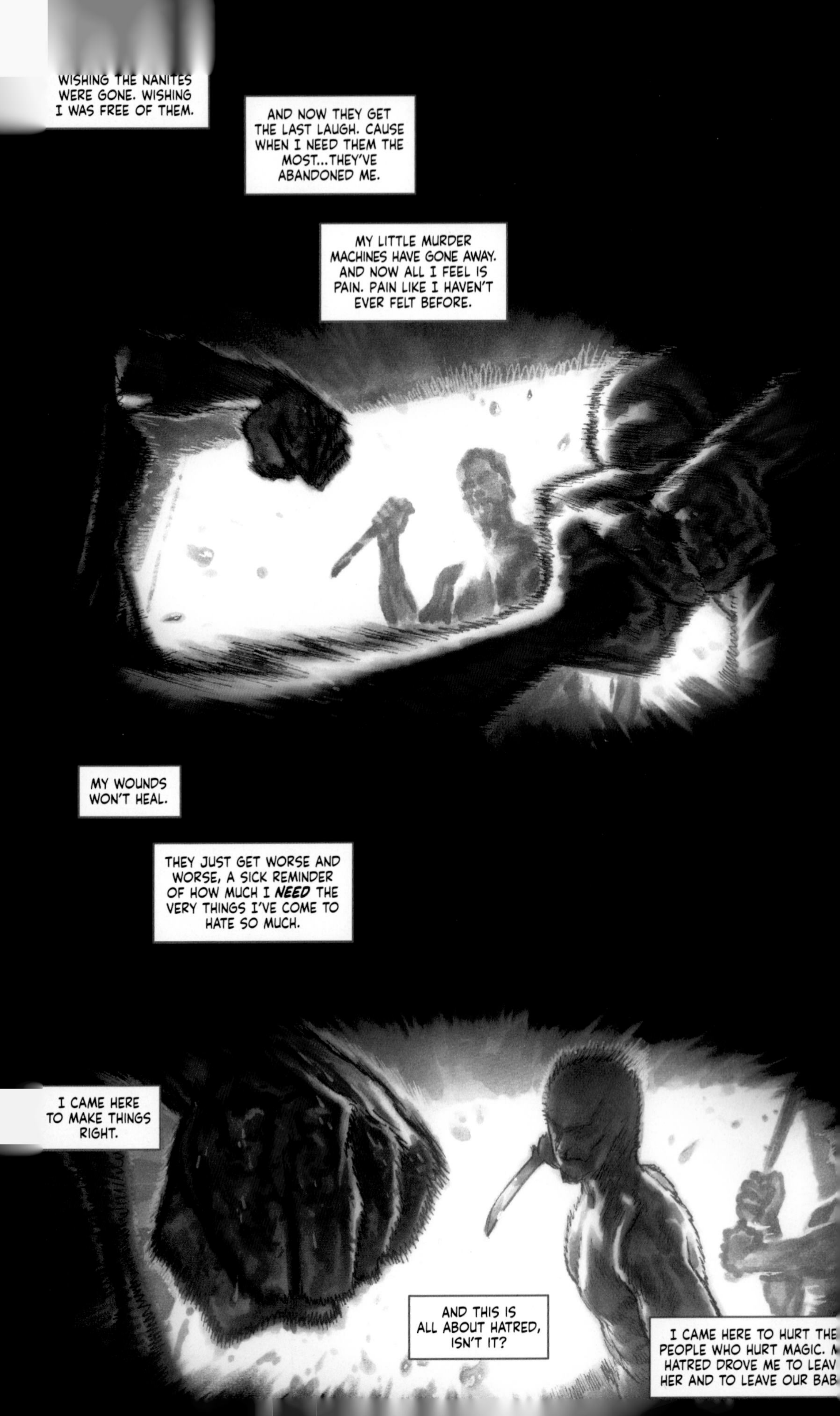
WISHING THE NANITES WERE GONE. WISHING I WAS FREE OF THEM.
AND NOW THEY GET THE LAST LAUGH. CAUSE WHEN I NEED THEM THE MOST...THEY'VE ABANDONED ME.
MY LITTLE MURDER MACHINES HAVE GONE AWAY. AND NOW ALL I FEEL IS PAIN. PAIN LIKE I HAVEN'T EVER FELT BEFORE.
MY WOUNDS WON'T HEAL.
THEY JUST GET WORSE AND WORSE, A SICK REMINDER OF HOW MUCH I ***NEED*** THE VERY THINGS I'VE COME TO HATE SO MUCH.
I CAME HERE TO MAKE THINGS RIGHT.
AND THIS IS ALL ABOUT HATRED, ISN'T IT?
I CAME HERE TO HURT THE PEOPLE WHO HURT MAGIC. HATRED DROVE ME TO LEAV HER AND TO LEAVE OUR BAB

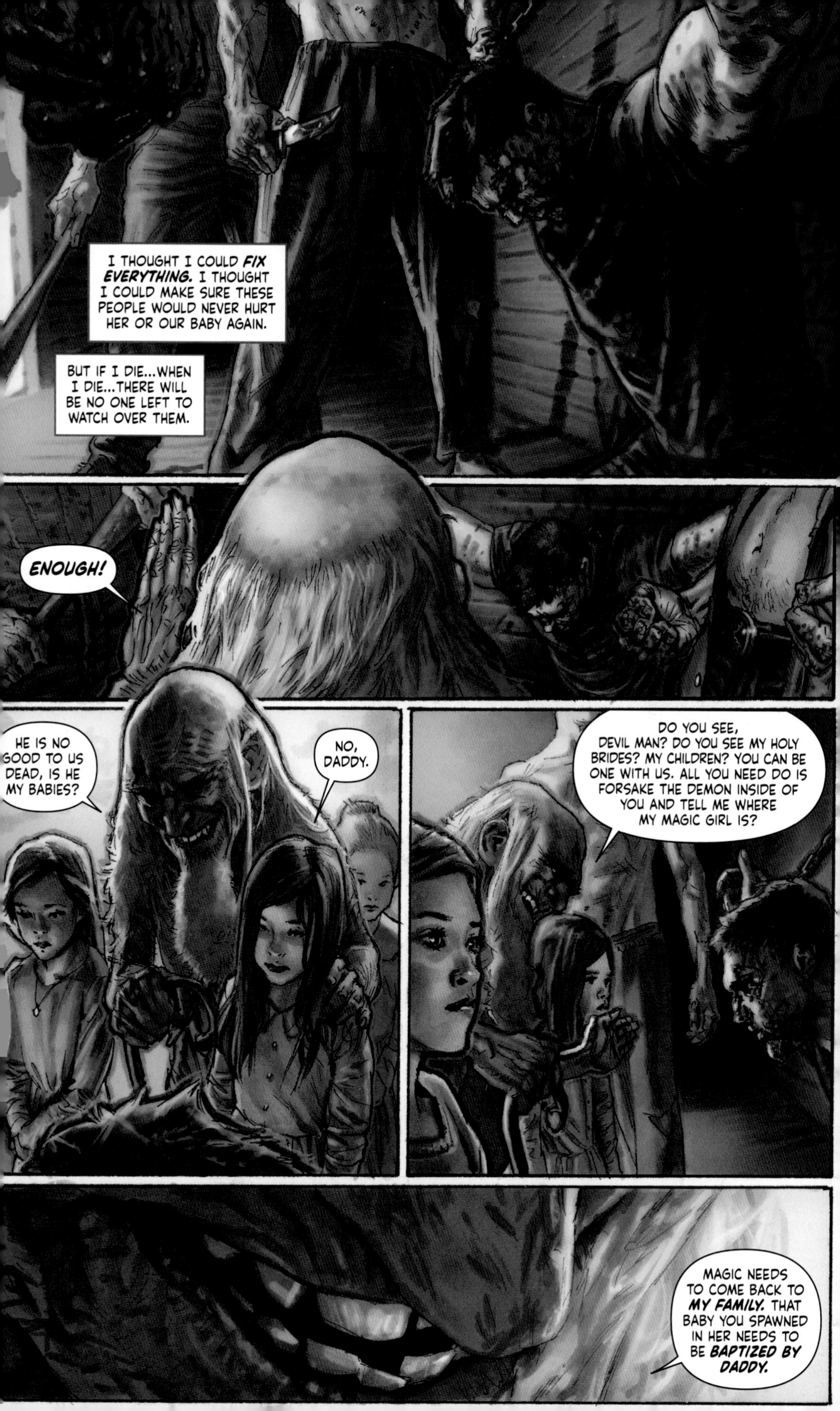
I THOUGHT I COULD FIX EVERYTHING. I THOUGHT I COULD MAKE SURE THESE PEOPLE WOULD NEVER HURT HER OR OUR BABY AGAIN.
BUT IF I DIE...WHEN I DIE...THERE WILL BE NO ONE LEFT TO WATCH OVER THEM.
ENOUGH!
HE IS NO GOOD TO US DEAD, IS HE MY BABIES?
NO, DADDY.
DO YOU SEE, DEVIL MAN? DO YOU SEE MY HOLY BRIDES? MY CHILDREN? YOU CAN BE ONE WITH US. ALL YOU NEED DO IS FORSAKE THE DEMON INSIDE OF YOU AND TELL ME WHERE MY MAGIC GIRL IS?
MAGIC NEEDS TO COME BACK TO MY FAMILY. THAT BABY YOU SPAWNED IN HER NEEDS TO BE BAPTIZED BY DADDY.

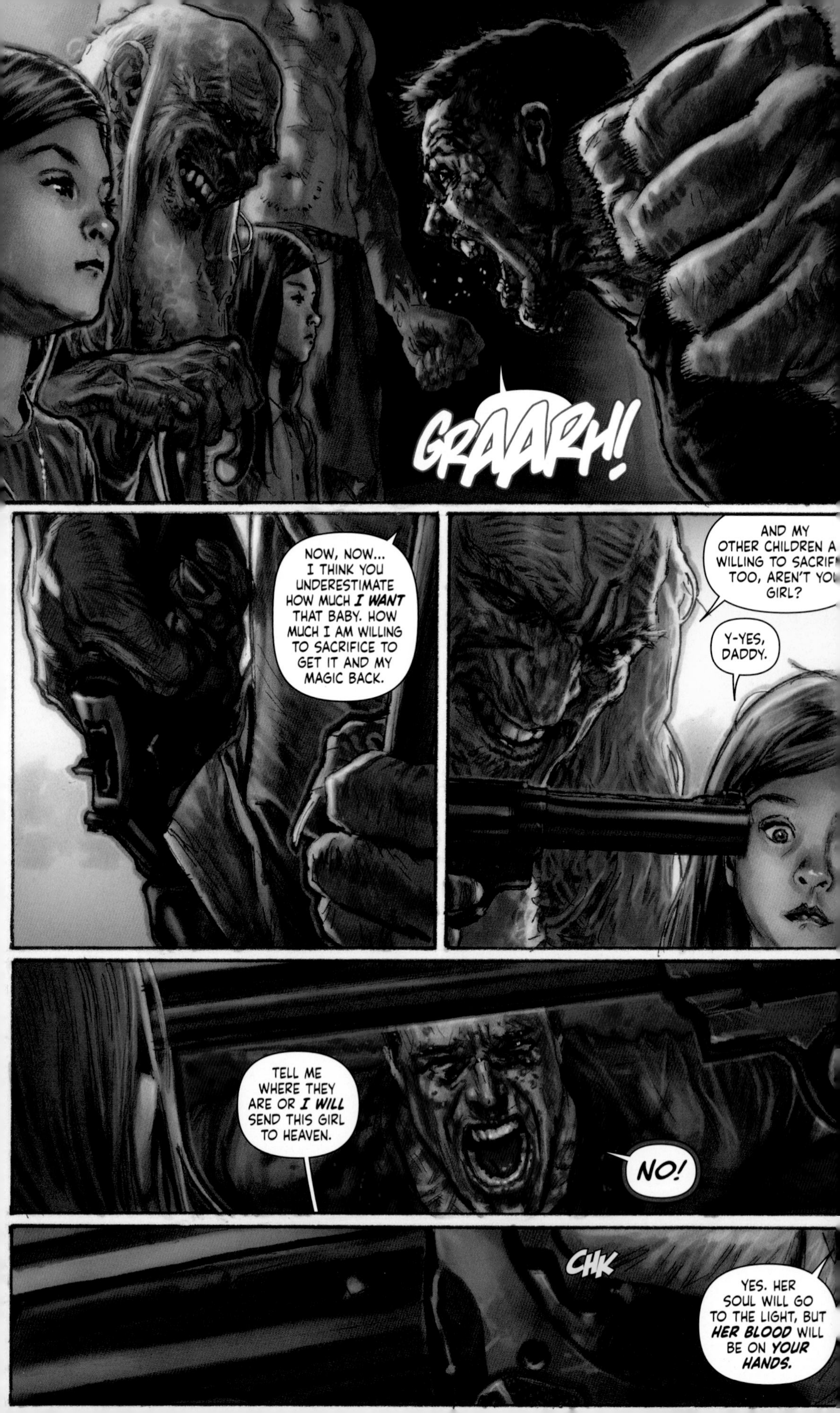
GRAAARH!
NOW, NOW... I THINK YOU UNDERESTIMATE HOW MUCH *I WANT* THAT BABY. HOW MUCH I AM WILLING TO SACRIFICE TO GET IT AND MY MAGIC BACK.
AND MY OTHER CHILDREN A WILLING TO SACRIF TOO, AREN'T YO GIRL?
Y-YES, DADDY.
TELL ME WHERE THEY ARE OR *I WILL* SEND THIS GIRL TO HEAVEN.
NO!
CHK
YES. HER SOUL WILL GO TO THE LIGHT, BUT *HER BLOOD* WILL BE ON *YOUR HANDS.*

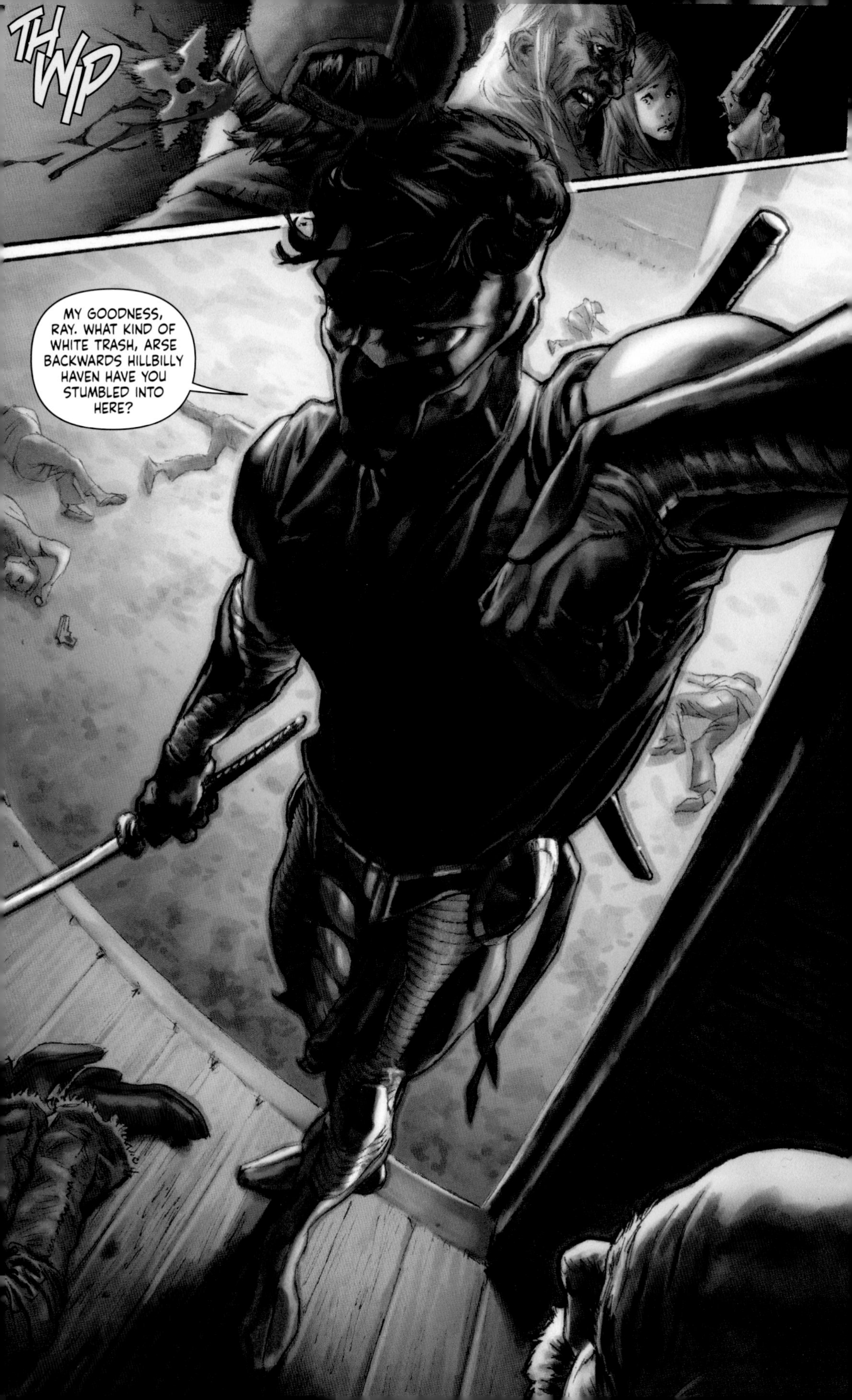
THWIP
MY GOODNESS, RAY. WHAT KIND OF WHITE TRASH, ARSE BACKWARDS HILLBILLY HAVEN HAVE YOU STUMBLED INTO HERE?

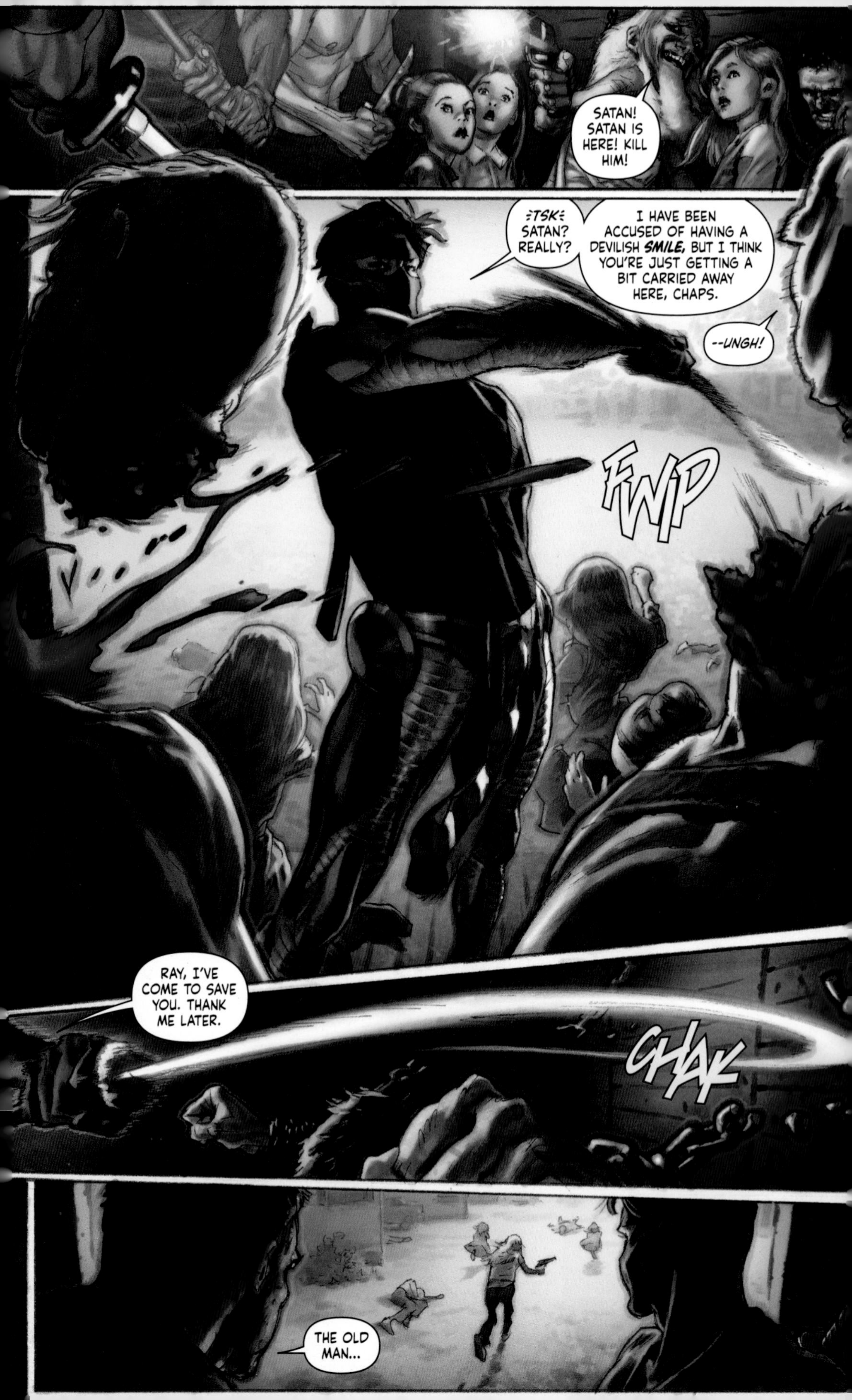
SATAN! SATAN IS HERE! KILL HIM!
TSK SATAN? REALLY?
I HAVE BEEN ACCUSED OF HAVING A DEVILISH SMILE, BUT I THINK YOU'RE JUST GETTING A BIT CARRIED AWAY HERE, CHAPS.
--UNGH!
FWIP
RAY, I'VE COME TO SAVE YOU. THANK ME LATER.
CHAK
THE OLD MAN...

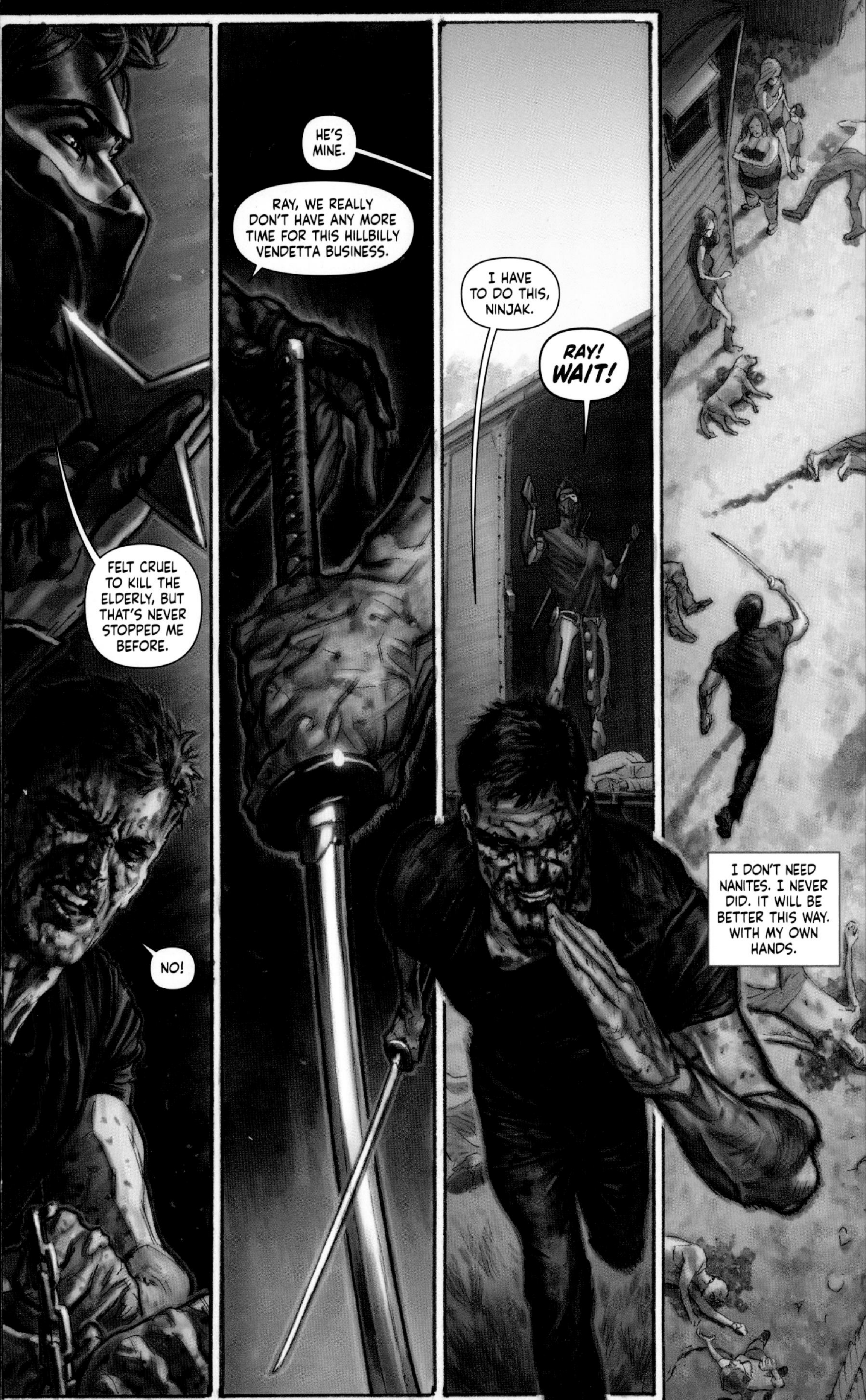
FELT CRUEL TO KILL THE ELDERLY, BUT THAT'S NEVER STOPPED ME BEFORE.
NO!
HE'S MINE.
RAY, WE REALLY DON'T HAVE ANY MORE TIME FOR THIS HILLBILLY VENDETTA BUSINESS.
I HAVE TO DO THIS, NINJAK.
RAY! WAIT!
I DON'T NEED NANITES. I NEVER DID. IT WILL BE BETTER THIS WAY. WITH MY OWN HANDS.

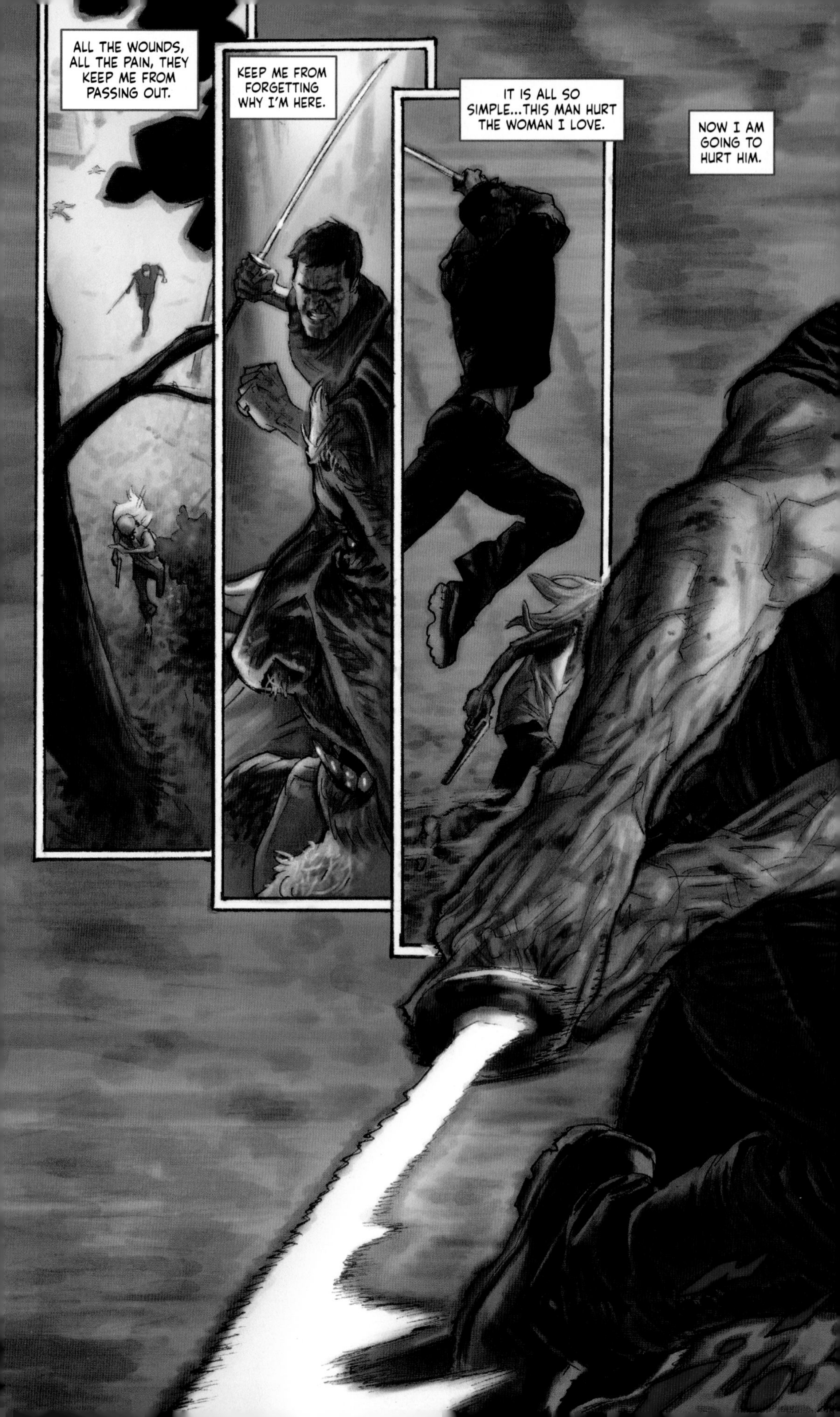
ALL THE WOUNDS, ALL THE PAIN, THEY KEEP ME FROM PASSING OUT.
KEEP ME FROM FORGETTING WHY I'M HERE.
IT IS ALL SO SIMPLE...THIS MAN HURT THE WOMAN I LOVE.
NOW I AM GOING TO HURT HIM.

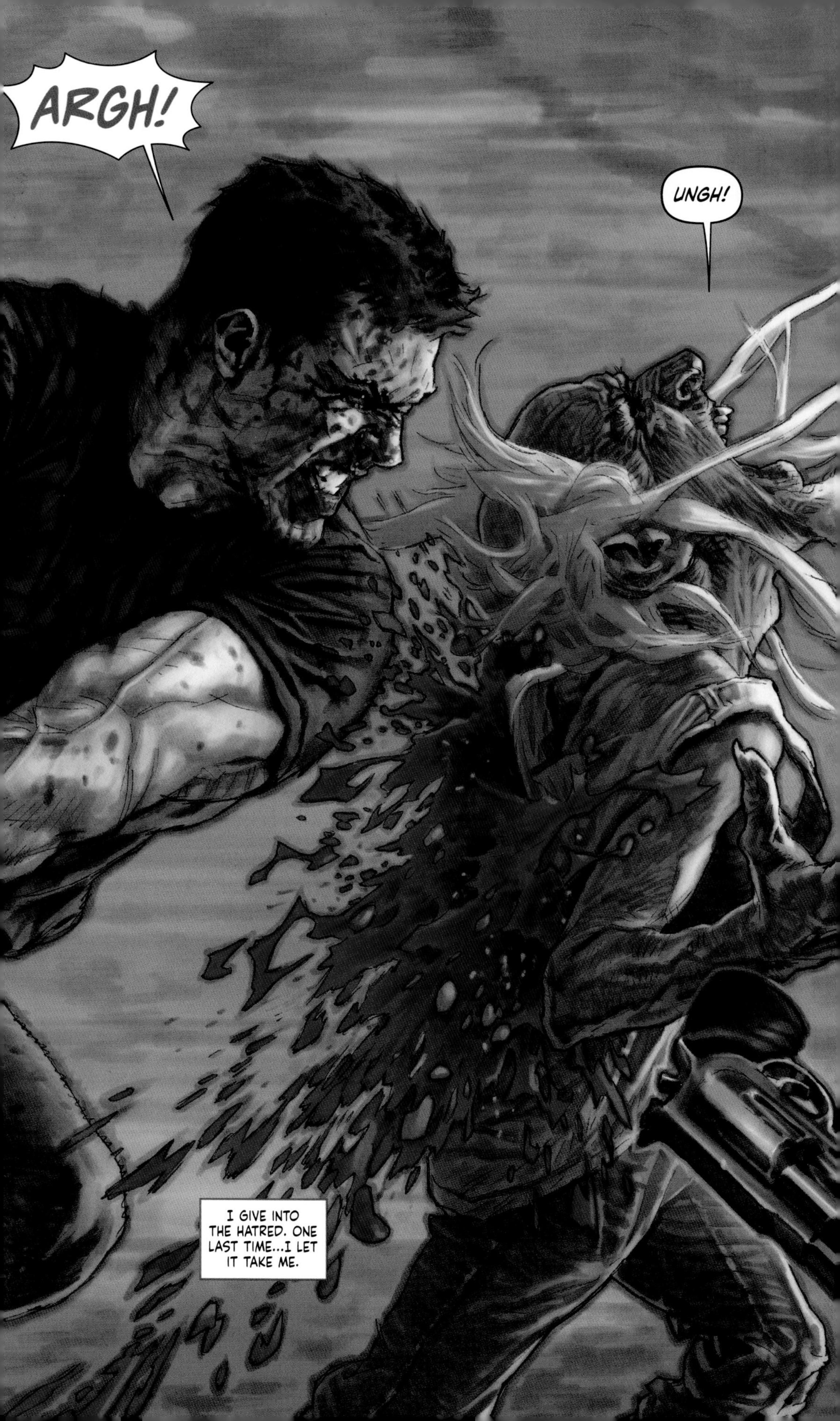
ARGH!
UNGH!
I GIVE INTO THE HATRED. ONE LAST TIME...I LET IT TAKE ME.

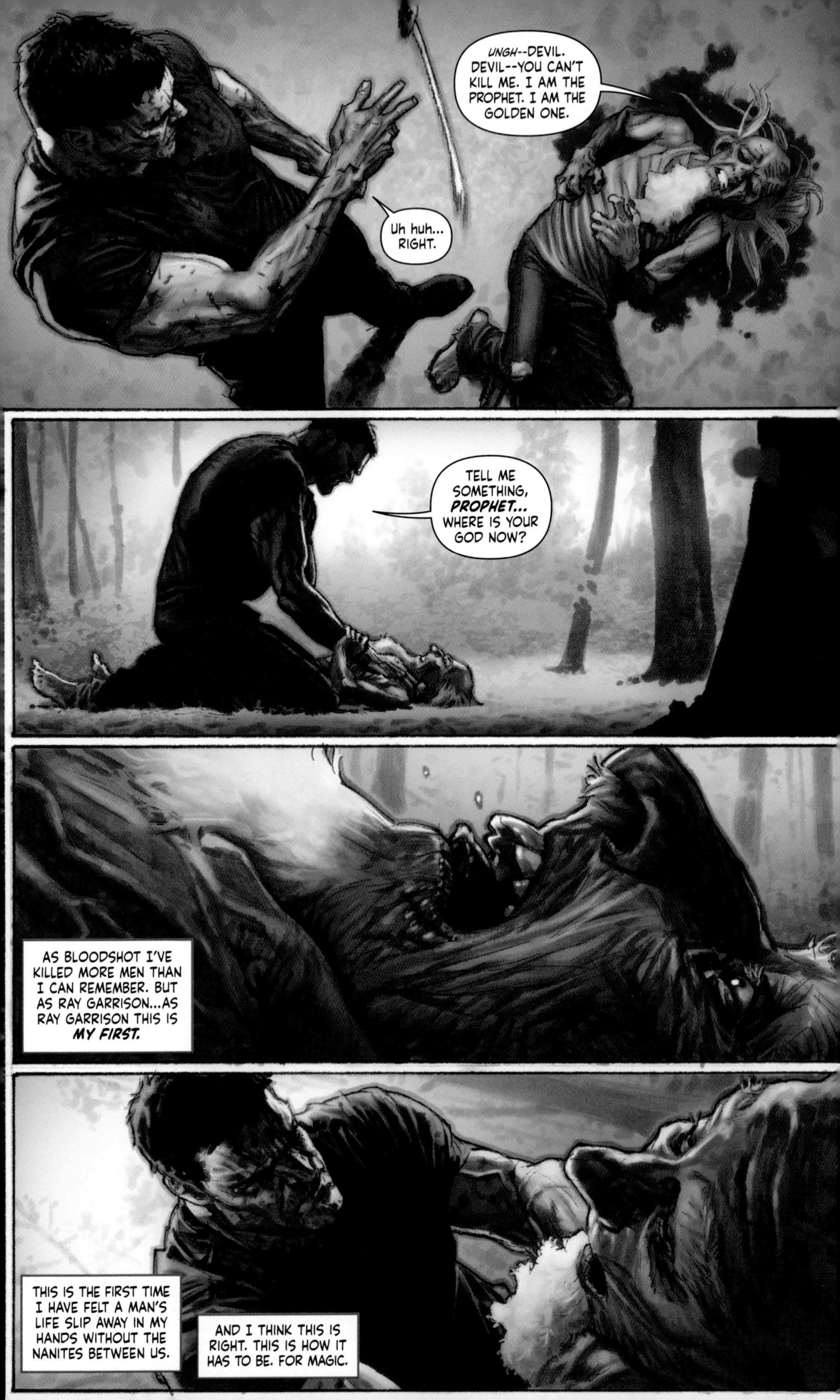
UNGH--DEVIL. DEVIL--YOU CAN'T KILL ME. I AM THE PROPHET. I AM THE GOLDEN ONE.
Uh huh... RIGHT.
TELL ME SOMETHING, PROPHET... WHERE IS YOUR GOD NOW?
AS BLOODSHOT I'VE KILLED MORE MEN THAN I CAN REMEMBER. BUT AS RAY GARRISON...AS RAY GARRISON THIS IS MY FIRST.
THIS IS THE FIRST TIME I HAVE FELT A MAN'S LIFE SLIP AWAY IN MY HANDS WITHOUT THE NANITES BETWEEN US.
AND I THINK THIS IS RIGHT. THIS IS HOW IT HAS TO BE. FOR MAGIC.

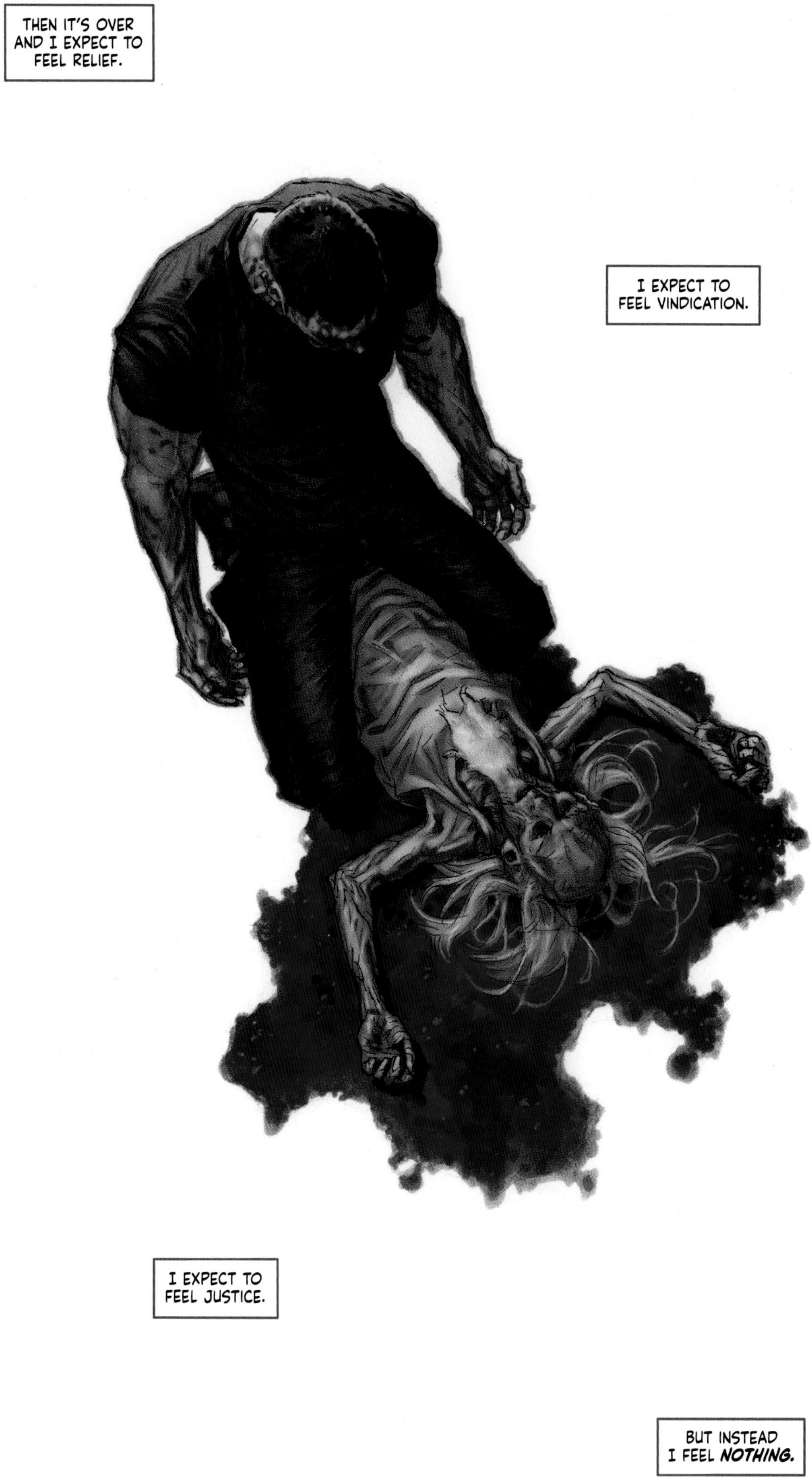
THEN IT'S OVER AND I EXPECT TO FEEL RELIEF.
I EXPECT TO FEEL VINDICATION.
I EXPECT TO FEEL JUSTICE.
BUT INSTEAD I FEEL ***NOTHING.***

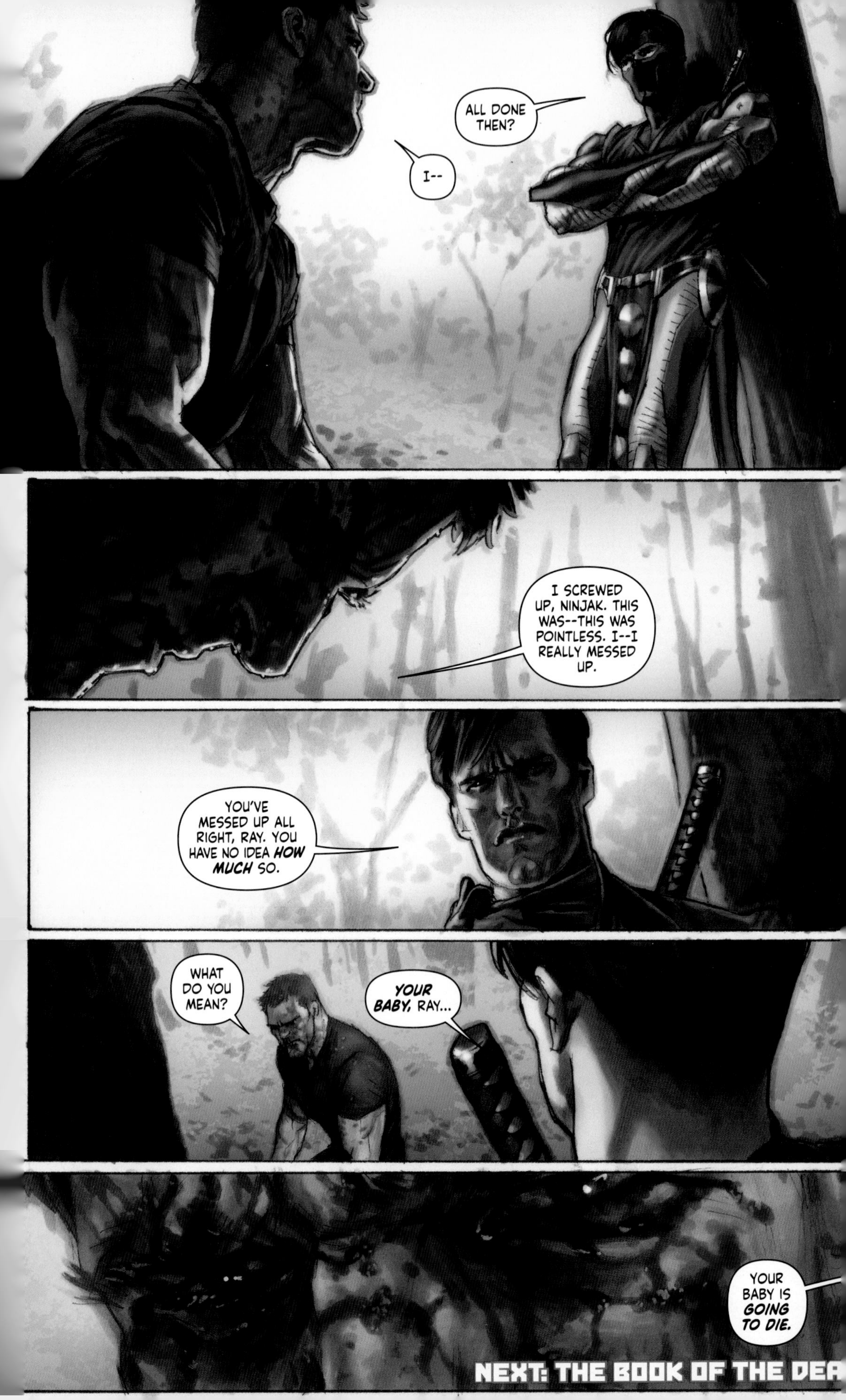
ALL DONE THEN?
I--
I SCREWED UP, NINJAK. THIS WAS--THIS WAS POINTLESS. I--I REALLY MESSED UP.
YOU'VE MESSED UP ALL RIGHT, RAY. YOU HAVE NO IDEA *HOW MUCH* SO.
WHAT DO YOU MEAN?
*YOUR BABY,* RAY...
YOUR BABY IS *GOING TO DIE.*
NEXT: THE BOOK OF THE DEA

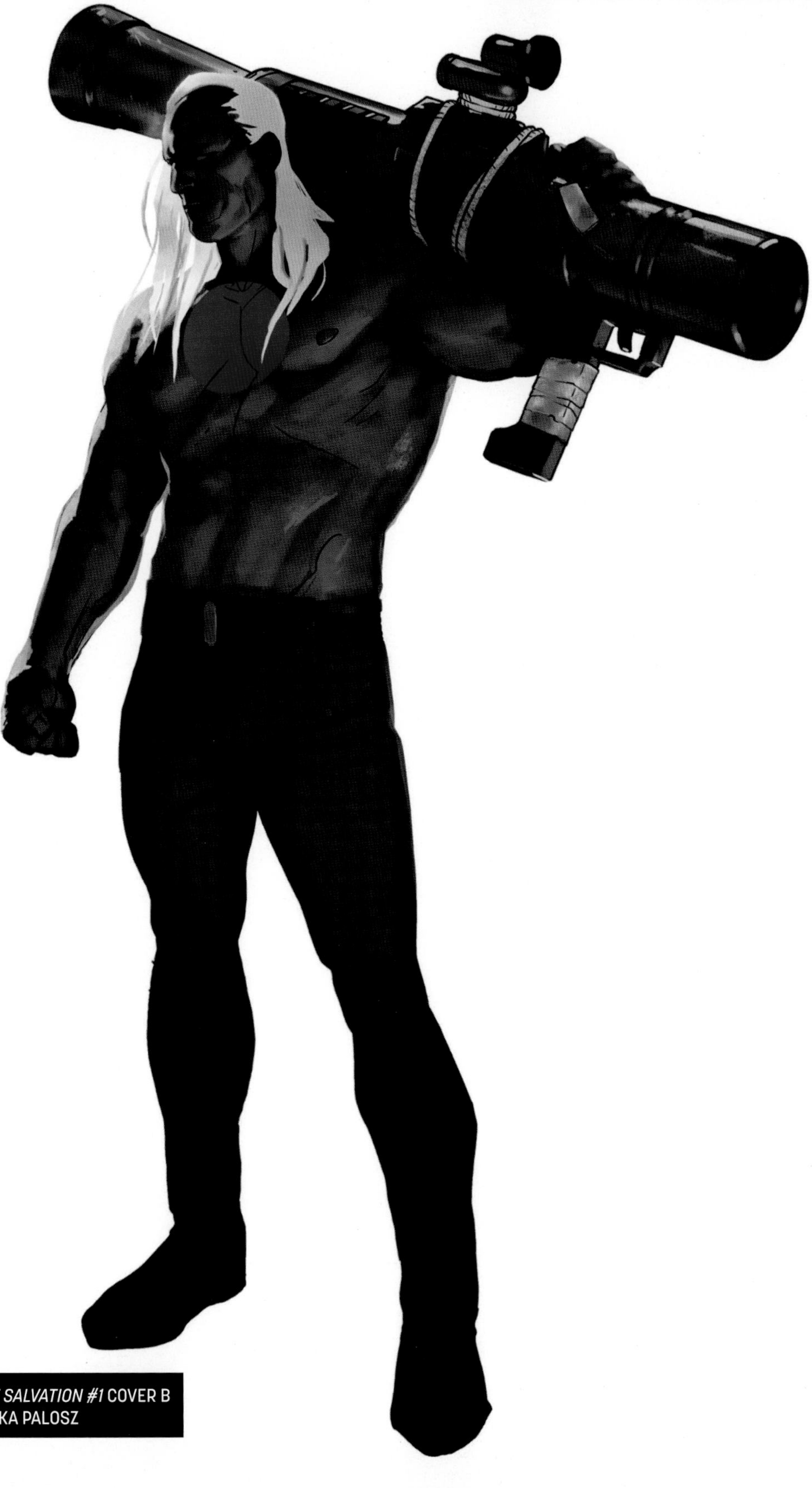

*BLOODSHOT SALVATION #1* COVER B
Art by MONIKA PALOSZ

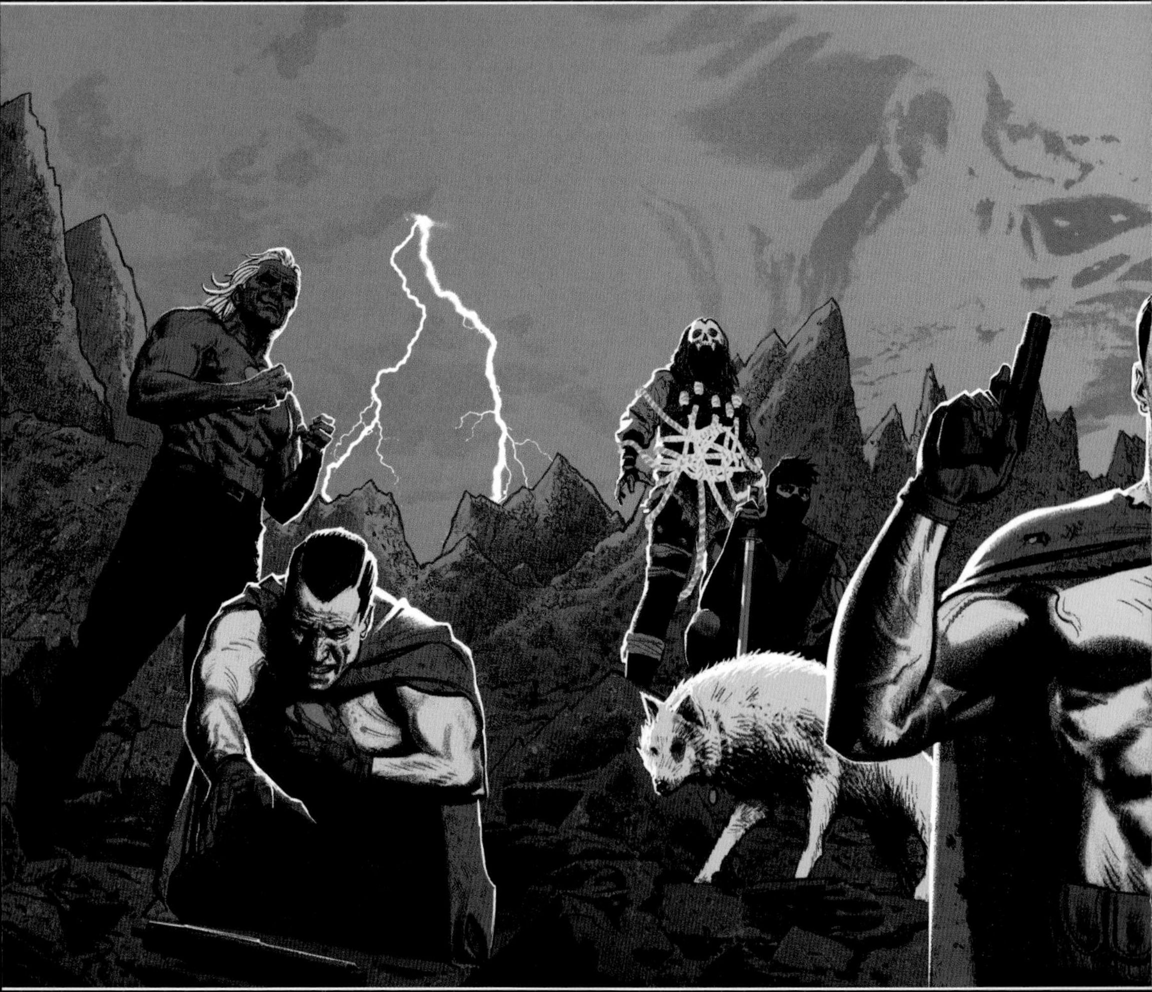

*BLOODSHOT SALVATION #1, 2, 3, and 5* INTERLOCKING VARIANT COVERS
Art by GREG SMALLWOOD

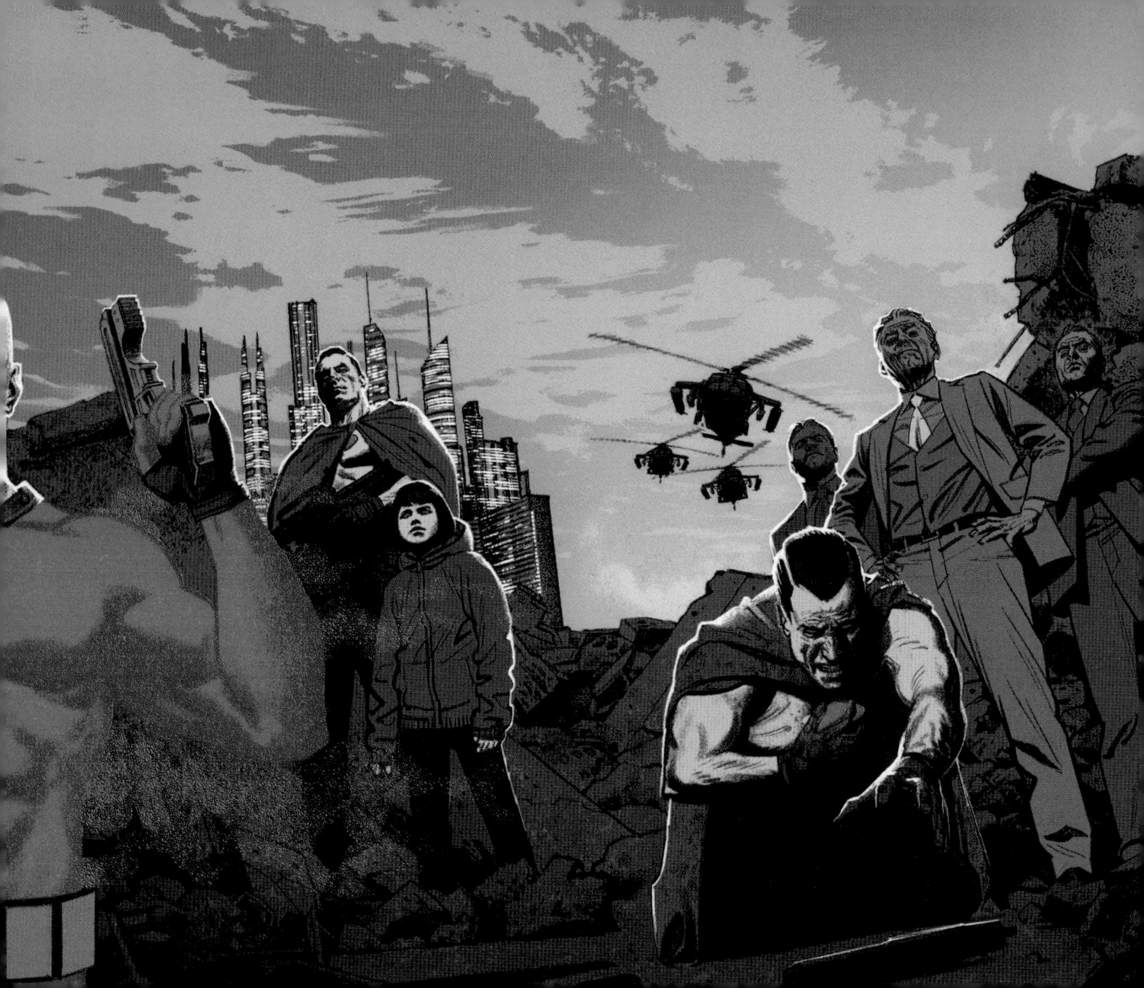

*BLOODSHOT SALVATION #2* ICON VARIANT COVER
Art by GLENN FABRY with ADAM BROWN

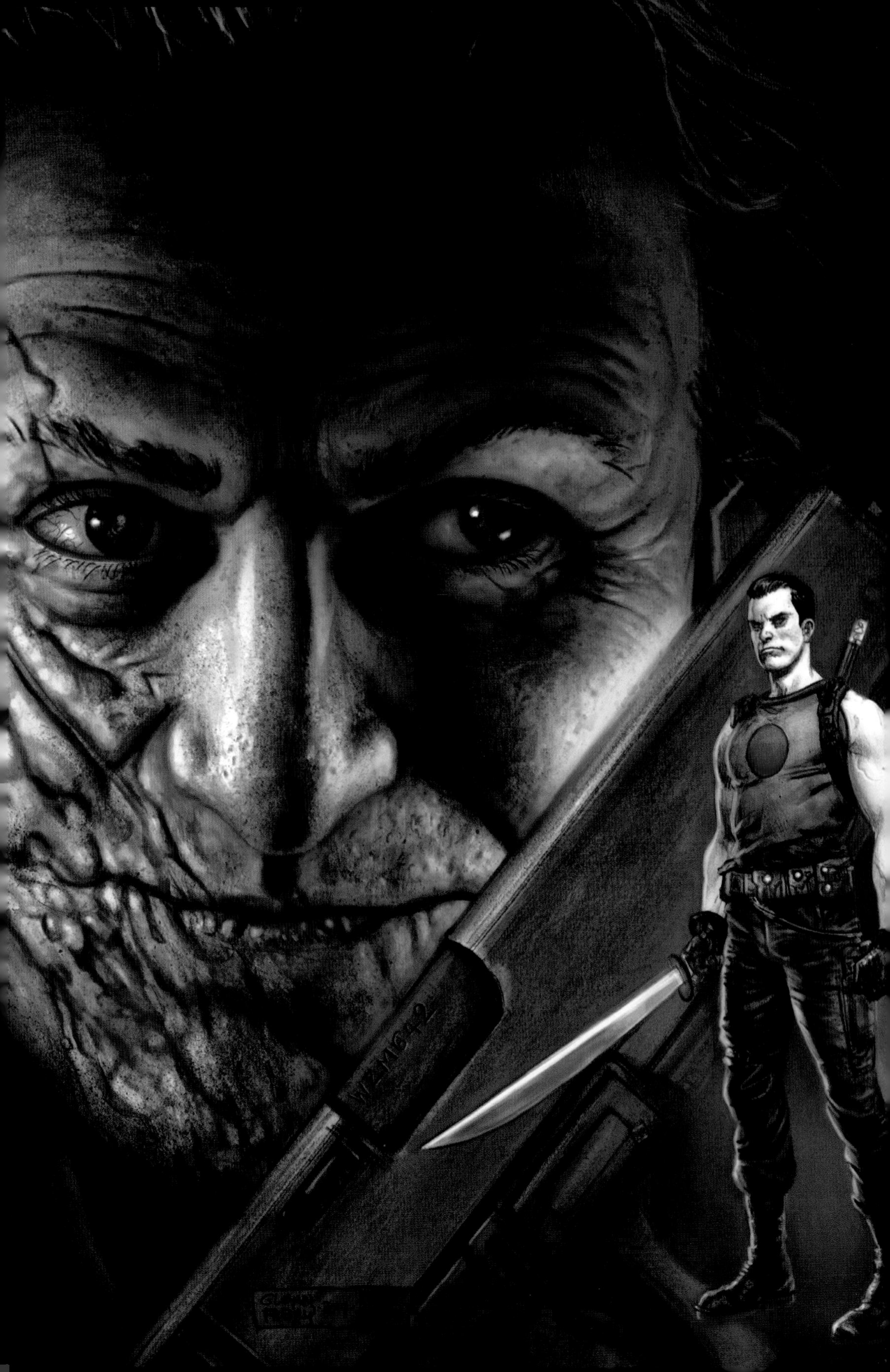

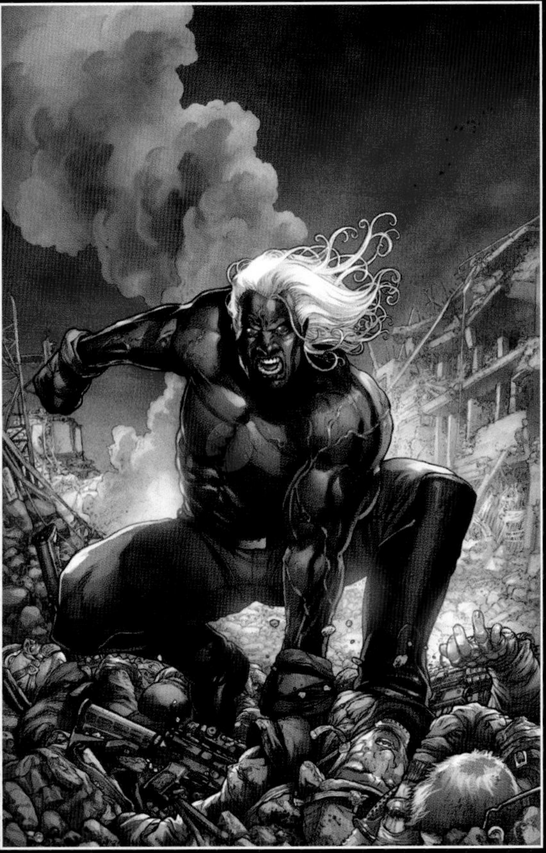

*BLOODSHOT SALVATION #4* COVER B
Art by JUAN JOSÉ RYP with ULISES ARREOLA

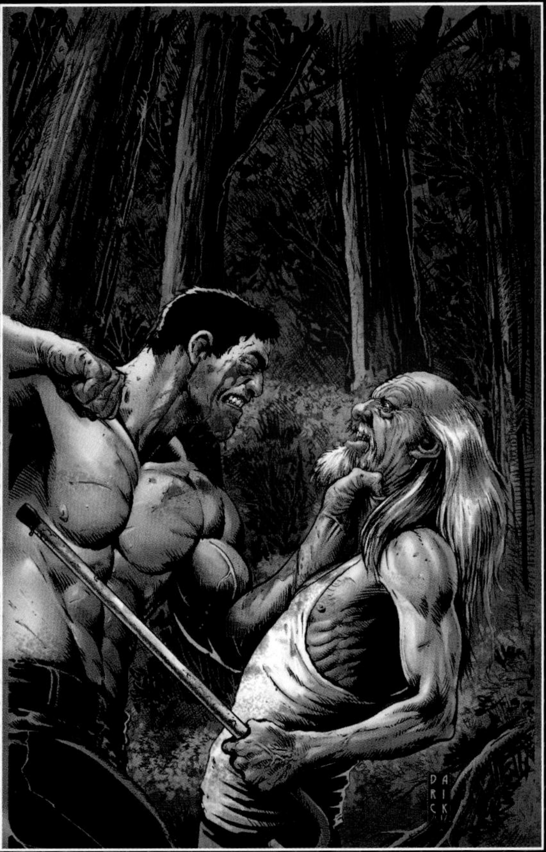

*BLOODSHOT SALVATION #5* COVER C
Art by DARICK ROBERTSON with DIEGO RODRIGUEZ

*BLOODSHOT SALVATION #1*, p. 1
Art by MICO SUAYAN

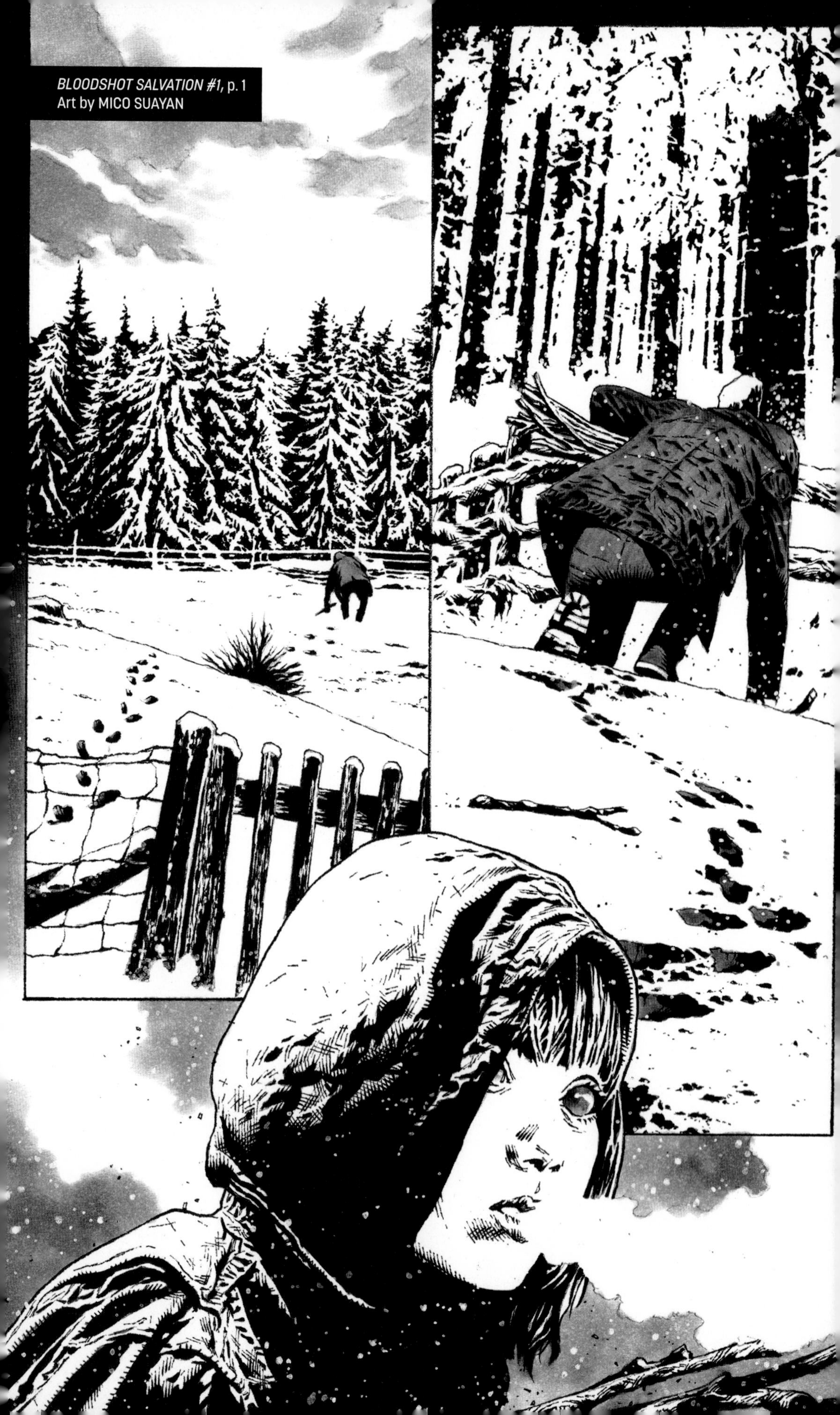

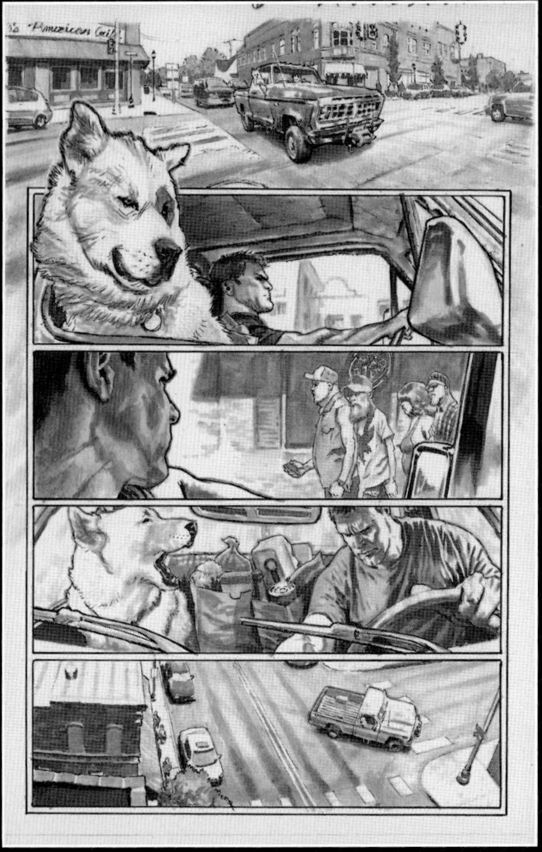

*BLOODSHOT SALVATION #1*, p. 8
Art by LEWIS LAROSA

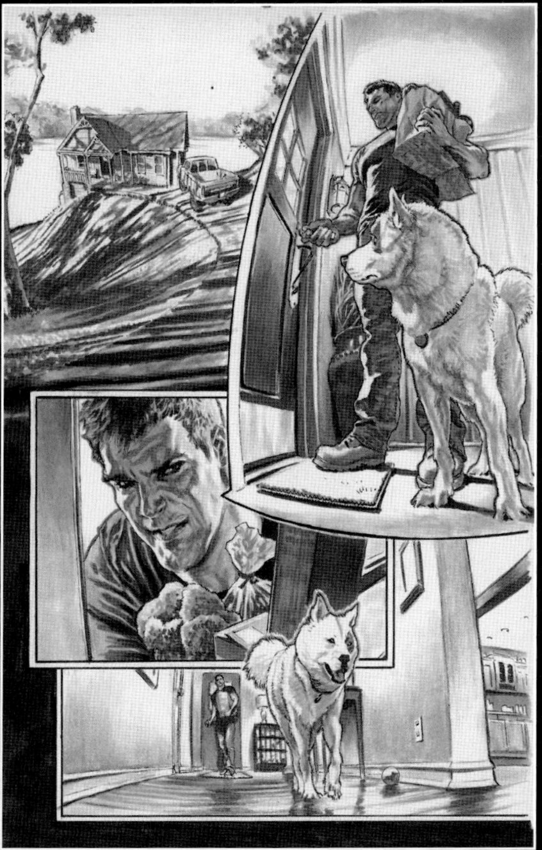

*BLOODSHOT SALVATION #1*, p. 9
Art by LEWIS LAROSA

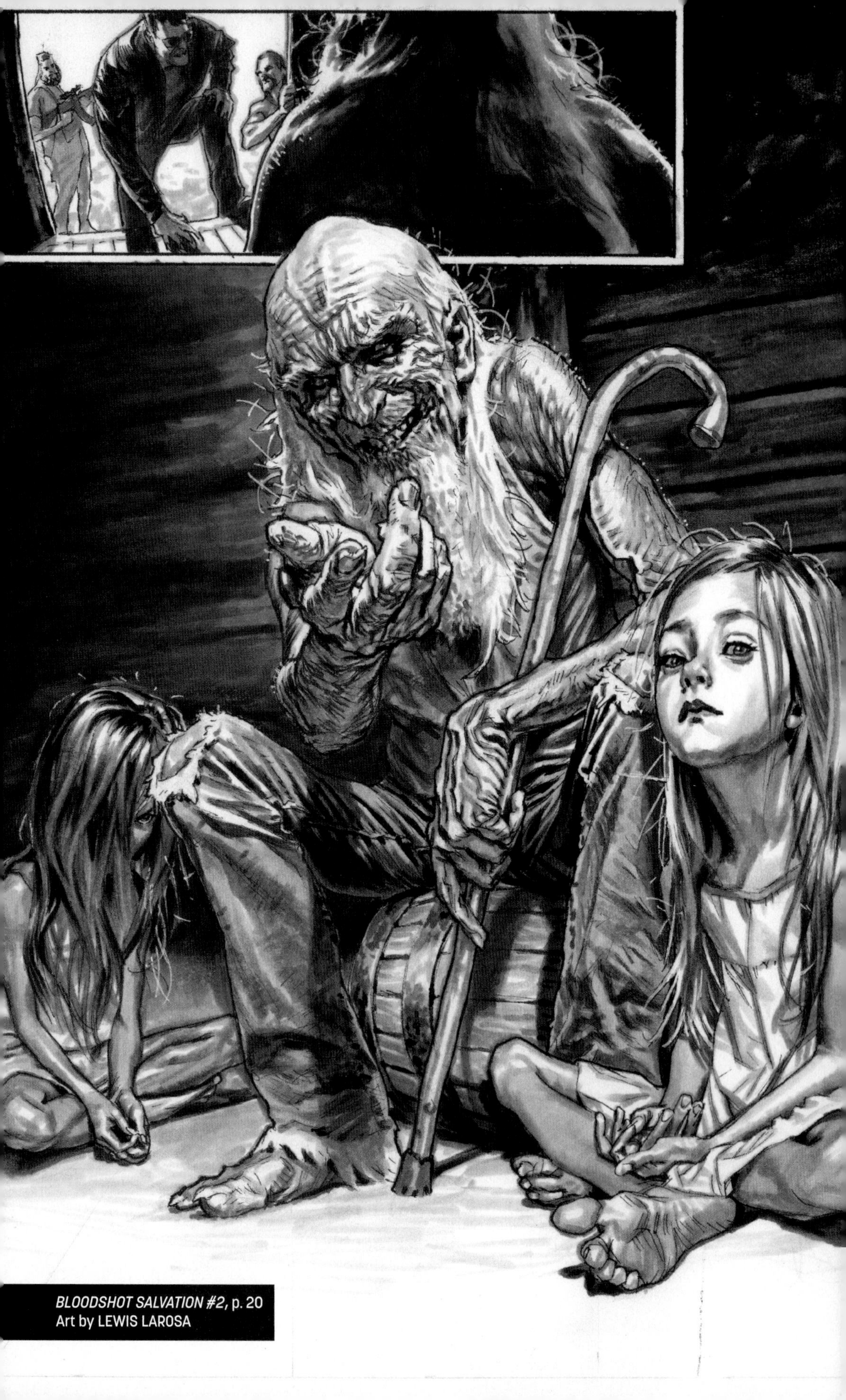

*BLOODSHOT SALVATION #2*, p. 20
Art by LEWIS LAROSA

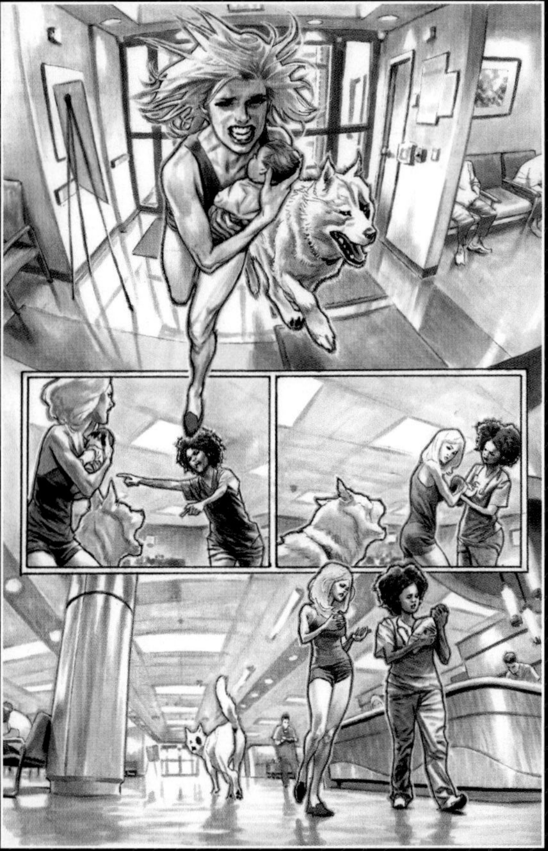

*BLOODSHOT SALVATION #2,*
Art by LEWIS LAROSA

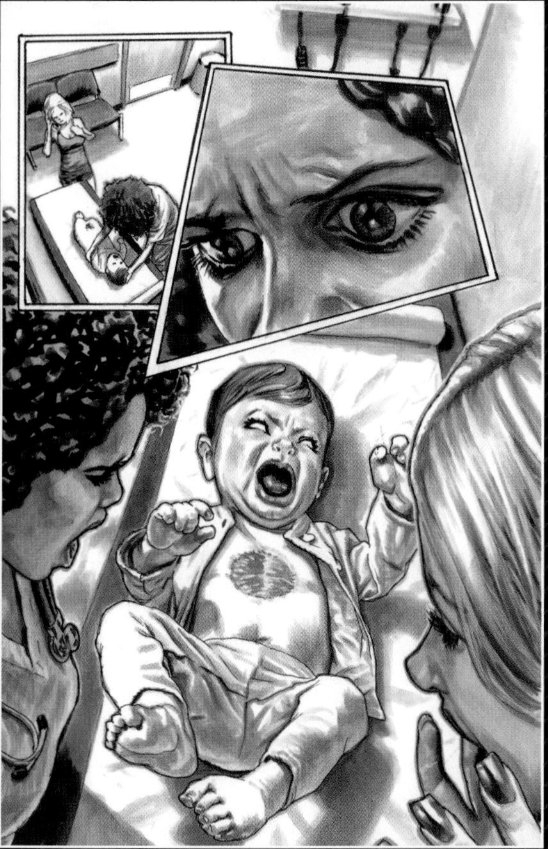

*BLOODSHOT SALVATION #2,*
Art by LEWIS LAROSA

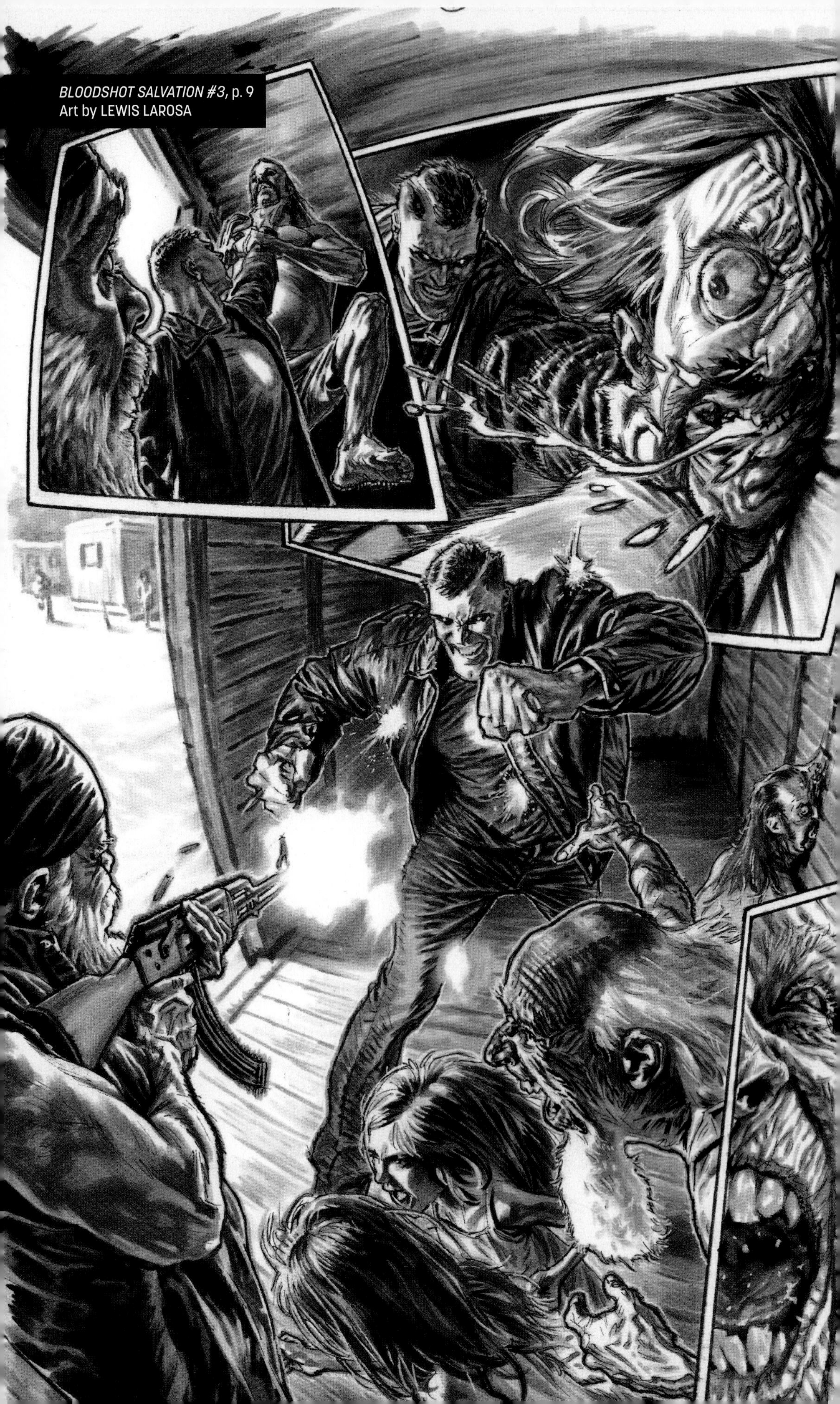

*BLOODSHOT SALVATION #3*, p. 9
Art by LEWIS LAROSA

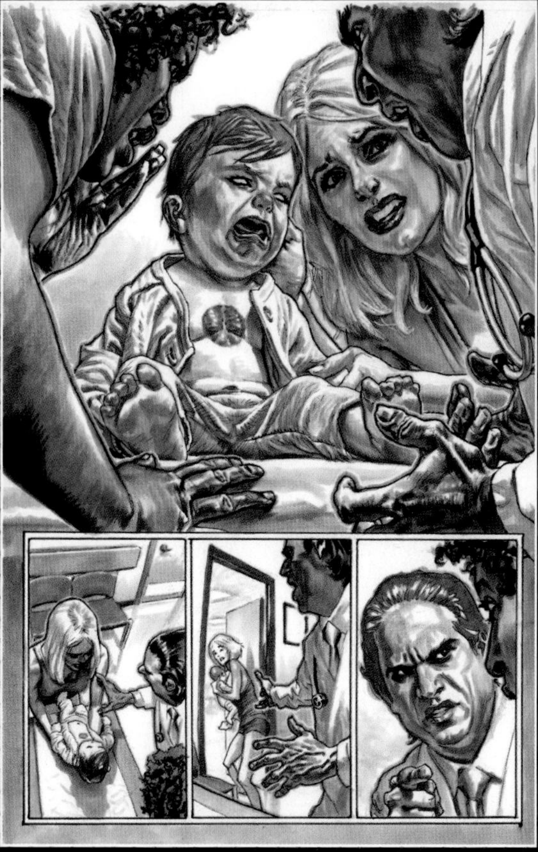

*BLOODSHOT SALVATION #3*, p. 10
Art by LEWIS LAROSA

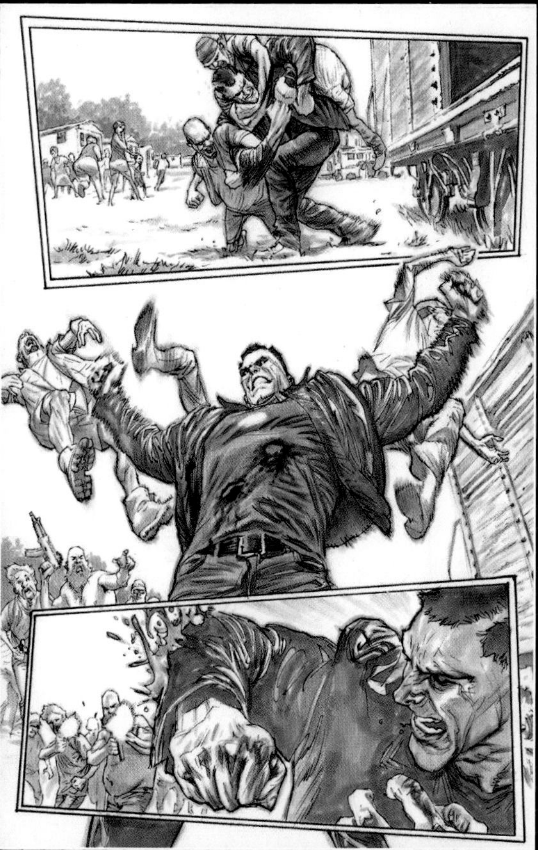

*BLOODSHOT SALVATION #3*, p. 16
Art by LEWIS LAROSA

# EXPLORE THE VALIANT UNIVERSE

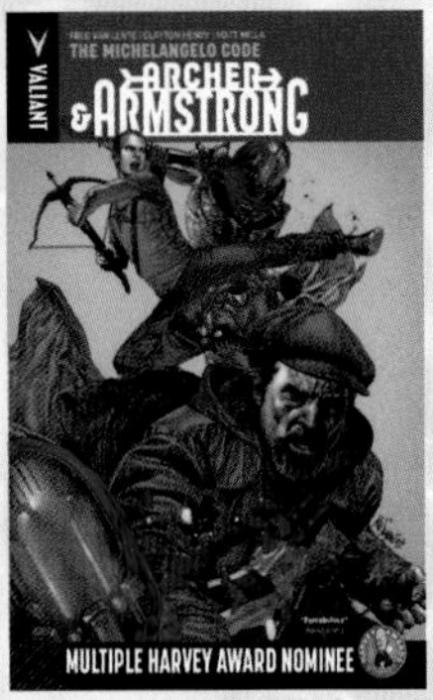
VALIANT
THE MICHELANGELO CODE
ARCHER & ARMSTRONG
MULTIPLE HARVEY AWARD NOMINEE

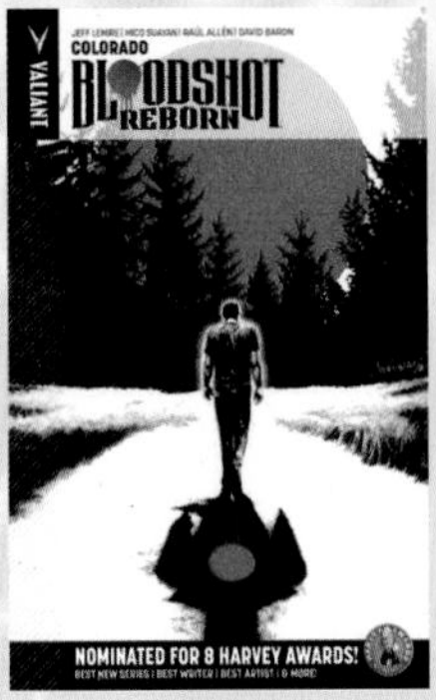
VALIANT
COLORADO
BLOODSHOT REBORN
NOMINATED FOR 8 HARVEY AWARDS!

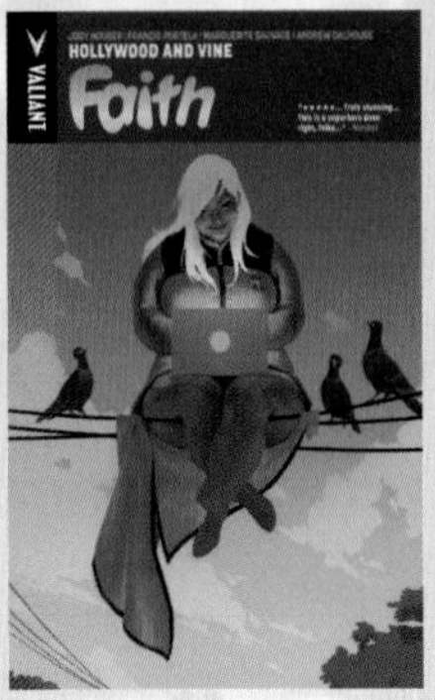
VALIANT
HOLLYWOOD AND VINE
Faith

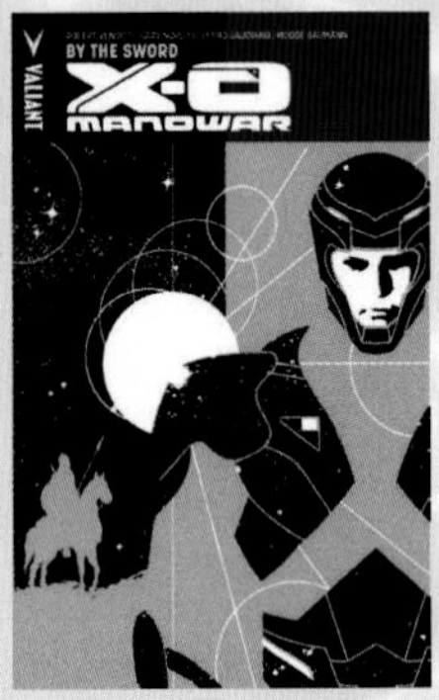
VALIANT
BY THE SWORD
X-O MANOWAR

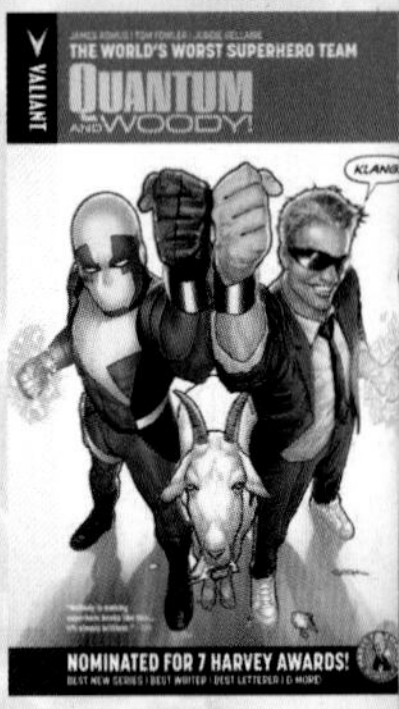
VALIANT
THE WORLD'S WORST SUPERHERO TEAM
QUANTUM AND WOODY!
NOMINATED FOR 7 HARVEY AWARDS!

## 4001 A.D.
**4001 A.D.**
ISBN: 9781682151433
**4001 A.D.: Beyond New Japan**
ISBN: 9781682151464
**Rai Vol 4: 4001 A.D.**
ISBN: 9781682151471

## A&A: THE ADVENTURES OF ARCHER AND ARMSTRONG
**Volume 1: In the Bag**
ISBN: 9781682151495
**Volume 2: Romance and Road Trips**
ISBN: 9781682151716
**Volume 3: Andromeda Estranged**
ISBN: 9781682152034

## ARCHER & ARMSTRONG
**Volume 1: The Michelangelo Code**
ISBN: 9780979640988
**Volume 2: Wrath of the Eternal Warrior**
ISBN: 9781939346049
**Volume 3: Far Faraway**
ISBN: 9781939346148
**Volume 4: Sect Civil War**
ISBN: 9781939346254
**Volume 5: Mission: Improbable**
ISBN: 9781939346353
**Volume 6: American Wasteland**
ISBN: 9781939346421
**Volume 7: The One Percent and Other Tales**
ISBN: 9781939346537

## ARMOR HUNTERS
**Armor Hunters**
ISBN: 9781939346452
**Armor Hunters: Bloodshot**
ISBN: 9781939346469
**Armor Hunters: Harbinger**
ISBN: 9781939346506
**Unity Vol. 3: Armor Hunters**
ISBN: 9781939346445
**X-O Manowar Vol. 7: Armor Hunters**
ISBN: 9781939346476

## BLOODSHOT
**Volume 1: Setting the World on Fire**
ISBN: 9780979640964
**Volume 2: The Rise and the Fall**
ISBN: 9781939346032
**Volume 3: Harbinger Wars**
ISBN: 9781939346124
**Volume 4: H.A.R.D. Corps**
ISBN: 9781939346193
**Volume 5: Get Some!**
ISBN: 9781939346315
**Volume 6: The Glitch and Other Tales**
ISBN: 9781939346711

## BLOODSHOT REBORN
**Volume 1: Colorado**
ISBN: 9781939346674
**Volume 2: The Hunt**
ISBN: 9781939346827
**Volume 3: The Analog Man**
ISBN: 9781682151334
**Volume 4: Bloodshot Island**
ISBN: 9781682151952

## BLOODSHOT U.S.A.
ISBN: 9781682151952

## BOOK OF DEATH
**Book of Death**
ISBN: 9781939346971
**Book of Death: The Fall of the Valiant Universe**
ISBN: 9781939346988

## BRITANNIA
**Volume 1**
ISBN: 9781682151853
**Volume 2: We Who Are About to Die**
ISBN: 9781682152133

## DEAD DROP
ISBN: 9781939346858

## THE DEATH-DEFYING DOCTOR MIRAGE
**Volume 1**
ISBN: 9781939346490
**Volume 2: Second Lives**
ISBN: 9781682151297

## THE DELINQUENTS
ISBN: 9781939346513

## DIVINITY
**Divinity I**
ISBN: 9781939346766
**Divinity II**
ISBN: 9781682151518
**Divinity III**
ISBN: 9781682151914
**Divinity III: Glorious Heroes of the Stalinverse**
ISBN: 9781682152072

## ETERNAL WARRIOR
**Volume 1: Sword of the Wild**
ISBN: 9781939346209
**Volume 2: Eternal Emperor**
ISBN: 9781939346292
**Volume 3: Days of Steel**
ISBN: 9781939346742

## WRATH OF THE ETERNAL WARRIO
**Volume 1: Risen**
ISBN: 9781682151235
**Volume 2: Labyrinth**
ISBN: 9781682151594
**Volume 3: Deal With a Devil**
ISBN: 9781682151976

## FAITH
**Volume 1: Hollywood and Vine**
ISBN: 9781682151402
**Volume 2: California Scheming**
ISBN: 9781682151631
**Volume 3: Superstar**
ISBN: 9781682151990
**Volume 4: The Faithless**
ISBN: 9781682152195
**Faith and the Future Force:**
ISBN: 9781682152331

## GENERATION ZERO
**Volume 1: We Are the Future**
ISBN: 9781682151754
**Volume 2: Heroscape**
ISBN: 9781682152096

## HARBINGER
**Volume 1: Omega Rising**
ISBN: 9780979640957
**Volume 2: Renegades**
ISBN: 9781939346025
**Volume 3: Harbinger Wars**
ISBN: 9781939346117
**Volume 4: Perfect Day**
ISBN: 9781939346155
**Volume 5: Death of a Renegade**
ISBN: 9781939346339
**Volume 6: Omegas**
ISBN: 9781939346384

## HARBINGER RENEGADE
**Volume 1: The Judgment of Solomon**
ISBN: 9781682151693
**Volume 2: Massacre**
ISBN: 9781682152232

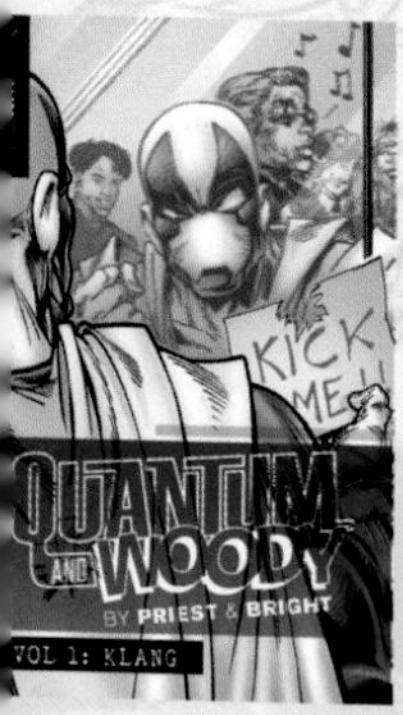
KICK ME!!
QUANTUM AND WOODY
BY PRIEST & BRIGHT
VOL 1: KLANG

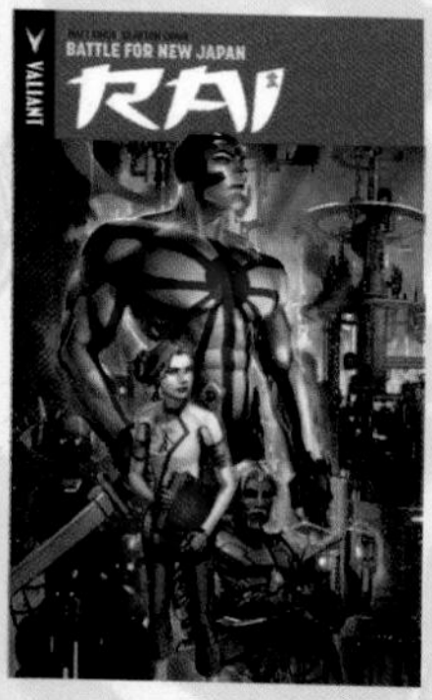
VALIANT
BATTLE FOR NEW JAPAN
RAI

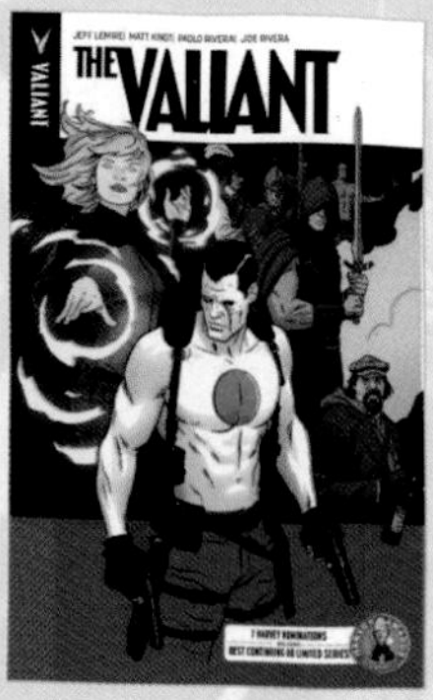
VALIANT
THE VALIANT

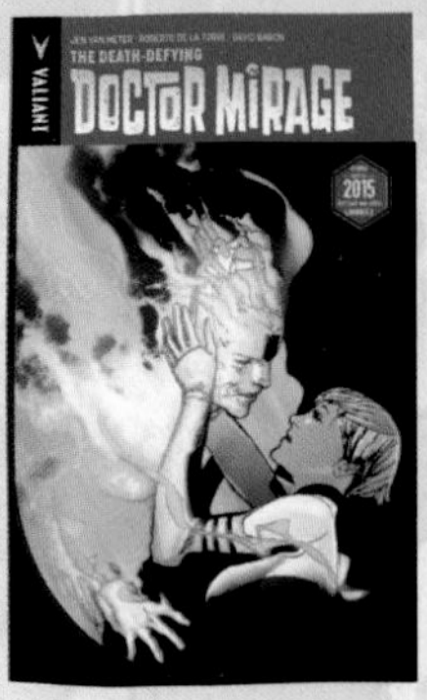
VALIANT
THE DEATH-DEFYING
DOCTOR MIRAGE

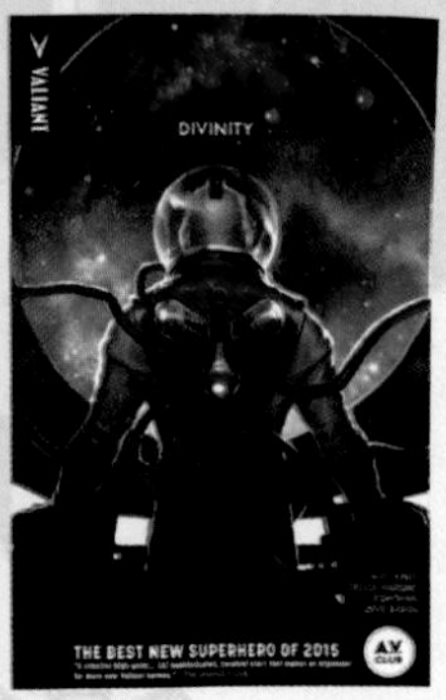
VALIANT
DIVINITY
THE BEST NEW SUPERHERO OF 2015

## ARBINGER RENEGADE
lume 1: The Judgment of Solomon
3N: 9781682151693
lume 2: Massacre
BN: 9781682152232

## ARBINGER WARS
rbinger Wars
BN: 9781939346094
oodshot Vol. 3: Harbinger Wars
3N: 9781939346124
rbinger Vol. 3: Harbinger Wars
3N: 9781939346117

## IPERIUM
lume 1: Collecting Monsters
3N: 9781939346759
ume 2: Broken Angels
N: 9781939346896
ume 3: The Vine Imperative
3N: 9781682151112
ume 4: Stormbreak
3N: 9781682151372

## INJAK
ume 1: Weaponeer
N: 9781939346667
ume 2: The Shadow Wars
N: 9781939346940
ume 3: Operation: Deadside
N: 9781682151259
ume 4: The Siege of King's Castle
N: 9781682151617
ume 5: The Fist & The Steel
N: 9781682151792
ume 6: The Seven Blades of Master Darque
N: 9781682152119

## ANTUM AND WOODY
ume 1: The World's Worst Superhero Team
N: 9781939346186
ume 2: In Security
N: 9781939346230
ume 3: Crooked Pasts, Present Tense
N: 9781939346391
ume 4: Quantum and Woody Must Die!
N: 9781939346629

## ANTUM AND WOODY PRIEST & BRIGHT
me 1: Klang
N: 9781939346780
me 2: Switch
: 9781939346803

Volume 3: And So...
ISBN: 9781939346865
Volume 4: Q2 - The Return
ISBN: 9781682151099

## RAI
Volume 1: Welcome to New Japan
ISBN: 9781939346414
Volume 2: Battle for New Japan
ISBN: 9781939346612
Volume 3: The Orphan
ISBN: 9781939346841
Volume 4: 4001 A.D.
ISBN: 9781682151471

## RAPTURE
ISBN: 9781682151891

## SAVAGE
ISBN: 9781682152256

## SECRET WEAPONS
ISBN: 9781682152294

## SHADOWMAN
Volume 1: Birth Rites
ISBN: 9781939346001
Volume 2: Darque Reckoning
ISBN: 9781939346056
Volume 3: Deadside Blues
ISBN: 9781939346162
Volume 4: Fear, Blood, And Shadows
ISBN: 9781939346278
Volume 5: End Times
ISBN: 9781939346377

## SHADOWMAN BY ENNIS & WOOD
ISBN: 9781682151358

## IVAR, TIMEWALKER
Volume 1: Making History
ISBN: 9781939346636
Volume 2: Breaking History
ISBN: 9781939346834
Volume 3: Ending History
ISBN: 9781939346995

## UNITY
Volume 1: To Kill a King
ISBN: 9781939346261
Volume 2: Trapped by Webnet
ISBN: 9781939346346
Volume 3: Armor Hunters
ISBN: 9781939346445
Volume 4: The United
ISBN: 9781939346544
Volume 5: Homefront
ISBN: 9781939346797
Volume 6: The War-Monger
ISBN: 9781939346902
Volume 7: Revenge of the Armor Hunters
ISBN: 9781682151136

## THE VALIANT
ISBN: 9781939346605

## VALIANT ZEROES AND ORIGINS
ISBN: 9781939346582

## WAR MOTHER
ISBN: 9781682152379

## X-O MANOWAR
Volume 1: By the Sword
ISBN: 9780979640940
Volume 2: Enter Ninjak
ISBN: 9780979640995
Volume 3: Planet Death
ISBN: 9781939346087
Volume 4: Homecoming
ISBN: 9781939346179
Volume 5: At War With Unity
ISBN: 9781939346247
Volume 6: Prelude to Armor Hunters
ISBN: 9781939346407
Volume 7: Armor Hunters
ISBN: 9781939346476
Volume 8: Enter: Armorines
ISBN: 9781939346551
Volume 9: Dead Hand
ISBN: 9781939346650
Volume 10: Exodus
ISBN: 9781939346933
Volume 11: The Kill List
ISBN: 9781682151273
Volume 12: Long Live the King
ISBN: 9781682151655
Volume 13: Succession and Other Tales
ISBN: 9781682151754

## X-O MANOWAR (2017)
Volume 1: Soldier
ISBN: 9781682152058
Volume 2: General
ISBN: 9781682152171
Volume 3: Emperor
ISBN: 9781682152355

# EXPLORE THE VALIANT UNIVERSE

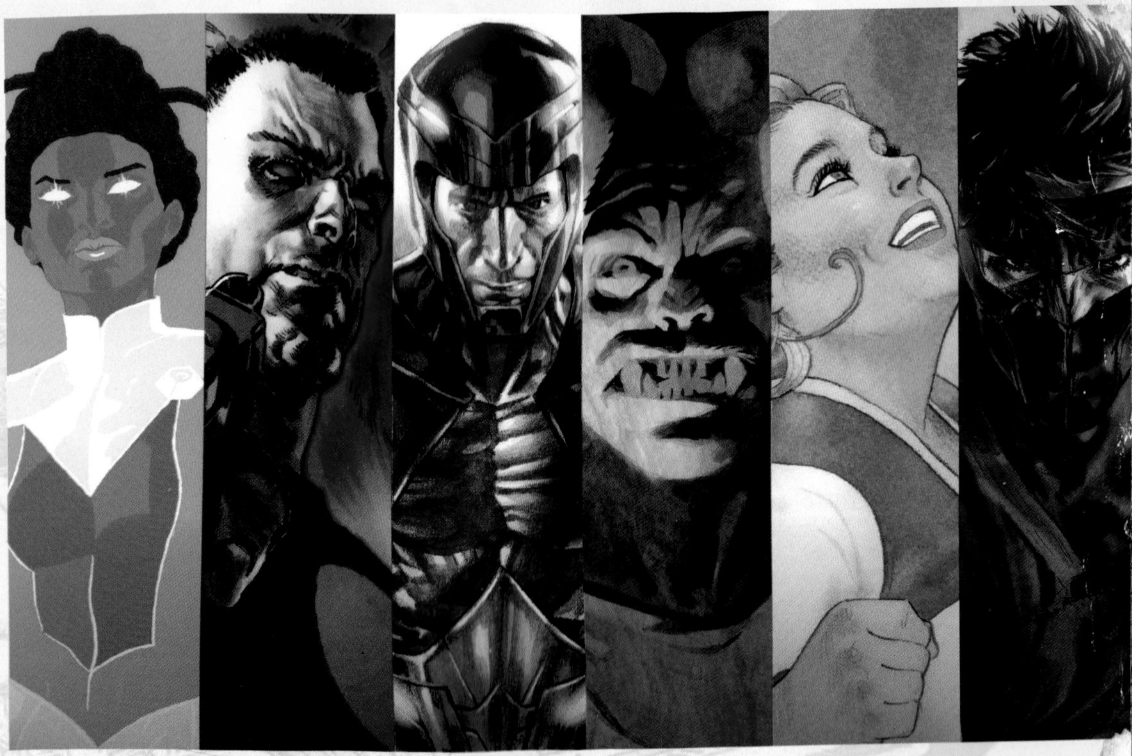

**4001 A.D. DELUXE EDITION**
ISBN: 978-1-68215-193-8

**ARCHER & ARMSTRONG DELUXE EDITIONS**
Book 1: ISBN: 978-1-939346-22-3
Book 2: ISBN: 978-1-939346-95-7

**ARMOR HUNTERS DELUXE EDITION**
ISBN: 978-1-939346-72-8

**BLOODSHOT DELUXE EDITIONS**
Book 1: ISBN: 978-1-939346-21-6
Book 2: ISBN: 978-1-939346-81-0

**BLOODSHOT REBORN DELUXE EDITIONS**
Book 1: ISBN: 978-1-68215-155-6
Book 2: ISBN: 978-1-68215-227-0

**BOOK OF DEATH DELUXE EDITION**
ISBN: 978-1-68215-115-0

**THE DEATH-DEFYING DOCTOR MIRAGE DELUXE EDITION**
ISBN: 978-1-68215-153-2

**DIVINITY DELUXE EDITION**
ISBN: 978-1-939346-92-6

**FAITH: HOLLYWOOD & VINE DELUXE EDITION**
ISBN: 978-1-68215-201-0

**HARBINGER DELUXE EDITIONS**
Book 1: ISBN: 978-1-939346-13-1
Book 2: ISBN: 978-1-939346-77-3

**HARBINGER WARS DELUXE EDITION**
ISBN: 978-1-939346-32-2

**IVAR, TIMEWALKER DELUXE EDITION**
Book 1: ISBN: 978-1-68215-119-8

**NINJAK DELUXE EDITION**
Book 1: ISBN: 978-1-68215-157-0
Book 2: ISBN: 978-1-68215-257-7

**QUANTUM AND WOODY DELUXE EDITION**
Book 1: ISBN: 978-1-939346-68-1

**RAI DELUXE EDITION**
Book 1: ISBN: 978-1-68215-117-4

**SHADOWMAN DELUXE EDITION**
Book 1: ISBN: 978-1-939346-43-8

**UNITY DELUXE EDITION**
Book 1: 978-1-939346-57-5

**THE VALIANT DELUXE EDITION**
ISBN: 978-1-939346-91-9

**X-O MANOWAR DELUXE EDITIONS**
Book 1: ISBN: 978-1-939346-10-0
Book 2: ISBN: 978-1-939346-52-0
Book 3 : ISBN: 978-1-68215-131-0
Book 4: ISBN: 978-1-68215-183-9
Book 5: ISBN: 978-1-68215-215-7

## VALIANT CLASSIC

**ARCHER & ARMSTRONG: THE COMPLETE CLASSIC OMNIBUS**
ISBN: 978-1-939346-87-2

**QUANTUM AND WOODY: THE COMPLETE CLASSIC OMNIBUS**
ISBN: 978-1-939346-36-0

**Q2: THE RETURN OF QUANTUM AND WOODY DELUXE EDITION**
ISBN: 978-1-939346-56-8

**VALIANT MASTERS: BLOODSHOT VOL. 1 - BLOOD OF THE MACHINE**
ISBN: 978-0-9796409-3-3

**VALIANT MASTERS: HARBINGER VOL. 1 - CHILDREN OF THE EIGHTH D**
ISBN: 978-1-939346-48-3

**VALIANT MASTERS: H.A.R.D. CORPS VOL. 1 - SEARCH AND DESTROY**
ISBN: 978-1-939346-28-5

**VALIANT MASTERS: NINJAK VOL. 1 - BLACK WATER**
ISBN: 978-0-9796409-7-1

**VALIANT MASTERS: RAI VOL. 1 - FROM HONOR TO STRENGTH**
ISBN: 978-1-939346-07-0

**VALIANT MASTERS: SHADOWMAN VOL. 1 - SPIRITS WITHIN**
ISBN: 978-1-939346-01-8

**X-O MANOWAR CLASSIC OMNIBUS**
Vol. 1: ISBN: 978-1-939346-30-8